THE CULTURE CONSUMERS

The Culture Consumers

A STUDY OF ART
AND AFFLUENCE
IN AMERICA

Alvin Toffler

Introduction by Eric Larrabee

VINTAGE BOOKS
A Division of Random House/New York

To Heidi

Contents

Introduction

THIS IS A BOOK OF MANY FIRSTS. IT WAS THE FIRST TO BRING TOGETHER information about the extraordinary increase of activity in the arts in the United States during the 1950s and 1960s. It was the first to show that the phenomenon was not a matter of isolated instances, but of a common and nearly universal pattern. It was, if not the first, certainly the most effective in arguing that this rise in quantity did not necessarily imply a lowering in quality but quite the reverse. And it was the first—and for that matter is still the only book—to assert that what has taken place is not superficial or transitory, but in fact constitutes a social revolution, a fundamental change in the relationship of the arts to society.

The Culture Consumers, that is, can now be read as a very different work from what it appeared to be on publication. For one thing, it was deceptively straightforward. Much of it— naturally enough, since it had originated in a magazine article— was given over to essentially journalistic reporting. Nor was the news it had to offer any great secret; the state of stepped-up performance and enlarged audience which Mr. Toffler described was evident on every hand. But to the readers of that time his book said several things they may not have wanted to hear. People who are concerned about the arts are notoriously reluctant to be consoled, and he was telling them that their country was beginning to take them seriously and request their services. He was also telling them that they were going broke—which is not always popular. With the benefit of hindsight they can now see how right he was: their services are now even more in demand and they *are* thoroughly and self-evidently broke.

Now that the revolution Mr. Toffler perceived is well advanced, the shape of it can be seen to have followed his outline. He characterized it as the transition "from cult to culture," which is an effectively condensed way of saying that the arts have moved from being the preoccupation of an elite toward becoming the possession of all, permeating the entire social structure. The author made it clear, too, he knew this message would not be wholly welcome, and knew also in what quarters it would alternately be denied and disparaged. He is less than gentle with those who tend to regard the arts as their personal possession, in danger of being soiled or misused if allowed to fall into other hands. The type is still with us, but either there are fewer of them or they are less eager to speak up, for Mr. Toffler's view is closer to the dominant one today.

Perhaps, also, some readers may have missed his meaning because of their distaste for treating something as sacred and sensitive as an art museum or a symphony orchestra as though it were (as it is) a business enterprise. The folk customs of American philanthropy die hard, and one of them has always required that the arts be regarded as so rewarding to the psyche that the artists and those who serve the arts need not be paid enough to eat. To mention money in connection with an artistic enterprise is therefore in bad taste. Furthermore, the boards of trustees were often men and women of considerable means who found it embarrassing to admit that any institution they supported could be in seriously deteriorating financial condition. A deficit was something you talked about once a year during the fund-raising drive; since it had always been there but the organization had somehow survived, it wasn't quite real.

Not unexpectedly for a man who was later to write a book called *Future Shock*, Mr. Toffler not only saw what was coming but understood why. One of his most ingenious formulations is what he calls the Law of the Inefficiency of Art, which holds that every increase in social or technological effectiveness will necessarily operate to the *comparative* disadvantage of the arts. A work of painting or music or theater has the strength but also the fatal weakness of being unique; it happens one at a time. There is no way of speeding up the process of creating or exhibiting or performing it. As society becomes more efficient, the arts stand still, held back by the very individuality and human directness which is their principal reason for being. In the years following publication of *The Culture Consumers* this iron law took hold with increasing severity as cultural institutions of every kind began to run deficits that were no longer trivial but threatened to consume endowments and exhaust the resources of traditional donors.

Mr. Toffler recognized that the times were calling for, and starting to produce, a new system of patronage. But he knew that no fully workable solution was available, and so it is not surprising that several of his suggestions have yet to be adopted. The commitment of American universities to the arts, for example, which was then an exciting prospect, has proved to be somewhat more ornamental than functional. That is to say, university arts centers proliferated and campuses are inundated with cultural offerings, but the incorporation of living and breathing processes of artistic creation into scholarship and teaching at a university level—on a par, say, with scientific research—still has a long way to go. The emergence of business patronage, as well, has lagged behind the hopes and expectations which could be entertained for it ten years ago. Yet Mr. Toffler's point that patronage should be pluralistic, if only to assure that no single piper could possibly call the tune, remains as central now as it was then.

For this particular reader, since I am presently involved in administering state funds for the arts, the most interesting passages to reread have been those concerned with government and politics. The arts council movement had at that time just begun, and the possibilities for funding on the substantial level that now seems achievable would then have been dismissed as illusory and probably dangerous. Many of us, with memories still fresh of the congressional attacks on State Department exhibits overseas for showing works by "communists," were afraid that any involvement of government in the arts would lead to interference or outright censorship. Others, like Russell Lynes (in a passage Mr. Toffler quotes), were even more concerned that governmental bureaucracy would operate in the arts to bring about a state of "creeping mediocrity."

If the worst of these fears have not been realized, the reasons why could scarcely have been foreseen. Mr. Toffler, while taking a gingerly approach to government subsidy, argued that it had worked in Western Europe without incurring "undue political pressure." This may be true enough, on the face of it, but in terms of cause and effect the European example has turned out to be subtly misleading. The pressure was there: it was simply pressure on the part of an artistic establishment of educated taste and sensibility so powerful that its judgments, in the event that they were not admirable, were self-confirming. Such is not the case, to put it mildly, in the United States.

Here the arts have hitherto been as innocent of politics as politics have been of the arts. That they get along at all is a surprise, but the real miracle is that political pressures—using "politics" in the good sense of the word, to mean the rights of every element in the community to be served—have paradoxically proved to be a liberating rather than a constricting force. The marble-pillared museum and the storefront in the ghetto approach government with needs of a totally different magnitude and kind but an equal degree of legitimacy. The existence of each validates the claim of the other. As long as it is called upon for assistance from all quarters, government is free to invoke the one standard it should adhere to anyhow, which is that of quality.

A theme that runs throughout *The Culture Consumers,* and might be said to animate it, is the interweaving relationship between excellence and equity. If the concerns of all are taken into account, what happens to the smaller number whose care is not for justice but for perfection? Mr. Toffler never loses sight of this question, and he answers it in a multitude of ways. He maintains, for example, that the amateur is not the enemy of the professional but an ally. He brings eloquent testimony to support his contention that the new audiences have proved to be more expert, and harder to please, than the old. He argues, in short, that the building of a wider base enables the peak to reach higher. Does the quality of American basketball suffer, he very properly asks, because there is a hoop in every backyard? Does the quality of Russian chess-playing suffer because the game is so ubiquitously played and enjoyed?

His case could be strengthened by another of the discoveries that have been made since he wrote. This is the unanticipated by-product of extending government aid in the arts to minority groups. To the black and Spanish-speaking communities, theater and music and dance irrefutably their own and no one else's are important out of all proportion to their numbers, precisely because a sense of heritage and cultural self-respect are the qualities they miss and must pursue. Moreover, in the effort to find an artistic style and substance unlike that of the dominant majority, they have provided a model for indigenous arts of all kinds to spring up in other neglected corners of society with problems of isolation and alienation not unlike their own. Something has been started, something rooted in the same soil from which the high arts of the past eventually grew, and the benefits may well be reaped for years to come.

In the end Mr. Toffler finds himself quoting Leverkuhn in Thomas Mann's *Dr. Faustus,* on the theme that art must find its way back to human beings and "once more see itself as the servant of a community, a community welded together by far more than education, a community that would not *have* a culture, but perhaps *be* one." To that aim he wrote this book and, so doing, raised a standard to which all of us can repair.

Eric Larrabee
Executive Director
New York State Council on the Arts

PART ONE

Art and People

1

The Culture Elitists

THE UNITED STATES SUFFERS FROM AN INFERIORITY COMPLEX ABOUT its culture. From colonial days on, Europeans have traveled among us, filled their notebooks, and returned home to write acid reports about our seemingly congenital inhospitality to the arts. Nor were the Europeans alone. This theme—that Americans are coarse and cultureless—has been echoed by generations of our own artists and social critics. It is repeated with blind assurance by our tastemakers today.

This book will not challenge the judgments rendered by de Tocqueville and others about what Americans were like in the distant past. Some of their judgments, however unfriendly, were painfully accurate. Nor is it my purpose to prove that we have created in the United States a finished culture, a splendid, shining pavilion of artistic excellence in which every exhibit is elegant and every performance brilliant. I do not contend that we are in the midst of a new renaissance.

I do contend, however, that it is high time Americans stopped feeling ashamed of the state of their arts. It is my purpose to prove that since the end of the last World War a series of astonishing, and on the whole healthy, changes have transformed the social base of the arts in this country. I contend that those critics who continue to utter the traditional cliches about American cultural backwardness are simply out of touch with the new reality. The time has come to question the stereotyped image of the uncultured American.

The changes of recent years, for want of a better term, have been called a "culture explosion." Nobody is certain of its exact meaning, but the phrase itself touches off controversy.

First, there are those who claim that no change has occurred. According to some critics, the "culture explosion" is no more than a smug fiction invented by the mass media. Whatever it is, no such thing has happened, they insist, and Americans are still as indifferent to the arts as they ever were. The arts, according to these observers have always suffered neglect in the United States, and still do. Americans are still barbarians, only richer. Nothing has changed. The term "culture explosion," therefore, signifies zero.

This book will prove otherwise.

A second group admits that something has, indeed, happened to the arts in the United States since the end of World War II. They acknowledge a growth, even an explosive growth, in the culture public. They agree that there are more people standing in lines outside theaters, museums and concert halls today than ever before. They argue, however, that the change is purely quantitative, and that the people on these queues are not driven by any genuine interest in or appreciation for art.

Thus Marya Mannes writes: "I know people who have gone to concerts every week of their lives and say they love music, but most of them can't tell Bach from Haydn or know what a grace note is. . . . Attendance, then, at a cultural event is alone not evidence of culture." She wonders aloud "whether . . . a greater *proportion* of our people cherish the arts than used to." Others are more definite. Poet Randall Jarrell writes about "the appalling taste of the age" and denounces so-called supermarket culture. He is echoed by legions of artists, critics, foundation executives and academics who are absolutely certain that the arts in America are skidding from a none-too-high plateau to a new nadir.

This book will dispute that charge.

Among those who echo the accusation that American culture is decaying are the culture elitists. These people contend that art has always been the special province of an elite, and that once it spreads beyond this elite its standards of excellence necessarily decline. The growth in culture consumption—i.e., the rise of mass public interest in the arts—threatens to swamp the elite or has already done so. Hence, the more Americans show an interest in music, drama, dance, painting or poetry, the more certain it is that the criteria of excellence erected by a cultivated elite will be trampled by a mob of eager ignoramuses.

The high priest of the art-for-elite ideology is that engaging gadfly, Dwight Macdonald, who laments that "While High Culture could formerly address itself only to the *cognoscenti,* now it must take the *ignoscenti* into account. . . . If there were a clearly defined cultural elite here, then the masses could have their *Kitsch* and the classes could have their High Culture, with everybody happy." In short, it is the culture consumer today who dooms art to mediocrity, the elitists declare, and the rise of culture consumption therefore makes it inevitable that the arts in the United States must deteriorate.

This book will test the elitist theory.

Finally, there are those who are simply befuddled by the existence (or non-existence) of the "culture explosion," and by its meaning (or non-meaning). A prime example of this befuddlement is Harold C. Schonberg, music critic of *The New York Times,* and by virtue of that position one of the country's more influential tastemakers. Mr. Schonberg it was who wrote a widely quoted article for the *Saturday Evening Post* under the title: "The National 'Culture Explosion' is Phony." To underscore his meaning, a subtitle rang out: "Hogwash, says a leading critic to the experts who brag that U.S. culture is booming."

Mr. Schonberg opened his article by saying:

"Culture! It is the new fad, the very latest status symbol. We Americans seem desperate to be told we are cultured. And so specialists are obliging us by leaping to rostrums, assuring us that the new renaissance is at hand."

All this would have been more persuasive had not Mr. Schonberg, himself, a short while before, vaulted to the rostrum, as it were, to assure us in the *Times* that:

"Compared with what used to be encountered 25 years ago, the last decade has been virtually a renaissance, and may be recognized as such in history."

Which are we to believe, Mr. Schonberg in the *Saturday*

Evening Post or Mr. Schonberg in *The New York Times?* Or neither? Confusion breeds confusion.

Seldom, in fact, has any non-event, or any event whose significance is zero, managed to stir quite so much confusion and controversy in the tastemaking confraternity. The truth is that there has been a historic shift in the place of the arts in American life. Moreover, this shift is important not only to Americans, but to other nations as well, for it is related to basic economic and class changes brought on by the emergence of industrial society into a stage of affluence. What is happening in the United States today is likely to find its parallel in other societies before long.

The changes to which I refer are complex, but at least some of them are immediately visible to anyone whose eyes are not blinded by theoretical precommitment or by the need to maintain a pose of critical superiority. Each of us has seen some of the signs of the new American attitude toward the arts. We have registered mild surprise, perhaps, on learning that the engineer next door spends one evening a week playing the cello with an amateur string quartet. We have noticed that the housewife down the block goes to an "art center" on Thursday afternoons to model clay. We, ourselves, have unaccustomed difficulty in getting the seats we want at the opera or ballet or theater, and we cannot help but notice that LP records and paperbacks are everywhere. It was not always this way.

For me, personally, the change is symbolized by a single contrast. When I was in college shortly after the war, I spent many hours wandering through the clean, silent galleries of the Museum of Modern Art, gazing at *Guernica* or sitting in the little film theater downstairs as Dr. Caligari went through his paces. Ordinarily there were so few other visitors that I felt the emptiness of the place. It was easy to imagine that the entire museum, with its magnificent collection, belonged to me. And with those other visitors, so few in number, I felt a subtle bond, as if our common presence set us defiantly apart from other Americans. Today the illusion of ownership is no longer possible. The sense of exclusivity is gone. The museum is crowded with "other Americans" and there may well be hundreds more queued up outside waiting to enter. The same is true all over the country, not only at museums, but at concert halls and theaters. The devotees of art have grown from a lonely handful to an army.

Where do they come from, all these people who, until recently, appeared to be indifferent to the arts? What do they want? What motivates them? Only after such questions are answered can one discuss intelligently the influence of the culture consumer on art, itself. Only then can the culture consumer be praised or damned.

In short, if we are to interpret a phenomenon, we must begin by studying its objective characteristics. If an increase in public involvement in the arts threatens our standards of excellence, it seems only sensible to ask how large that involvement is. How many Americans are, in one way or another, interested in the arts? We can never really tell how much the arts mean to an individual or a nation. But we can observe the behavior of that individual or nation and draw appropriate conclusions from it. The man who says he loves to read but hasn't the time for it, must be judged by his actions, not his words. Similarly, the amount of money and time a nation invests in the arts offers us at least a clue to the national attitude. Before we begin to opine about the state of the arts, or of the American psyche and its shortcomings, we ought, in other words, to examine the observable facts. And yet, for all the theorizing and fulmination, this simple thought seems not to have flitted through the brains of those most exercised about the alleged decline of American taste. They prefer dealing with unverifiable generalities. Facts, are, after all, hard to come by. Opinions are more cheaply collected and more easily sold.

Similarly, there is evident on the part of many of the most vehement critics a geographical myopia that can most politely be described as provincialism. They limit their observations to Manhattan Island on the bland assumption that nothing west of the Hudson is of any cultural importance. This may, perhaps, have been true at one time—an arguable point—but it is not true any longer, and if we are to generalize at all about the level of national taste, we ought to have some notion about what is going on in Lincoln, Nebraska, as well as Lincoln Center.

This doesn't mean that an assessment of the health of the arts in America can be based entirely on objective or documentable data. Aesthetic judgments are non-scientific, and even if this were otherwise, intuition must do where information is unavailable. But those who claim concern for the arts have an obligation to review the information that is available before hurling their denunciamentos. They ought to examine the culture consumer before they bait him.

I shall begin, therefore, with a chapter on quantity. I shall attempt to give a rough idea of the amount of culture consumption in this country and how it has changed since the late 1940's. With this as a setting, we focus on the culture consumer. If it is true that the future of taste in this country is in his hands, then we should know more about him. We should study his passions and his foibles, his income, his education, his taste in food, drink, and travel. The more we know about him, the better we will be able to judge his likely impact on the arts.

After we have scrutinized the culture consumer and his motives, as best we can, we shall look at some of the little-noticed changes associated with his rise. One of these is a colorful revolution now sweeping through the boardrooms of our museums, orchestras, and similar institutions, replacing an old elite-minded leadership with a young guard committed to anti-elite objectives. We shall enter these boardrooms to meet the combatants.

No great expansion in culture consumption could occur without changing the relationship of the arts to other segments of our society. Thus we shall examine the altered juxtapositions of art and the university, art and business. We shall also visit some of the great new art centers springing up around the country and probe the rise of a new class of culture bureaucrat.

Shifting to the artist, we will try to find out exactly how garret-poor he is or isn't. We will then sketch the eccentric economics of art, showing why the cost of culture is so high, and why the culture consumer's price of admission is bound to get even higher in the future. If this is so, we can expect that the patron will begin to play an even more central role in art than he now does. Who are the new patrons? How do they differ from the famous patrons of old? How has the patron-artist relationship been transformed in recent years? And what, if any, role should the federal government play in the arts?

A debate over federal aid to the arts is almost a ritual at convocations of artists and art lovers. Yet the debate itself is usually conducted in ritual fashion, with a handful of threadbare arguments rehearsed over and over again. On the one side we are warned that if the federal government does not come immediately to the support of the arts, our entire cultural machine will screech to a halt. On the other, we are warned that federal support of culture is tantamount to socialism—or worse. Seldom does the debate rise above this primitive level.

What makes such discussions so boring and bootless is that anyone feels qualified to participate in them without reference to fact. Everybody from Senator to saxophonist considers himself an expert about federal aid. But almost nobody considers it necessary to develop his expertise by first taking an objective look at what is really happening around the country. This we shall do before, not after, suggesting the proper role of the federal government in the arts.

Finally, we shall return to the aesthetic issues raised by the elitists and others. We shall attempt to test the theory of elitism against reality, to arrive at some estimate of the probable impact of the cultural consumer on taste. Only in this way can we come to conclusions that will be useful in shaping public policy and the day-to-day decisions that determine the direction of movement in our cultural life. Only in this way can the public discussion be raised above the level of airy generality.

It is clear, if we are to travel this path, that a few qualifications and definitions are in order. The term "consumer," for example, has so many contradictory connotations in our society that its use requires comment. I shall define it later on. For the present it is only important to note that I shall employ it throughout in a neutral, non-pejorative sense. By speaking of the culture consumer, moreover, I do not mean to compare him in any simplistic way with consumers of tires or toothpaste or tobacco. Not only is art different from all other commodities or services, but, unlike the consumer of such items as toothpaste, the culture consumer does not necessarily use up that which he consumes. A million people may file past a painting in a museum: they do not in the least reduce its beauty or power. Similarly, they may fill the seats of theaters or concert halls without "devouring" or "destroying" the works of art performed for them. Indeed, the contrary is true: they form by their presence and response a living partnership with the performers.

Nor does the term, as I shall use it, imply passivity. Millions of culture consumers are active amateurs. They paint. They play music. They dance. However we may regard their work, it is clear that they are more than passive receivers. Moreover, the concert-goer or balletomane may sit stock still in his seat, moving only his eyeballs on occasion, and still not be "passive." Certainly there is a high potential for intense activity in examining or apprehending the structure of a sonata or the symbolism of a play. We have no way of knowing or measuring how much activity is going on inside his skull or in the synapses of his nervous system, and it is pointless to speculate. It is presumptuous to term him "passive."

As for the term "culture," it is clear from what I have already written that I am not using the word in its anthropological sense as a synonym for "society." Nor am I using it in the sense employed by sociological analysts of the mass media; I am not talking about what they call "mass culture." I use the term more or less colloquially as a synonym for the fine arts—what the elitists like to call High Culture. Thus I mean by it painting, music, drama, sculpture, dance, literature and the art film. In what follows I do not concern myself, except tangentially, with television, Hollywood, mass magazines or jazz, and only that sector of radio broadcasting that is primarily devoted to classical music will interest us here.

Furthermore, I shall not eschew the term "culture explosion," and I shall, hereafter, drop the quotation marks around it. It is true that Americans are given to linguistic excess, and that the explosion image has been sadly overworked. Still, to the degree that the word explosion connotes change, formless but powerful, it is an apt way of describing the transformation that I believe has taken place in the cultural life of the United States since the late 1940's. The rise of the culture consumer is only the starting point, for his emergence on the scene has brought with it a train of aesthetic, sociological and economic consequences. The phrase culture explosion is a shorthand way of summing up all these changes at once. The phrase may be tired, but no other serves as well.

I shall also refer here and there to the "culture industry," by which I shall mean the entire machinery, physical and social, both commercial and non-profit, that is devoted to producing or distributing the goods and services of artists. Most of us do not like to think of art in such frostily unglamorous terms. But, even though art may be produced by men of genius oblivious to its market potential, once it is communicated beyond a circle of intimates, it becomes a social product. It needs channels of distribution. It requires investment, not only of imagination, but also of measurable time and money. This is true under all economic systems, not only our own, and we cannot begin to understand the relationship of art to society if we insist on blurring this reality.

Lastly, it is a premise of this book that art is less mysterious than the culture elitists would have us believe. At its best, art may be indescribably complex. But it is not divorced from the society around it. Indeed, its content, its typical forms, its quality are all indirectly affected by such mundane considerations as a tremor on Wall Street or a ruling of the Internal Revenue Service. This book will offer no easy rules for understanding modern dance or for pricing a Picasso; but it will explore the links between art and the affluent society in a way that, I believe, has not yet been attempted elsewhere.

This exploration will lead us inevitably back to the charge that aesthetic excellence is incompatible with democracy. Mr. Macdonald assures us that "the conservatives are right when they say there has never been a broadly democratic culture on a high level." That may be so. But it does not prove there cannot be. We live in a strange and wonderful epoch, in which the unprecedented has become commonplace. The truth is that the presumed antithesis of art and democracy has never until now been put to the test in an affluent society in which leisure and education are broadly distributed. The results of that test may happily surprise us.

Let us begin, then, to take our own measure. Let us look at this new and peculiar fascination with the arts—at its outer manifestations, its bulk and weight, its shape and movement, and its kaleidoscopic color.

2

The Quantity of Culture

THE AMERICAN ATTITUDE TOWARD THE ARTS HAS COMPLETED A 180-degree turn since the end of World War II. From one of apathy, indifference, and even hostility, it has become one of eager, if sometimes ignorant, enthusiasm. The distance traveled, and the speed of movement, have been startling, even in an age of rapidly shifting values.

In the beginning there was contempt. In the mid-seventeenth century in England, anti-vagrancy ordinances lumped "rogues, vagabonds, stage-players, and sturdy beggars" in a single breath, and the Puritans shuttered the theaters that only a few generations before had bred Shakespeare and Marlowe. For the card-carrying Puritan, work was sacred, idleness evil, and art, at best, a waste of "God's precious time." It is hardly surprising that this disdain for the arts should have been transplanted to the wilderness on this side of the Atlantic. Even in Virginia, more liberal at the time than the New England colonies, three men were haled into court in 1665 for having had the temerity to mount a play. (It was thus, snarled in litigation, that theater first entered American history.)

In 1700 we find Pennsylvania passing statutes to prohibit "stage-plays, masks, revels." Six years later Cotton Mather was heaping contumely on those who dared to engage in "stage-plays and Mixed dancings," along with readers of "unprofitable" books, and other sinners, including smokers, cardplayers, drinkers and dicethrowers. And when, in 1714, Judge Sewall of Boston heard rumors that a play was to be presented in the council chamber, he harrumphed: "I do forbid it. . . . Let not Christian Boston go beyond heathen Rome in the practice of shameful vanities."

The subsequent slow development of the arts in America cannot be laid wholly at the door of Puritanism. Americans were busy hacking their way through primeval forest. Truly urban communities, essential for the nutrition of the arts, had not yet sprung up. In Washington's time New York had only 33,000 inhabitants, and in all the colonies only 200,000 people lived in communities of 2,500 or more. Moreover, as England's offspring, the colonists brought with them a veneer of culture from the mother country. As de Tocqueville suggested, this relationship made it possible for Americans "to neglect these pursuits (science, literature, and the arts) without relapsing into barbarism."

At the same time, it is a mistake to assume that until recently America was totally innocent of culture. Theater, music, and painting all had begun to take root in the U.S. before 1800, in towns like Charleston, South Carolina, in what is now Winston-Salem, in Philadelphia and New York. The 1840's even saw a boomlet in public interest in painting. The American Art Union, which each year ran a grand lottery with engravings and paintings as prizes, found agents in four hundred cities before a court order put it out of the lottery (and consequently out of the art) business in 1851.

In literature, Melville, Whitman, Emerson, Hawthorne and Poe flourished in the middle of the last century. With the rise of great fortunes after the Civil War the pursuit of culture, at least in its European manifestations, had become part of the status maneuvering of the rich. And by 1904 the traveling Chautauqua, that colorful mixture of culture and uplift under canvas, was a familiar part of the American scene, homogenizing art and oratory along with home economics, vaudeville, and pulpit-pounding.

Still, the psychological force of puritanism persisted long after the demise of Puritanism as an organized movement. The gospel of work and its concomitant contempt for culture remained deeply embedded in middle-class attitudes. When Babbitt snorted, "I may not be any Rockefeller or James J. Shakespeare, but I certainly do know my own mind, and I do keep right on plugging along in the office," he was expressing puritanism's essential hostility to art and leisure, as well as his personal resentment against a son who wanted to be an actor.

And despite the tentative advances of culture in the country, as recently as thirty-five years ago Mencken could accurately characterize vast stretches of the U.S. as a "Sahara of the Bozart" and comment that "the leading American musical director, if he went to Leipzig, would be put to polishing trombones and copying drum parts." Ross of the *New Yorker* could jibe at the philistinism of "the old lady in Dubuque." Even as late as 1945 there was a contemporary bite to such complaints. By the mid-'fifties, however, America's traditional contempt for culture had already begun to change. Indeed, a great surge of public interest in the arts had begun shortly after World War II. Gathering momentum, it has burst forth in recent years with the energy of long-suppressed desire.

Today, instead of contempt, there is craving, and the alacrity with which Americans rush to act in a community theater, to daub at canvas, manipulate clay, practice the piano, or merely to enjoy some "unprofitable" hours in a library or museum, would no doubt give old Judge Sewall a bad case of dyspepsia.

This new appetite for the arts manifests itself in varied ways. It showed itself in President Kennedy's appointment of an official advisor on culture. It is reflected in the culture festivals held in Enid, Oklahoma, Nashville, Tennessee, and scores of other communities. It is manifested in the new liturgical movement that, in the words of one report, "is using plays and musicales to relate religion to contemporary life." It is to be seen in the conference called by the AFL-CIO in 1963 to discuss "the constructive use of free time." It is found in the requirement that when builders work for the Philadelphia Redevelopment Authority they must commit "no less than one per cent" of the contract dollars to the purchase of sculpture and art. And, alas poor Judge Sewall, it is evident in the 200 theatrical productions mounted in a single year in his own Christian Boston.

Just how strong this new tide of culture hunger runs is suggested by how much money Americans invest in it. Nobody can determine this with precision—too much depends on arbitrary definition, and what figures can be pulled together are fragmentary. Nevertheless, within an area of rough agreement the figures are eye-opening. In 1961, in an article for *Fortune,* I reported:

"Americans in 1960 spent nearly $300 million just to operate their 620 art museums. How much more they poured into . . . historical, scientific, and other non-art museums is an unknown but clearly sizable sum. Americans also laid out over $300 million to run their public libraries. They spent some $200 million to buy paintings, prints, color reproductions, and art materials for professional and amateur fine-arts use. They bought $90 million worth of recordings of classical music; they also spent $590 million for musical instruments and $26 million to operate their symphony orchestras—not counting those connected with schools and colleges. Their bill for books ran to at least $1 billion, a figure large enough to leave an impressive sum even after subtracting all the textbooks, westerns, and whodunits. They spent about $375 million at theater, opera, and concert-hall box offices.

"Exactly how much more they spent for art and music education in the schools, or for watercolor instruction and ballet lessons outside the schools, is impossible to know. And no one knows how many millions are being spent to run the literally hundreds of art centers . . . that have sprouted up in wild profusion across the nation in the past decade. Americans spent or donated, all together, a rock-bottom minimum of $3 billion for culture last year, a figure that excludes public funds and business gifts. The significant point is that this sum is 70 per cent more than the comparable estimate for ten years ago." This rate of growth was nearly four times greater than the rate of population growth during the decade.

I might have added, with so much concern voiced nowadays about the power of the mass media, that $3 billion is more than the amount spent each year by the entire broadcasting industry, radio and television both. It is more than is spent on newspapers, and more than twice the amount spent each year to produce our major mass magazines. The figure is no justification for smug pride, but it helps put the overall "bulk" of cultural activity into some kind of perspective.

Moreover, since I wrote that, the figures have been soaring.* The figure for book expenditures now is closer to $1.6 billion than to $1 billion although only a very short time has intervened. Recently, the Stanford Research Institute reported, "The image of the uncultured American has been shattered by a statistical bludgeon." Arnold Mitchell, the S.R.I. economist responsible for this report, predicted that "the trends toward culture will create a total arts market of about $7 billion by 1970." Adds Mr. Mitchell: "I find it somehow quaint that more servicemen visiting New York go to the Museum of Modern Art than to any other attraction except for the Empire State Building."

Mr. Mitchell's servicemen are not oddballs. Americans have become a nation of museumgoers, as foreign visitors note with surprise when they make the tourist rounds. A survey of 21 museums alone showed an aggregate attendance of 19,370,000 in 1958. Within two years this had climbed to 21,360,000—a gain of more than ten per cent. Across the country museums are making room for unaccustomed crowds.

Libraries, too, are doing a thriving business. The number of volumes in public libraries has shot up from 143,000,000 in 1950 to 210,000,000 in 1960. Nor were these volumes merely gathering dust. Total public library circulation reached a record high of 677 million volumes in 1958, and the number of individual borrowers has probably gone up fifty per cent in the past ten years.

The audience was avidly buying books, too. The 'fifties saw the occurrence of the so-called "paperback explosion" which brought inexpensive editions of books on poetry, music, aesthetics, and art within easy reach of the consumer, and the reading jag that this both stimulated and reflected is bound to continue. The National Book Committee, in a recent report, used the words "culture fever" to describe the new situation. A survey conducted by the Committee indicated that in the past five years

* The only important exception, to my knowledge, is a drop in the dollar volume of classical record sales. The decline, in all likelihood, represents a temporary dip in a curve that has been climbing irregularly for a decade or more.

book sales and library circulation have increased three times more rapidly than the population.

Americans have been delighting their ears as well as nourishing their minds. According to the American Symphony Orchestra League, the increase in symphony attendance in recent years has been nothing short of "phenomenal," with the League now receiving more reports of sold-out concert halls than at any time since it began keeping records. Typically, the Detroit Symphony watched its attendance rise from 300,000 to 700,000 per year in a decade. With this kind of encouragement, new symphonies have formed at a rapid rate and old ones have increased the length of their seasons. There were approximately eight hundred symphonies in the U.S. in 1950. Today there are about twelve hundred and fifty and most of the new ones have cropped up in cities with 50,000 population or less. In all, it is estimated that these orchestras played to an aggregate attendance of ten million.

In opera a similar splurge has occurred. The Metropolitan Opera Association has doubled the number of performances it gives each year in New York and is playing to virtual capacity. Nor is the Met alone. There are 710 opera-producing groups, mainly amateur, in the U.S., and more starting all the time. The Detroit Opera Theatre, born only a few years ago, scored notable success in staging professional chamber opera, including such off-the-beaten-path works as Douglas Moore's *Gallantry,* and Donizetti's *The Night Bell,* both of which played to SRO audiences. Chicago formed a professional opera company in 1954. Dallas organized one in 1957 which is already putting on an eight-performance season in a 4,200-seat hall.

At the same time, culture consumers were thronging record stores, taking home with them each year about 17.5 million discs of what not long ago was derisively termed "long hair stuff." Housewives have been buying classical LP's along with their frozen vegetables at the nearby supermarket. Moreover, the 'fifties saw a spectacular rise in amateur music-making. According to the American Music Conference, the number of amateur instrumentalists jumped from 19 million in 1950 to 35.5 million in 1963 and the dollar volume of instrument sales soared more than 175 per cent.

The boom in music sprang from a popular base that was already fairly broad. In contrast, ever since the rise of the camera put the small-town journeyman portrait painter out of business in the last decades of the nineteenth century, American painters and their admirers had more or less huddled in a New York ghetto bounded by Fifty-seventh Street on the north and Greenwich Village on the south. For this reason, the mushrooming of mass interest in painting is even more startling than the surge of musical activity.

In 1950 there were about 150 art galleries in New York and perhaps an equal number spread thinly across the country, mostly in its larger cities. Today there are over 300 galleries in New York alone, and nobody has been able to count up the hundreds that have burgeoned in places like Flint, Michigan, and Quincy, Illinois. In Phoenix, Arizona, there were two galleries in 1950, four in 1955. The four did a combined business estimated at $100,000. Five years later there were at least fifteen galleries with an estimated volume of $1,500,000. In Rochester, New York, a small, well-designed gallery exhibits highly professional work on the mezzanine floor of a downtown shopping plaza.

Galleries range from old and richly impressive Fifty-seventh Street emporiums like Wildenstein's, where it is not surprising to see a Rembrandt change hands, to a new kind of surburban or semi-suburban gallery like the Raven, which opened its doors in Detroit in July, 1960. The Raven is a storefront operation nestled in a quiet residential neighborhood. Started on a shoestring of $5,000 by an art-loving former printer named Herbert Cohen, the tastefully laid-out gallery sells sculpture and paintings for from $10 to $2,300, all the work of Michigan artists. To attract the public, Cohen stages chamber music recitals and discussions on cultural subjects for broadcast on WQRS, a local FM station. He serves patrons sandwiches and cafe espresso. In its first year, The Raven counted 40,000 visitors. Such turnouts are no longer uncommon. It is true that the mortality rate among such small (and often under-capitalized) galleries is high. They come and go. But for every one that closes, several new ones spring up to serve the growing army of small collectors.

The new passion for paintings has encouraged other establishments to get into the act. The District of Columbia in 1959 was forced to crack down on a bistro which sold paintings off its walls in violation of local liquor regulations. In Detroit a Buick dealer has used exhibits of original paintings, prints, and etchings at prices from $200 to $300 to lure customers in for automobiles, and a home builder has been selling paintings off the walls of his model homes. More and more organizations, from Junior Leagues to Tammany Clubs, are holding art sales as fund raising events, and the quintessence of this new mania for pigment was probably reached not very long ago when inmates of a California prison put on their own exhibition billed by officials as "the nation's largest—and perhaps finest—prison art show."

Beneath this mass interest in the graphic arts lies an amateur movement that, like the amateur movement in music, began a long, powerful upswing after the war and has not yet crested. The National Art Materials Trade Association estimates that the number of Sunday painters has risen from 30 million in 1950 to 40 million in 1960, perhaps a million of whom are actually taking lessons. Such statistics are necessarily spongy, but the new public attitude they reflect is unmistakable. The breadth and variety of the amateur movement is illustrated by what happened in 1957 when a young woman producer suggested that KQED, a San Francisco educational TV station, air a half-hour program about Japanese brush painting. Since it was to be a "how-to" program, she conceived the idea of selling brush painting kits. Accordingly, she bought 300 sets and exhibited them at the end of the program. "Frankly," says James Day, general manager of the station "I was skeptical. I told her I hoped she had made arrangements to return all the sets she couldn't sell." The station eventually sold 14,000 sets at $3 each, and the program has since been sold to fifty-three other TV channels around the country.

Like painting, the professional theater in America was, until the current breakthrough began, constricted within a tiny area in mid-Manhattan. Today, despite the mournful cries issuing from the offices of Broadway producers, the theater in America is bubbling with vitality. Not since the death of vaudeville has the average American had more opportunity to enjoy live drama.

While audiences for high-cost Broadway productions dwindled during the 'fifties, a new theater has sprung up right next door which has not only developed scores of talented actors, directors, and producers, but has introduced to the nation the work of significant modern playwrights whom Broadway until recently ignored. This is, of course, the off-Broadway theater which has grown from a handful of houses in 1950 into thirty-two playhouses in 1964 and which, according to Paul Liben of the League of Off-Broadway Theaters and Producers, annually takes in an estimated $3 million from nearly one million theater-goers. The success of off-Broadway has been a factor in encouraging the formation of professional resident acting companies of extremely high quality in cities like Minneapolis, Pittsburgh, Milwaukee, Houston, Washington and San Francisco.

The 'fifties witnessed the organization of scores of other professional and hundreds of semi-professional and amateur groups. According to *Variety*, there are now about 5,000 non-professional theater groups in the U.S., plus about the same number of college theaters, and perhaps 15,000 more groups in clubs, churches, and schools. It estimates that 500,000 amateur productions run up an attendance of about 100 million each year.

The rise of a mass interest in the arts is reflected in the structure and programming of the mass media as well. In the late 'forties, there were about a dozen movie houses—half of them in New York—that regularly screened so-called art films, foreign films, movie classics and experimental shorts. Since then the audience for these has swelled to the point at which today it supports an "art circuit" of some 500 theaters. Some films imported for showings in this circuit have attracted so much public attention that they have gone on to play more than 5,000 downtown and neighborhood houses. The quality of films shown in the art circuit is uneven, and many, if not most, art houses mix what the trade bluntly calls "exploitation films" (read "sex") in with their art. But the rise of the art film—mostly imported footage—is highly significant, coming as it did during a decade that saw overall movie attendance drop from 60 million a week to 40 million. It is not accidental that Americans are laying out a conservatively estimated $125 million a year for tickets to these films.

Similar changes are to be found in broadcasting. Witness the rise of FM radio stations devoted almost entirely to broadcasting classical music, discussions of art, literature, and related subjects. There are today more than 400 FM stations of this type with a large and faithful body of listeners. WFMT in Chicago, which doesn't hesitate to broadcast all four-and-a-half hours of Wagner's *Parsifal* without interruption for commercials, in 1958 broke into the "Top Ten" list of Chicago stations according to size of listenership. WFMT sells 25,000 subscriptions to its monthly program guide to its more devoted listeners who pay $5 a year to find out when they can hear a performance of a suite by Telemann or a reading of T. S. Eliot's poetry. Commercial television, once described by former Chairman Newton Minow of the FCC as a "wasteland," has made only very tentative probes in the direction of cultural programming, but there are minor portents pointing in this direction. Moreover, the number of educational TV stations has been increasing, and if pay-TV becomes a reality and lives up to its advance billing, it might provide the kind of specialized programming that FM and art theaters provide for their public.

Such facts merely skim the surface of the culture surge. They only suggest its scope and force. Yet the objection is often heard that statistics mean nothing in matters of art. Perhaps so. Perhaps numbers can tell us nothing about art. But they can tell us something about society. And art, after all, is what happens between an artist and his society. Those who deny the importance of such facts forget that quantitative changes have a way of becoming qualitative. A quantitative rise in temperature changes the qualitative state of matter. A quantitative increase in the firepower of weapons has altered qualitatively the entire meaning of war and race survival.

August Heckscher, director of the Twentieth Century Fund and the man President Kennedy chose as his Special Consultant on the Arts, has said: "When all has been said in the way of caution and disparagement, the fact remains that numbers *are* important. The United States today is in the midst of a vast quantitative expansion of its cultural life. Where so much is happening, at least some of it must be good." This not to argue that these quantifiable changes have made us overnight into a "cultured nation"—whatever that scintillating abstraction signifies. It is merely to say that something has happened, something quite revolutionary.

What this represents is not merely money, but a massive investment of time, energy, and emotion. Millions of Americans as consumers and participants, hundreds of thousands as members and volunteer workers, are putting a little bit of their lives not merely into a search for aesthetic satisfaction, but into building and leading the institutions needed to produce and distribute culture in America. To proclaim an interest in the arts is no longer to make oneself an outcast. In many circles it is, indeed, a passport to status. The boorish businessman nowadays who jibes at "James J. Shakespeare" feels a twinge of guilt in doing so. And conversely, for the first time in our history millions of individuals are experiencing—without guilt—some of the exquisite pleasures of good music, dance, drama, painting and sculpture. For the arts have been liberated from their prison cell and brought into the sunlight. In the process, they have lost some of their charisma. They appear now to be less mystifying, less "special," less exalted than in the past. There they are, as it were, on the supermarket shelf, and what could be more natural?

Culture is now, for many people, an altogether everyday affair, capable of yielding intense joy, but no longer awesome. Perhaps something has been lost in this process, some sense of the majesty of accomplishment of truly great art. Yet this loss, if indeed it has occurred, need not be permanent, and there are ample reasons to be optimistic. We are busy freeing the arts in our society from their dependence upon a tiny, cult-like following. We are converting, as it were, from cult to culture.

3

The Culture Consumers

"POETS DO NOT WRITE FOR POETS ALONE, BUT FOR MEN," DECLARED Wordsworth. But for what kind of men? Maoris? Edwardians? Hoboken stevedores? Throughout history artists have been influenced, consciously or unconsciously, by the character of the audience for their works. Not only the content, but the form of art works, reflect, at least in part, the cultural audience of their time. Certainly, the kind of flash that occurs between a work of art and its apprehender is conditioned by the character of the apprehender or "consumer." An audience of Papuans hearing Bach's *Goldberg Variations* for the first time clearly must experience something different than an audience consisting solely of Juilliard students. If we are concerned with the impact of the culture explosion on art and the artist—or, conversely, with the impact of art or artist on audience—we must ask ourselves a single central question: Who is the culture consumer? Who are these millions who, to the discomfiture of the elitists, are crowding our museums and concert halls and theaters nowadays?

Culture in America was never as tightly monopolized by a few as it was in countries having a feudal heritage. Yet the overall audience for the fine arts has been so small, relative to the size of the population, as to have created a monopoly by default. Moreover, this tiny audience was hardly a representative cross-section of society as a whole. No scientific basis exists for analyzing the culture-consuming public of a generation or two ago. Nevertheless, three main components of the audience can be identified. There was, first, the Europe-oriented rich. Next there were the alienated intellectuals, often bitterly critical of what they viewed as a crassly materialistic society, followed by artists and would-be artists, a small but important part of the total. The audience was also, if we can believe contemporaneous accounts, heavily female. The woman traditionally was responsible for bringing culture into the home. Finally, it was decidedly adult. The composition of the culture public shifted, of course, from time to time, place to place. But by and large the audience lacked any strong delegation from the great middle class of America, or from its masses of working people and farmers.

The recent growth of a mass audience for the arts has changed all this dramatically. Millions of Americans have been attracted to the arts, changing the composition of the audience profoundly. This change has been praised and damned as a "democratization" of the arts. A major step toward democratization has, indeed, been taken. Yet we would be sorely deluded if we jumped to the conclusion that all Americans today are equal participants in the culture boom. The culture public today is still by no means a neat cross-section of the total population. It is far more representative than the arts audience of the past, but there are extremely large sectors of the American population that remain untouched by the new wave of interest in the arts. It is important, therefore, that we determine, as best we can, just how far the process of democratization has gone, and where, for all practical purposes, it stops. To do this we must begin to paint, as it were, a portrait of the culture consumer.

This is not easy. Consumer research has been able for years to tell us in mind-numbing detail what the average American automobile purchaser or soap user is like, what he earns, how many bathtubs, television sets, or educational degrees he has, and where his warts are located. There has been no comparable body of data about the culture consumer. Nevertheless, in the past few years a number of pioneering attempts have been made to accumulate data on the arts audience. The market researchers themselves have begun to evince an interest in the culture consumer. By pulling together such fragmentary statistics as do exist, by attempting a few educated guesses, and by calling upon the impressionistic evidence of well-placed observers, we can begin to trace the outlines of the portrait.

The first problem is definitional. There is no agreement as to what a truly cultured person is. There never has been. It is easier, however, to speak of a culture consumer. Let us arbitrarily say that, for our purposes, a culture consumer is a person who listens to classical music, or attends concerts, plays, operas, dance recitals or art films, or visits museums or galleries, or whose reading reflects an interest in the arts. Let us also include by definition all those who participate, as either professional or amateur, in what we loosely call artistic activity—i.e., the painters (of both the Sunday and weekday varieties), the actors, dancers, musicians, etc. Let us also include the millions of children who are "consuming" art or music lessons at home or in school. It is obvious that this is a jaggedly crude definition. It is full of unanswered questions. But it is better than none at all. It permits us to begin.

The initial question in any discussion of the arts audience in America must be that of size. Just how large a mass of people is involved? What figures can we start with as a base upon which to build? We know, thanks to the market researchers, that in any average week about 3,500,000 individuals listen to classical music broadcasts over the stations of the Market One network alone. We have, for what it is worth, *Variety's* estimate that attendance at amateur theatrical productions runs in the neighborhood of 100 million per year. How often did each individual attend? Few amateur companies mount more than half-a-dozen productions a year, and even if we assume every individual attended all six in his or her community (an unlikely assumption) we would come up with a minimum figure of between 16 and 17 million individuals. Similarly, if we take the fact that American museums ticked off a total attendance figure of between 200 million and 250 million in 1962, we can attempt the same kind of crude extrapolation. No one knows what the average frequency of attendance was, but if we assume, not too unreasonably, that the average museum attender did not attend more often than four times a year, we arrive at a total of at least 50 million individuals who set foot in a museum.

Let us arbitrarily reduce that number by half, inasmuch as many museums are devoted to subjects other than art. Let us take into account the estimate that 35.5 million Americans play musical instruments and the estimate that 40 million daub at a canvas now and then. Let us allow some factor for those who buy records or attend art films and who are not otherwise accounted for in the above enumeration. Performing similar statistical arabesques with other attendance figures, allowing wide margin for error, and checking them against income and education figures which, as we shall see, are important in any consideration of the arts audience, we arrive at a frankly unscientific, but nevertheless reasonable, conclusion that within the total 185 million population in the United States there is a sub-group of between 30 million and 45 million individuals who fit the rough definition given above.

This figure of 30–45 million individuals will unquestionably bring a gasp of indignation from many. It sounds ludicrously high. It will seem less so, however, if we bear two points in mind. First, while we have spoken of these people as culture *consumers,* we must remember that much of the culture consumed is free of charge. Most museums, for example, charge no admission. Music and art lessons are available free in many communities, not only to children but to adults as well. A good many concerts are open to the public at no cost, as are plays, dance recitals, and similar events. Second, we must remember what this figure is not. It emphatically does not mean that there are that many "cultured Americans." Within this vast pool are some people for whom the arts are, indeed, a way of life. But the overwhelming majority, we may quite safely assume, are only casually interested in one or another of the arts. Still and all, if our rough guess is correct—even give or take several million—it provides a clue to the location of the arts in the geography of American life. It tells us that, while cultural activity, broadly conceived, is not something in which a majority of Americans engage, it is nonetheless a part of the lives (albeit, perhaps, a small part) of a very substantial minority.

Simply in terms of mass, therefore, we are justified in speaking of a democratization as having occurred. This many people are no longer a cult. If these figures are at all correct, they mean that anywhere from one out of six to one out of four Americans is involved, in one way or another, with what we might call the culture industry. This is a degree of diffusion that few societies, past or present, can match.

Before we can move on, however, to determine to what degree these masses of people are representative of the total population, we need to know more about them. Fortunately, even with the very limited data available, we can begin to draw certain conclusions. For example, it is safe to say that since the end of World War II there has been a sharp increase in the proportion of men in the culture public. In pre-war days father had to be coerced to attend a concert. Yet today a visit to the concert hall, or to a museum or theater, will reveal a more or less even division between men and women. A survey conducted in 1955 by the Minneapolis Symphony Orchestra already showed that 42 per cent of its audience was male. Among readers of *American Artist,* a magazine for amateur painters, 40 per cent are male. And a recent study of the audience of the Tyrone Guthrie Theatre in Minneapolis reflects about the same distribution: 55 per cent female, 45 per cent male. On Broadway, where theater-going sometimes comes under the heading of business entertainment, the audience is predominantly male. A survey conducted by Thomas Gale Moore of the Carnegie Institute of Technology among the audiences of eight Broadway shows turned up a ratio of 63 per cent men to 37 per cent women. The old Maggie and Jiggs stereotype of the husband who is dragooned to the theater or concert hall by force is anachronous. An American male is no longer regarded as a "sissy" if he shows an interest in the arts. What this shift in numbers will mean eventually in terms of the psychological response of audiences, the kind of programming preferred, the tastes for color, sound, or form, the appreciation or lack of appreciation for such qualities as subtlety—all these remain to be discovered. But it is clear that a striking change has occurred.

This shift toward increased male participation in the culture market has been accompanied, I think, by a drop in the average age of the culture consumer. Here the data is more fragmentary and decidedly impressionistic. But a surprising number of professional administrators in the arts, who have an opportunity to observe the audience first-hand, report being struck by the presence of youth in its midst. Alfred Barr, director of museum collections at the Museum of Modern Art, has remarked that when he was a young man, "I didn't know any girl at Vassar and only one girl at Smith who would go to a gallery. And it's possible," he adds wryly, "that she went only because I wanted to." Today, he says, "it's a cheering and amusing experience going through the galleries with my daughter. She sees her friends and is saluted by them. They used to be teen-agers. Now they are in their twenties."

Barr's personal impression is supported by that of Perry T. Rathbone, director of the Boston Museum of Fine Arts, who says his museum now draws more people in the 20–40 age bracket than it did in years past. In Richmond, Leslie Cheek, director of the Virginia Museum of Fine Arts, calls attention to the increasing number of "young marrieds" on his membership list. He has suggested that after a young couple settle down and have their first child, they turn to the museum as a relatively inexpensive yet satisfying way to invest their leisure time.

Similarly, Harry Abrams, a leading publisher of art books, in appraising his market, concludes that the largest part of it lies with customers in the 25–45 age bracket, a group, he says, that is particularly alert to new trends.

In music, the Minneapolis orchestra survey showed that 54 per cent of its attendance was 35 years or under, and when a reporter asked managers of a number of Boston-area opera groups to describe their audiences, they, too, emphasized the young set, people 30 and under. They commented about seeing a large number of students on dates. Even more striking is the estimate by Bryan Halliday of Janus Films, a leading distributor of art movies, that as much as 90 per cent of the audience for foreign art films is under 40.

One can hardly be dogmatic about the evidence, but it would seem that young people are more important in the arts audience today than at any time in memory. This should not surprise us. The median age of the American population as a whole is plummeting. It has been estimated that by 1966 fully 50 per cent of the total population of the country will be under 25 years of age. This, of course, is an astonishing fact by itself. Yet its implications for art are still to be explored. They will be immense. Ask any actor or musician whether or not he senses a difference when he performs for young people. The answer will be "yes." The increasing youthfulness of the culture consumer will affect programming deeply. For one thing, the younger the audience, the more receptive it is likely to be to all forms of innovation and experiment.

In terms of sex and age, therefore, it can be said that the culture public has become more truly representative of the total population than ever before. It is when we begin to examine the economic and educational characteristics of the arts audience that we see just how far the process of democratization has advanced, and how far from complete it is. Before World War II it was still possible to refer to the culture public as an elite audience. In most communities, especially the smaller ones, its core was the wealthy, old-stock, conservative upper stratum of the population. Today the locus has shifted definitely and irretrievably downward. But not all the way. What has happened is the rise of a new class to importance in the arts: the "comfort class."

In 1947 only 30 per cent of all American families and unrelated individuals had an income equivalent to $6,000 or more in 1962 dollars. By 1962, a brief fifteen years later, fully 48 per cent were in the $6,000 or more category, and one family in five had an income of more than $10,000 per year. This statistical fact has brought about dramatic changes in the structure of American society. It is not enough for our purposes to refer to the growth of the "middle class" or to, as David Riesman puts it, the "middle millions." For "middle" implies that part of the group earns more and part earns less than the median income of the nation. But the median income of the nation as late as 1962 was lower than $6,000. Thus the group referred to here was, by definition, above the national income norm. It could be termed the "upper half" or, more traditionally, "the upper middle." Yet both of these terms are unsatisfactory because they focus purely on the economic characteristics of the group. The term "comfort class" is more apt. It suggests something not merely about the group's economic condition, but about its psychological outlook.

There is a certain income point, different in each community but lying somewhere between $6,000 and $10,000, beyond which a family need no longer concern itself solely about "basics." It becomes, as it were, comfort-oriented. It shifts its attention from quantity to quality. It begins to reach out for the minor luxuries.

It begins to care about "the better things of life"—meaning, very often, non-material things. The comfort class is not the rich-rich. Neither is it the poor or middle-income group. It lies halfway between middle and rich-rich. It is aggressive. It is moving up the scale. Its horizons are widening every day, both economically and psychologically. It is interested in comfort, in fulfillment, in nicety, not just necessity. The last decade and a half has seen an explosive growth in the number of families in this category, a tremendous spread of the new attitudes of this "comfort class." And it is from among these that the new culture public is drawn. The rich, of course, are still with us. They still own paintings and go to concerts. But numerically they form a relatively small part of the total audience. The culture consumer is, most often, a member of the comfort class.

What evidence supports this assertion? Let us begin with income. Between October, 1960, and October, 1961, *Playbill*, a publication distributed to Broadway theater-goers, conducted a survey of the audience at 368 different Broadway performances. It concluded that the median family income of those attending the theater was $10,032. During 1961, *Bravo*, a comparable publication that is distributed to the audiences at subscription concerts throughout the country, surveyed concert-goers in 81 cities. Median household income turned out to be $10,419.

The only other comprehensive data on the income of the culture consumer comes from readership studies made by magazines whose readers can be assumed to be culture consumers. *Theatre Arts*, for example, claims that its readers have a median income of $15,000. *The Saturday Review*, readers of which may be presumed to be interested in literature and music, claims a reader income figure of $13,090. *Show*, which calls itself "The Magazine of the Arts," reports a median of $13,049. For *Dance*, the leading magazine in its field, the figure lies between $9,000 and $10,000. And the readers of *American Artist* run up a median of $9,910.

Let us make appropriate discount for error or inflation; let us agree that these surveys represent soundings taken at different times, different places, under different circumstances, and with differing degrees of skill and scientific responsibility. Granted all this, the degree of concurrence is still remarkable.

In a country in which the national median income lies between

$5,000 and $6,000 we find the lowest reported median for one of these cultural audiences to be about $9,000. Making all due allowances for error, we still find that the typical culture consumer is far above the national norm in income. Sociologists and economists tell us that the model of American society is no longer that of a pyramid with a broad base of low-income families, a small middle-income group, and a tiny aristocracy, but that of a diamond. If so, the culture consumer is clearly a part of that trapezoid that sits just above the center bulge.

Our culture consumer, it will be no surprise to learn, is also far better educated than the man in the street. He may not have completed college, but the odds are roughly four out of five that he has had at least some exposure to higher education or that the head of his household has. The *Bravo* concert hall study and the Guthrie theater audience study both found that between 80 and 83 per cent of those in their audience had attended college or were members of families headed by a person who had been to college. Only *Playbill*'s Broadway audience differed somewhat. Its survey found that 66 per cent of the total had attended college. Once again, with the exception of the *Playbill* results, we have a remarkable concurrence. Even allowing for the *Playbill* figures, the weight of evidence is overwhelming.

This does not mean that there are not in our country some poorly educated Italian shoemakers who nourish a passion for grand opera or some denim-clad ditch-diggers with an appetite for abstract expressionism. What it does mean is that they form a small part of the total culture public. The culture consumer is, by American standards, a well-educated person. In fact, there is evidence that education is the single most important indicator of a person's cultural status, more important even than income. In short, an educated person without money is more likely to be a culture consumer than a rich person without an education. But these are the extremes. In most cases, education and income go hand in hand.

If we analyze the culture consuming public by occupation we find further supporting evidence. Thus we discover that families in which the head of the household may be termed a professional or technical employee form a heavily disproportionate part of the culture public. In April, 1962, the U.S. Department of Labor found that, of all employed persons, only 12.8 per cent fell into the category it calls "professional, technical and kindred workers." Each of the arts audience studies uses a somewhat different category. But the high proportion of professional-technical people is noticeable throughout. In the Guthrie and Minneapolis Symphony studies and in the *Bravo* survey the correlation is within a few percentage points. All three report that between 32 and 35 per cent of their attendance fall into the professional or technical classification.

The most interesting breakdown is provided by the *Bravo* study of concert hall audiences which not only asked the occupation of the attender but of the head of the household. Thus students and housewives were asked to report the occupation of their family breadwinner. The survey found that 43.6 per cent of the total audience households were headed by professionals. It went on to show in what proportions:

Education	
(Professors, teachers, school administrators)	13.1%
Scientists	
(Engineers, chemists, architects, mathematicians, etc.)	10.8%
Medicine	
(Doctors, dentists, pharmacists, etc.)	7.3%
Lawyers, judges	2.1%
Accountants, auditors	1.9%
All other	
(Including clergymen, artists, librarians, nurses, editors, medical technicians, etc.)	8.4%
	43.6%

If professionals and their families make up the single largest occupation block in the audience, they are followed by what might loosely be called businessmen or executives and their families. Some studies simply lump the business and professional categories together. Thus the *Playbill* study claims that 57.1 per cent of Broadway theater-goers are in families headed by someone in the business-executive-professional class.

It must be emphasized again that these studies are fragmentary at best and that they are, unfortunately, not directly compatible with one another. In consequence, the figures should not be taken literally. But they appear to indicate the relative orders of magnitude correctly, and they add up to the finding that the culture public is a selective, rather than representative, slice of the U.S. population, with the professional-technical component playing a central role.

Ethnically, too, there is evidence that the culture audience is still far from being an accurate mirror of society. For example, although there is no statistical data that even attempts to analyze the racial or religious background of the arts public, conversations with gallery directors, orchestra managers, and other arts administrators in many cities lead one to conclude that the culture public contains a higher than proportionate number of Jewish people. Jews, of course, have always been prominent as artists. (Count the number of Jews among the world's finest violinists, for example.) But, except perhaps for New York, where the Jewish population is very large, the Jewish community has probably not been disproportionately represented in the culture audience until recent years. The breakdown of anti-Semitism in society at large, and the general process of cultural democratization that we have been describing, along with the acceleration of assimilation among Jews, are all reflected now, it would appear, in increasing culture consumption by American Jews.

The extension director of a university in California, in discussing the rising level of cultural activity in Los Angeles, cites the growth of the Jewish population there as a causative agent. A museum director in San Antonio says: "The vast majority of collectors here are Jewish." In Dallas the arts attract considerable support from the Jewish community. Detroit, as we shall see later, has witnessed a very perceptible change in the degree of Jewish involvement in community cultural life since the war. So enthusiastically have American Jews taken to the cultural explosion that some Jewish leaders have begun to complain that this interest in the arts is diverting their money and attention from more traditional pursuits.

Sam Freeman, an official of the National Jewish Welfare Board, has been quoted as saying that "Jewish [community] activities tend to get overshadowed by the enormous appeal of creative activities in the general community." And *The Reconstructionist,* a Jewish magazine, complains, perhaps melodramatically, that "whereas public concert and lecture halls report 'standing room only' at many programs . . . Jewish [community centers], even the newest and most elaborate, are usually shrouded in darkness."

There is still another discernible characteristic of the culture consumer that is worth noting: his relatively high mobility. The class we have been describing tends, in general, to travel more, to move more often, to progress up and down the social scale more rapidly than most Americans. Many of the young executives, professionals, and technicians who with their families form the backbone of the culture public, are in fact modern-day migratory workers transplanted from community to community by their corporate employers. Many of them who come from larger cities suddenly find themselves living in small towns with limited or underdeveloped cultural resources. The newcomers, who not infrequently arrive en masse, promptly enroll in existing arts organizations, generate a good bit of cultural activity, and help form the audience. An excellent illustration of the process is to be found in Winston-Salem, North Carolina, where Western Electric opened a large new installation after World War II. The new plant brought with it a large body of professional, technical, and white-collar employees. In 1960 a survey found that seventeen per cent of all the names on the mailing lists of the city's primary arts organizations were those of Western Electric employees or their relatives.

If these observations are generally correct, then we may begin to sum up the distinguishing marks of the new culture audience: It is youthful. It is almost evenly divided between the sexes. It is financially comfortable. It is well-educated. It has a high proportion of professional, technical or executive families in it. There is a perceptible degree of Jewish participation in it. And it is relatively mobile.

This summary, by inference, also tells us who is not a part of the culture public. Thus, every survey so far conducted bears out the finding that blue-collar and service workers, for example, form only a minuscule part of the total. Despite the progress of democratization, the fact remains that the mass of American workers and farmers are not participants in the culture boom.

The Minneapolis Symphony Orchestra study in 1955 showed that of the audience in attendance the night of the survey, a bare two per cent could be classified as workers. Seven years later the Guthrie study in the same city showed only 3.1 per cent in the category that included "craftsman, foreman, laborer, farmer, etc., plus unemployed." Clearly this is a generalization. The degree to which workers and their families are part of the audience varies with such factors as the price of admission, the complexity of the material presented, the amount of mass-media advertising or publicity surrounding the attraction, the social traditions of the community, the posture of the particular arts organization or institution toward the public and toward the lower income groups specifically. It no doubt varies also from one art field to another. Nevertheless, there is little doubt that the worker and his family are badly under-represented in the total culture public.

Similarly, as might be expected from these results, the number of Negroes in the culture audience is infinitesimal. The question of the racial composition of the culture public is complicated by the continued practice of segregation in a good many theaters, concert halls, and other arts facilities. Actors' Equity, the theatrical union, has instructed its members to refuse engagements in segregated theaters. But the policy is by no means airtight, and there are many actors and actresses who do not belong to Equity. In music, when pianist Gary Graffman not long ago refused to perform in a segregated auditorium in Jackson, Mississippi, the German pianist Hans Richter-Haaser stepped forward to fill the engagement, commenting that "as a foreigner" he saw no connection between music and the race issue. One wonders at a conception of music that excludes any consideration of who the audience is. Nevertheless, the fact remains that even where segregation policies do not bar Negroes, indeed, even where Negroes are actively welcomed, they form only a tiny part of the audience.

In Detroit where a special effort was made to attract blue-collar workers and Negroes to a series of city-wide arts events, the results were dismal. In Waterloo, Iowa, where the community arts center is municipally supported and is located in the heart of the Negro district, hardly a handful of Negroes make use of its activities. In some cities, of course, such as Winston-Salem, Negroes have their own amateur theater, art classes, and the like.

Many Negro colleges run active cultural programs and the appearance of Leontyne Price in a concert hall will attract a sizable Negro turnout. Nevertheless, the evidence is heavy that, percentagewise, the culture boom is still very much a white man's affair.

The culture consumer, as part of the rapidly growing comfort class, shares with others a particular style of life. A man who has made a considerable effort to study this style is a balding, voluble market researcher named Emanuel Demby, president of Motivational Programmers, Inc. Demby works for many of the nation's large broadcasters, publishers and manufacturers. In the process he has compiled what he calls a research bank of data about the tastes and idiosyncrasies of precisely that population slice from which the culture public is so largely drawn. Hedging his remarks because of the looseness of the definition of the culture consumer, and because so many of the salient statistics are simply nonexistent, Demby nevertheless begins to fill in the portrait of the culture consumer with what must be regarded as speculative, though provocative, detail.

"If you looked into the home of your culture consumer," he says, "you would almost certainly find in it some kind of equipment for reproducing music—a record player or tape recorder. Between 70 and 95 per cent of your families would own them. Owning a phonograph or tape recorder obviously doesn't make a person a culture consumer. But almost all culture consumers own them. Far more of them proportionally than the public at large." In contrast, Demby says, they probably own fewer television sets per hundred families than the general public.

Several years ago the Opinion Research Corp. of Princeton, New Jersey, made a provocative study of what it called *America's Tastemakers*. Its interest was not in aesthetic taste, but in the degree of acceptance of new products. In short, it wanted to know which individuals were most likely to be the first ones on their block to adopt a new consumer item, thus setting a pattern for their neighbors. It came to the conclusion that a high degree of mobility, as measured on seven different scales,* coincided with a receptivity to new ideas or products. Demby uses somewhat differ-

---

* The seven scales measure mobility in terms of geography; education; economics; social relations; kinship relations; occupation, and intellect.

ent terms, but he agrees with the general drift of the tastemaker theory, and says, "the culture consumer is likely to have a great many convenience appliances in his home long before, even years before, their use becomes general. You will find electric can openers, automatic slide projectors, electric dishwashers and garbage disposals far more often in the home of the culture consumer than you will outside this group." This same willingness to take a chance can be observed in a higher readiness to use air travel. Of course, there is an important economic factor at work. Air travel is expensive. But, according to Demby, the families in the culture consumer category are twice as likely to fly to their vacation site as the run-of-the-mill American family. They differ radically from the public, too, in what they would consider an ideal vacation. Most Americans, given their preference, would go to Hawaii for a holiday, Demby believes. The culture consumer, in contrast, lists Europe as his number one choice.

Mobility suggests what might be called "automobility." Culture consumers, Demby is persuaded, buy more new cars than used cars, whereas the reverse is true of the public in general. And one out of five autos parked in the carports or garages of culture consumer families is likely to be of foreign make. They use these cars to get to their summer homes very often, because, if Demby is accurate, as many as one out of every four families in this group owns a second home. More than half also own at least a small portfolio of stocks, bonds, or mutual fund shares.

In purchasing major household appliances, the culture consumer tends to buy the same name brand items as most other Americans—G.E., Kenmore (Sears), Westinghouse, etc.—Demby asserts. But when it comes to food and drink he is likely to lean toward premium brands. Thus, Demby says, "Canadian Club is probably his favorite blended whiskey; Smirnoff his vodka; and Old Grandad and Jack Daniels his choice among bourbons. His scotches are probably Cutty Sark and Ballantines." Nor should it be assumed that the culture consumer is abstemious. Gallup has found that professionals, executives, and white-collar groups, as a class, are relatively big drinkers. Culture consumers, as a class, also are, according to Demby. This goes for beer as well as distilled spirits. Those who still conceive of beer as a plebian beverage may be surprised to learn that, at least according to Demby, beer is likely to be found in the refrigerators of more than half of all culture consuming families. Their favorite brand, he says, is Budweiser.

Another characteristic of this group is its exposure to communications. The culture consumer, Demby says with some certainty, spends the better part of an hour with his daily newspaper, and a slightly longer time each day with a magazine. He listens to the radio, perhaps with only half an ear, for about an hour and a quarter. But if he owns an FM tuner the period spent listening to radio rises sharply. He may play his FM set for an hour and a half in the evening alone, plus another hour and a quarter divided between morning and afternoon. He is, through one medium or another, more "tuned in" to the world around him than his non-culture-consuming counterpart.

Being "tuned in" implies more than just passive receptivity. It implies active interaction with the world around them. This would appear to be a characteristic of the culture public—and especially of its hard core. Thus we may assume that readers of *Harper's* and *Atlantic* are, in general, also members of the arts audience. This finding is supported not merely by their choice of magazines, both of which devote a considerable part of their editorial content to "cultural" matters, but also by other known data about them, such as their high proclivity to purchase classical records, FM tuners, and other indicative goods. In 1962 these two magazines tried to find out, not how their readers differed from the general public—this they already knew; the pattern was clear, as described above: median income over $10,000; extremely high percentage of college graduates; and so forth—but to determine how their readers differed from other people in roughly similar economic circumstances. Thus they sent questionnaires to a selected group of readers and to their next-door neighbors. Would there be any pattern to differentiate readers of *Harper's* and *Atlantic* from their next-door neighbors? A number of distinguishing characteristics were uncovered. But one of the most interesting had to do precisely with the issue of "activism." The popular image of the reader or culture lover pictures a sedentary, home-centered person. Quite the opposite tended to be true. The readers of these two magazines, it turned out, were far more active in community, business and cultural affairs than their next-door neighbors were.

The pattern was consistent. Whether it was a country club or golf club, a Red Cross organization or YMCA, a business or professional organization, a lodge or service club, a political party or a cultural committee like a symphony association or an art gallery group, the *Harper's-Atlantic* readers showed a higher percentage of memberships than their next-door neighbors. The only category in which the next-door neighbors were more active was "Church or Religious Organizations" and here the difference was less than one percentage point.

Being more active, these people also tended toward community leadership. A higher percentage of those in the *Harper's-Atlantic* group were officers and directors of the above organizations than were their neighbors. This was true in every single category of organization but one: "Country or Golf Club."

They were active recreationally, too. Almost 30 per cent reported playing golf; a like number played tennis; a similar proportion participated in boating; and 18 per cent skied. In all these sports the *Harper's-Atlantic* group outnumbered their neighbors. Only in hunting and bowling did the neighbors show a higher percentage of participation. The same pattern was repeated in the field of hobbies. Only in woodwork, outdoor cooking, and photography did the neighbors show higher participation. There was a clear and consistent pattern, too, in civic participation. The subscriber group wrote more letters to elected officials and newspaper editors; they addressed more public meetings; they worked more in election campaigns.

It would be too facile, of course, to project these findings over the whole culture consuming public. Although the magazine subscriber group showed more direct participation in cultural activities, the neighbor group also included culture consumers within it. But it may not be outlandish to assume that culture consumption and activism in general go hand in hand.

It is clear from the foregoing that the culture consumer is a new breed. He is a man in mid-passage. He is not part of the old, settled aristocracy, certain of its place in the world and confirmed in its interests, its judgments and its tastes (often quite bad, although we tend to remember only its examples of good taste). Nor is he part of the shrinking world of the blue-collar worker or the farmer. Yet neither is he the sadly limited, provincial middle-class man of the past. He is, for one thing, too educated. He is also too traveled. When it is not uprooting him and his family and moving it cross-country, his company is forever dispatching him to a convention in New York, a technical meeting in Boston, or a government hearing in Washington—even, if he is lucky, to a session with the branch manager in Brussels or Zurich or Rome. His wife has probably attended college and may well be taking adult education courses in international relations or poetry or ceramics. In any event, she is no longer home-bound. She has an automobile available to her and time for activities outside the house. She may well, for that matter, have a job, not from economic necessity but in many cases from choice. If not, she is probably active in one or more community or arts organizations. She has some ties with the outside world. Her husband is no longer Mr. Babbitt. And she is not Mrs. Babbitt.

This is not to romanticize the new comfort class or the culture consuming sector of it. The culture consumers have their decided limitations. But it is altogether too easy to make fun of the ballet lessons they give their daughters or their efforts with easel or brush. Amateurism has always been an easy mark for the satirist, as has the nouveau riche. It is also easy to shrug off their interest as mere status climbing. It is much harder to analyze the true complexity of their motives. The rise of a mass public for the arts can, in its way, be compared with the rise of mass literacy in the eighteenth century in England. It must have amused the nobility to find their social inferiors struggling with their ABC's. Yet mass literacy has been one of the really fundamental advances achieved by mankind in its long and gory history. The rise of interest in the arts by a mass public in the United States could, despite all the humor it provides to the caricaturist and the critical establishment, despite all the tinsel and tomfoolery it entails, herald something quite important in the social development of modern man.

4

Beyond the Status Drive

"MOST OF THIS CULTURE FOOLISHNESS IS SOCIAL. PEOPLE WANT TO dress up and be seen. Culture has damn little to do with it." So says a New Orleans bookseller asked by a reporter to explain the increase in arts activity in that city. Vance Packard in *The Status Seekers* tells of the university official who, wishing to impress visitors with his intellectuality, ordered "good" books from a local bookstore and proposed to pay for them by the yard. Moreover, anyone who has observed copies of *Horizon* artfully left lying around a coffee table (unread) for the visitors to notice, or the nameplates of patrons on the backs of the seats in Philharmonic Hall at Lincoln Center, cannot but be aware that culture and status aspirations are somehow related.

There is no doubt that some members of the new culture public are attracted to art more by the desire to impress others than by any passionate longing for the aesthetic experience. Going to a foreign movie, attending a chamber music recital or toting a conspicuously esoteric paperback in one's purse carries with it a certain social cachet in fashionable circles in the comfort class. But status is not the only non-aesthetic cause for culture consumption.

Museum directors show a healthy skepticism about the motives of their swelling audience. It is a private joke among them that if someone were to build free public toilets across the street from their institutions attendance figures would plunge. That the yen for culture is not always what it seems was demonstrated also, not long ago, when an official of a Tennessee penal farm held an investigation to find out why mountains of books and records were suddenly turning up in the prison's incoming mail. He found that the inmates were enrolling in book and record clubs, peddling the bonus selections they received for joining, and systematically defaulting on their pledges to buy four or six more books or records per year. Mammon raises its unartistic head in the art gallery as well, for buying an original painting is not merely the chi-chi thing to do, it may have important economic consequences. There are art collectors—one gallery owner dubs them "the mutual fund school"—who buy paintings in wholesale lots, warehouse them, and wait patiently for their value to rise on the highly inflationary art market. And it took a crackdown by the Internal Revenue Service to put an end to a sleight-of-hand operation under which a "collector" bought a painting for, say, $10,000, then had it appraised by a friendly evaluator who would announce that its "real" worth was $50,000. The owner could then contribute it to a museum and claim a giant tax deduction, often worth more to him than the original price of the painting.

Then there are the culture hucksters. These are the commercial operators who, noting the public's new interest in the arts, attach themselves parasitically to it. Thus we witness the Bach and Beethoven sweatshirt fad; we find galleries offering to sell "genuine original oil paintings" by mail, sight unseen; we see the formation of a club called The Escoffiers Inc., membership in which automatically "marks you as a taste maker." Such highly publicized gimmicks, intended to appeal to the remaining rubes in America, exploit the public's new interest in culture by cheapening it. The attendant ballyhoo lends a sulphurous odor to the cultural explosion, and the culture elitists, eager to justify their snobbism, act as if these manifestations were the guts of the matter. Crassness, commercialism, and status striving clearly exist. Yet the cultural explosion will be totally misunderstood if one assumes that it is nothing more than these, that it is powered only by fad or fashion. Its causes lie deeper in the American psyche.

A few small-minded hucksters cannot create a social movement. Nor can any single or simple cause. A development that has all the surging dynamism, all the internal variety or forward thrust of our culture boom, must result from a complex of causes. It can come about only when a number of deep-lying social trends suddenly converge to propel it forward with their cumulative impact. This is exactly what has happened to cause America's cultural breakthrough.

We spoke briefly in the last chapter about the remarkable growth since the end of World War II of that group we have labeled the comfort class. The rise in the earning power of the American worker, and especially of what have been called "the moneyed intellectuals," is beyond dispute. The fact that certain groups, Negroes, unskilled workers, the unemployed, have not shared equally in the general prosperity cannot cancel out the fact that most Americans today have more money than they ever had before.

Add to this the ramifying impact of the shorter work week, which has declined within our lifetime from roughly seventy hours to about half that, and some of the implications become clear. Americans have not only, by and large, moved past the subsistence level, they have been changing their entire psychological attitude toward work and leisure. For along with having more money they are beginning to rethink the Puritan ethic that insisted on work and frowned upon play, relaxation, and the muses. With the declining need to work people are liberated to spend, enjoy sensual satisfaction, to search for new and different delights—and they have increasing time to do so.

A third long-range trend flows into the gathering momentum created by the first two. At the turn of the century only two per cent of the population stayed in school past the age of fifteen. Today that two per cent has grown to 60 per cent. And college enrollments have soared so rapidly as to create a crisis on the campus. In 1950, 2,286,000 Americans were attending college. By 1960 this number had swelled to 3,583,000—an increase of about 57 per cent. This decade was the same one in which the cultural explosion began, and the facts are not unrelated. Moreover, the public is not merely better educated in a general sense, it is specifically better educated than ever in the arts. Both music and art have been part of the curriculum of many elementary and secondary schools since the 1920's and earlier. But since the second World War, with the consolidation of many small school districts, more and more school systems have been able to initiate specialized instruction in these subjects, and out-of-school instruction has increased even more rapidly. One indication of this is the startling growth in membership of the Music Educators National Conference from 20,000 members in 1950 to 42,000 members 13 years later. The number of children receiving musical instruction either at home or in school rocketed upward 340 per cent between 1947 and 1963—from 2,500,000 to 11,000,000. There is no question but that education in a very direct way makes possible greater mass consumption of the arts.

Even education that bears no direct relationship to art helps prepare the individual for artistic appreciation. The reasons for this are explained by psychiatrist Donald F. Klein, who points out that "the ability to appreciate art is linked to the ability to think abstractly. There is evidence that imagination, too, is related to this. Why does a child say 'Tell me a story'? He says it mainly because he cannot tell himself a story. Despite all the popular notions to the contrary, children do not, as a rule, possess good imaginations. In fact, they are quite literal or concrete-minded. What they have are direct and untutored responses to the world around them. But this is different from imagination, which we might define as the ability to view a situation and see a variety of potentials in it. This ability stems from the ability to abstract, and that is precisely what education develops in the child. Abstracting is a skill that education teaches. And every time it is applied successfully to solving some problem, the skill is reinforced."

This skill, Dr. Klein suggests, is further reinforced by the existence of choice in the individual's life. When a person is confronted with a situation that allows of no choice, he can rely on rote behavior. Abstraction is not particularly helpful, for example, for the man whose job it is to tighten every bolt moving down along the assembly line. He has no choice in the matter. It is the presence of choice—multiple possibilities—that encourages the growth of the skill to abstract. In this way, we get a self-reinforcing situation for some people. Education teaches them the skill. By so doing it prepares them for a better job, a wider choice of jobs, a wider spectrum choice. This, in turn, furthers the development of the skill once more.

What is true of the child—that he is literal minded—tends also to be true of adults with little education. Thus David Riesman says that workers have "an adherence to the tangible." This is simply another way of saying that they tend to be incapable of far-ranging abstraction.

This is directly related to the ability to enjoy art. "The low brow," Dr. Klein observes, "has a very concrete view of his own problems. Such a person tends to appreciate what we might term sub-art—Mickey Spillane, the Beatles, rock-n-roll, the Beverly Hillbillies. Here the appeal is simple and direct. It doesn't take much skill to discern the relationship in a June-moon rhyme, and since he sees his own life in relatively simple terms he can identify with the simplistic characters presented to him by such art. As people learn to view their own lives in more abstract fashion, they demand art that is more adequately representative of their new situation. This means a higher degree of complexity, and subtlety. It means art instead of sub-art."

The ability to detect patterns and to relate symbols back to their referents lies at the very root of the development of aesthetic taste, whether it is in music, literature, drama or the dance. And it is precisely this capacity that education and affluence foster. Pump education and affluence into a whole broad stratum of the population and, at the very least, a potential is created for increasing public participation in the cultural life of the nation.

Money, leisure, education. These are the obvious preconditions for a cultural explosion. But alone they do not adequately explain what has occurred. They explain why a member of the comfort class is increasingly capable of appreciating the arts; they do not explain why he is actually impelled to do so. Granted that the new millions in the culture public are not devoting themselves exclusively to the arts. Art remains for most of them a relatively minor concern fitted interstitially into their lives along with tennis, travel, and other activities. But why is it present in their lives at all? What is there in the life of the contemporary American of the comfort class that drives him to seek some form of fulfillment in the arts? It would appear that art serves some purpose for which nothing else can substitute.

To identify these needs, and the way in which culture serves them, we must first look at some of the hidden pressures that operate in modern life. One of these, impossible to ignore, is pervasive standardization. Max Lerner has written that, "Most American babies . . . are born in standardized hospitals, with a standardized tag put around them to keep them from getting confused with other standardized products of the hospital. Many of them grow up either in uniform rows of tenements or of small-town or suburban houses. . . . They spend the days of their years with monotonous regularity in factory, office, and shop, performing routinized operations at regular intervals. . . . They are drafted into standardized armies, and if they escape the death of mechanized warfare they die of highly uniform diseases, and to the accompaniment of routine platitudes they are buried in standardized graves and celebrated by standardized obituary notices. Caricature? Yes, perhaps a crude one, but with a core of frightening validity in it."

Standardization is not merely a characteristic of machine-made products. It is not merely a matter of one can of Campbell's tomato soup resembling the previous can. Lewis Mumford, for example, has pointed out that "The first characteristic of modern machine civilization is its temporal regularity. . . . As the scale of industrial organization grows, the punctuality and regularity of the mechanical régime tend to increase with it." Life is sensitively regulated by the clock so that we not only work at certain hours, but eat, travel and make love at more or less predictable moments.

Standardization exists, too, in the repetitive jobs most Americans perform and in the organizational environment within which they live. Bigness, whether the bigness of General Motors or of the AFL-CIO, or of the Pentagon, appears to be essential not only to economic efficiency but to political efficacy as well. The growth of bureaucracy was sufficiently advanced before World War I for Max Weber to make his pioneering studies of it. But the degree of rationalization in society has increased markedly since then, and with the recent introduction of the computer, operations research and other sophisticated tools, the structure of bureaucracy in American society has become ever more elaborate and refined. Bureaucracy, like the factory, has profound effects on the individual who labors in its toils. Thus Robert Merton writes: "The bureaucratic structure exerts a constant pressure upon the official to be 'methodical, prudent, disciplined.' If the bureaucracy is to operate successfully, it must attain a high degree of reliability of behavior."

To achieve this reliability, bureaucracy depersonalizes human relationships and encourages conformity. Standardized rules kill the spontaneity of natural human relations. Jobs are defined neatly. Lines of authority are spelled out with exactitude. Communication in the organization becomes increasingly formalized. A memo world is created. Paper stockades begin to fence people in. The results of this process were depicted in the flood of fiction and popular sociology that rained down upon Americans in the 'fifties and early 'sixties: *The Man in the Gray Flannel Suit; The Status Seekers; The Organization Man; The Lonely Crowd.* The mid-century American, we learned, was being suffocated by the all-enveloping standardization. "It is our belief," wrote sociologists David Riesman and Howard Roseborough in 1955, that "a general lowering of barriers is going on: between the age grades, between the sexes, between regions of the country, and between social classes, with the prospect in view of a fairly uniform middle-majority life style. . . ."

It is my conviction that too much has been made of the sameness and drabness of American life. There is, I believe, mounting evidence that when machine civilization reaches a certain level of affluence it begins to reverse the process through which it imposes conformity in its earlier stages. We may, indeed, stand on the threshold of an age of variety and spontaneity such as we have never known. Nonetheless, there is little doubt that standardization, conformity, and depersonalization have been powerful forces until now and that they have taken their toll.

Industrialization is a tool man uses to subdue nature. But the complexity of the tool is so great that he begins to lose touch with the purpose of his work. Division of labor splinters the job so that he comprehends, at best, only a fragment of it. Unlike the craft worker, he never has the opportunity to watch the work-object "grow" into its final form, and he is robbed of the special feeling, even fondness, that the craft worker can develop for his tools and materials. He is cut off, purposeless. Thus alienation becomes a dominant theme in the literature and art of industrial society. Benny Profane, a character in Thomas Pynchon's remarkable novel, *V.*, was always, so it seemed, walking into a landscape where nothing lived but himself. "Turn a corner . . . and there he'd be, in alien country." Or else, he would be walking "the aisles of a bright, gigantic supermarket, his only function to want."

It may be that novelists, sociologists, and existentialist philosophers exaggerate the prevalence of such *angst*. Nevertheless, unless all the evidence is skewed, multitudes in Western industrial society do, in fact, at one time or another, experience something akin to it. According to Ernest G. Schachtel, the psychoanalyst, "They no longer feel certain who they are . . . they are alienated from nature, alienated from their fellow men, alienated from the work of their hands and minds, and alienated from themselves. . . . When the lack of a sense of identity becomes conscious, it is often experienced—probably always—as a feeling that compared with others one is not fully a person." They experience what Robert MacIver has called "the great emptiness."

This void is accentuated by the mobility that has become such an increasingly important aspect of American life. Each year one American in five changes his place of residence. When we remember that many of the disadvantaged millions in America are the least mobile families, the miners glued to their mining town despite the fact that the mine has played out, the farmers whose livelihood is literally rooted in one place, it means that those we have described as the comfort class probably move, on the average, even more often. They are moving in other ways, too, up and down the economic and social scale, further away from their parents and relatives, from their religious origins, from their original occupational skills. And they are moving in autos, trains, planes and ships more than any other people moved before. Moreover, they are doing this in a world that is itself changing, moving, so rapidly that events, objects and values lost their solidity.

One would think that so much motion would numb the senses, the intellect and the ego. But quite the reverse occurs. Often it brings with it, instead of numbness, a sharpened hunger for new stimuli. Dr. Gerald Gurin, in *The Worker in the New Industrial Environment,* a study published by the Foundation for Research on Human Behavior, states that 80 per cent of those employed as professionals or technicians, certainly among the most mobile of Americans today, report that they gain ego-satisfaction from their work—that is, they satisfy certain needs having to do with interest and variety, use of their skills, expression of responsibility, etc. This contrasts with only 39 per cent of clerical workers and 29 per cent of unskilled workers who find these values in their work. This, by itself, is not surprising. What is, is his finding that "People in the higher status jobs, despite the much greater ego-gratification in their work, also express a greater degree of frustration of ego-needs. It appears that people in higher status jobs not only get more ego-gratification in their work, but seek such gratifications more."

Let us summarize, then, what this brief cruise through contemporary hell reveals: 1) standardization and gray sameness; 2) conformity and loss of individuality; 3) doubt about identity; 4) high mobility; and 5) a hunger for new stimuli. This gloomy catalog, it is true, expresses only partial reality. Life is not that grim for most of us. If it were, it would be intolerable, and most of us prefer tolerating it to ending it. One could match a whole series of advantages made possible by industrialism—from penicillin to flush toilets—that pessimists neglect to take into account. But the listing is useful, for it suggests some of the contemporary cravings that art may assuage.

Not merely that art may assuage, but that art can assuage more effectively than almost anything else. Football, stamp collecting, motor boating, golf, playing bridge—all such activities offer certain gratifications. But none of them dovetail quite as tidily with contemporary psychological needs as art.

If life is gray, art is vivid. If life is clock-bound, art is spontaneous and, at least in appearance, uninhibited. On a very superficial or sensuous level, art brings color, variety, and "differentness" into life. The costumes and settings of the opera or theater, the subtle, different, or outrageous colors in a painting, the strange psychological states of characters in a contemporary novel, the unusual combinations of sound in fine music—all these counteract the colorlessness of daily life. The same is true in the emotional realm. Psychologist Rudolf Arnheim reminds us that "much of the so-called emotional experience of daily life is very thin. It occurs within a very narrow band ranging from a pleasant tickle to mild irritation. These are, in a sense, retail emotions. But in art you are exposed to genuine emotional experience that reaches far beyond the ordinary. You go to a theater and you see a person—Hamlet, Oedipus, or even Willy Loman—profoundly upset. The problems of life are brought to a head. You are profoundly moved. To be profoundly moved is one of the most healthful sensations a human can experience. Art adds color to the emotional palette. It gives one a sense of being alive." On both the sensory and emotional levels, therefore, the arts stand in antithesis to the standardization of contemporary life.

They are also an antidote for conformity. Riesman and Roseborough, in the essay previously quoted, point out that sameness or conformity is expressed essentially in the "standard package" of material goods used by the family. This consists of such items as furniture, appliances, food and clothing. "It is in the leisure area beyond the package, for which the package is only a home base, that greater differences exist," they say. In short, it is through one's tastes in leisure pursuits and culture consumption that one is best able nowadays to differentiate oneself from others in like circumstances. Selecting a painting for the living-room wall, buying a classical record, or producing even an amateurish work of sculpture at the local art center class, are, whatever else they may be, defiant expressions of individuality.

It is affluence that makes such individuation possible. Thus the Stanford Research Institute, in a study of consumer values, was able to report perceptively, that "It now seems evident that the better-off and better-educated groups are consciously turning away from mass conformity. This is evident in the consumer field in the number of product innovations readily accepted, in the advent of radically different automobiles, in widespread acceptance of exotic foods, in rising foreign travel, and even in the broadening interest in avant-garde literature, music and art. The trend away from conformity toward individuality and self-expression should gather impetus . . . as levels of affluence rise." There are a finite number of automobiles for a consumer to choose from, a finite number of exotic meals that he can eat, and even a finite number of places to which he can, at the moment, travel. Art, by contrast, is infinite in its variations and possibilities. It is for this reason the broadest of all possible fields within which the individual can express his one-and-onlyness.

This one-and-onlyness lies at the heart of identity. The man who doubts his own identity searches for some revelation of himself. Whether this sign is reflected back to him from his individualized consumption of culture, or through his own production of art as a professional or amateur, art remains a helpful way to "find oneself." The kind of culture consumption in which he engages is a reflection of his individuality. And, to the degree that it is truly individual, it stands as reassuring evidence of his own essential uniqueness. Producing art, even bad amateur art, helps him to see himself. As Rudolf Arnheim observes, "whether you stand back and look at a painting you have just completed, or hear the music you are playing, it is self-revealing. It's like seeing the face of your own child. It helps define your identity to yourself in a way much more powerful than intellectual understanding alone." It is no accident that painting, music, and drama have all been used as specialized tools of psychotherapy. They can have a powerful effect on the personality.

In the matter of mobility, too, art offers certain special gratifications. In a world in which objects, events, and even values are increasingly transient, millions of deracinated individuals yearn for some sense of stability, certainty, and rootedness. Whether this yearning is healthy is an issue that might be debated at length. But the fact that it exists is indisputable. In colloquial, if clichéd, terms, the question is put: "What can a person hold on to?" For a variety of reasons, the arts are one answer to this question.

In a seemingly chaotic world, they possess and represent order. In a world that permits the worker to do only part of the job, and in which our ties with other people, with places and things, are continually being ruptured, the work of art has a completeness about it that is reassuring. Futhermore, the consumption of culture is an act that identifies one with an age-old tradition of excellence. Even when the subject matter of art is anti-traditional, the act of appreciating it remains traditional. People have been doing it for millennia. They have not been punching clocks, or taking their coffee in Lily cups, or speeding through space in metal tubes for very long. Art, not merely because it sometimes transmits the values of a past age, but because it has been a part of human society since the beginning, is an anodyne for rootlessness.

Finally, art assuages the hunger for stimuli. Art is different from other forms of experience because it involves symbolism. Even the most literal and representative painting or poem, the most non-abstract music or dance, is an "imitation" of reality as well as an aspect of reality. It is a symbol. And it is in the nature of symbols, it is the power of symbols, to engage the human psyche on multiple levels simultaneously. An effective symbol in a work of art sends out a storm of stimuli, emotional, intellectual, sensory. It is the symbolic content of art that arouses those ineffable emotional states that almost nothing else seems able to produce. A population that seeks new stimuli is bound to discover and respond to cultural products.

There are many subtler ways in which art serves the individual. What I have tried to show here, however, is that in a number of respects it is peculiarly suited to meet the cravings set up by contemporary industrial society. These volatile cravings have existed for a long time, of course. They have been detonated, as it were, by the income-leisure-education boom of the 'fifties. When we add them all up, combine them with the rise in education, leisure, and affluence and add, still further, America's profound passion for self-improvement, it becomes evident that the mushrooming, spectacular growth of culture consumption has not been a simple or surface matter. It cannot be explained away merely by the words "status seeking" or in any other unitary way.

We are compelled to view the cultural explosion, therefore, as something that reaches deeply into the core of American life, as something that reflects the changing temper of the American population, hitherto so all-absorbingly occupied with the nuts and bolts of life, with acquisition and material satisfactions. Indeed, it may be that what we call the cultural explosion is an early symptom of a basic change in the psychology of contemporary man in the most advanced of industrial societies.

Professor Ferdinand F. Mauser, in a provocative article in the *Harvard Business Review,* writes: "Through the ages, people placed value on ownership because there were not enough goods to go around. . . . In the new world of technological affluence, the principle of ownership of material possessions by individuals is fast becoming an anachronism." He supports this startling contention by citing the spread, in recent years, of rental plans and similar contractual arrangements in industry. He calls attention to such examples as the large appliance manufacturer that has announced it will rent refrigerators, dishwashers, freezers and air conditioners; the boom in auto rentals; and the department store in Washington, D.C., that advertises hundreds of items for rent such as baby bassinettes, linens, china, power tools and wheelchairs. He might also have mentioned the rise of art rental plans, and such off-beat examples as the company that rents mink coats to ladies who want to get all dressed up for a night.

This seemingly minor development may be symptomatic of something quite far-reaching. Thus, according to the Stanford Research Institute consumer study, "Of particular significance during the 1960's is the probable emergence of a large group of prosperous, pace-setting families who will reject materialism as their way of expressing self-betterment and replace it with individualistic 'self-realization.' This group may well shun efforts to emulate the very wealthy simply because status attainment through consumption will be so easy as to be pointless. Rather, this group is likely to turn to less conspicuous forms of consumption—perhaps to intellectual activities, to experimentation and variety of experience, to work in the public interest, and to the pursuit of excellence in general."

This same movement away from traditional goals has been termed "a revolutionary shift" by business consultant Edward T. Chase. Writing in the *Atlantic Monthly,* he explains: "Most Americans still care mightily about money, to be sure, but a different perspective is observable. To an unprecedented degree, things are being decided on nonmonetary criteria. . . . The new appreciation of noneconomic values is the key to many of our political differences; to misunderstandings between the older generations and the new one" and, among other things, a key to the culture boom, itself.

"A decline in the marginal urgency of goods," he continues, "means at the very least that a young man today need not, as in past ages, be limited to a struggle for survival, nor even that he must feel compelled to embrace some conventional money-making career if he wishes to enjoy standard creature comforts. He has more choices." Mr. Chase entitles his article, "Money Isn't Everything." This tendency has been discussed further in *Business Week*, which cites as an example the case of two young people who have pooled their incomes. One works for a year, then takes the next year off and lives off the other's income. Time free to pursue one's own individuality is, for many Americans, becoming more important than additional income.

This notable shift in values might be frightening to those concerned with practical dollars-and-cents in the economy, if it did not contain within itself a delightful paradox. For the change arrives at a time when many economists are coming to the conclusion that a nation's cultivation of its intellectual and cultural resources has much to do with its ultimate economic development. These economists have begun to devote increasing attention to investment in the creation and distribution of knowledge. One of the seminal thinkers in this field is the Princeton economist Fritz Machlup, author of *The Production and Distribution of Knowledge in the United States*, an imaginative, scholarly volume that defines "knowledge" broadly to include education, the mass media, research and development, as well as culture and other fields that are "non-productive" in the ordinary use of that term. Machlup asserts that the "knowledge industry"—of which the culture industry is a part—has been expanding at a rate about 2.5 times faster than the gross national product. Moreover, there is evidence that this sector of the economy will increase rapidly in the years ahead. It has been estimated that technical, professional, and managerial workers—"knowledge workers" as they are coming to be called—will constitute half the total American work force by the early 1980's. Education—of which culture, in this country, is sometimes a tributary—will become, in Peter Drucker's words, "the outstanding 'growth industry.' "

Indeed, we have already seen how education, along with leisure and income, are the principal preconditions for culture consumption. We now know that all three of these are in for massive expansion. The roughly 4,000,000 college students of today will be 7,000,000 by 1970 and 8,500,000 by 1975. The 48 per cent of our families with incomes of $6,000 or more will probably be 65 per cent by 1973. The work week will shrink, and even though the work force may grow numerically, the number of youngsters, retirees, and others who do not work will increase more rapidly. The total volume of free time will expand until it deluges Americans in oceanic quantities.

This is not the place to sketch the economic and technological outlines of the next generation as they are perceived by social science researchers. It is enough that we understand what such trends mean for the culture of this country. The rate of expansion of the culture industry may slow down percentagewise as the base becomes larger. But in absolute terms, we have only begun to see its growth. The cultural explosion of the last few years is the beginning, not the end, of something profound, colorful, and exciting. Nothing short of war or economic collapse can halt this progression. For in that super-industrial civilization of tomorrow, with its vast, silent, cybernetic intricacies and its liberating quantities of time for the individual, art will be not a fringe benefit for the few, but an indispensable part of life for the many. It will move from the edge to the nucleus of national life.

PART TWO

Trends

5

The Revolt of the Comfort Class

ONE WARM SPRING NIGHT NOT LONG AGO THE LIMA, OHIO, SYMPHONY gave a special performance. The concert was sponsored by the Women's Guild of the orchestra. The music was performed in a large, modern hall owned by a local of the United Automobile Workers of America. The orchestra included a Negro violinist, a bank vice president, and the mayor of a nearby village. The Women's Guild was headed by a young Jewish woman, wife of a professional man who, the year before, had served as president of the orchestra. The program ranged from songs of Rodgers and Hart to a Mozart horn concerto. Billed as a "carnival concert" of special interest to children, the event was decidedly informal. The walls were decorated with gay drawings of giraffes and lions. Between selections, clowns scampered up and down the aisle amusing the kids. Six hundred people sat along tables set up in the hall. They munched popcorn and potato chips and drank soda pop. The music produced by this community orchestra (composed of amateurs and a sprinkling of professional musicians hired from major orchestras in Midwest cities just for the one night) was, of course, not up to the standards of the New York Philharmonic. But it was live, at times good, and for the warm and appreciative audience, it was more than that: it was real. What such events, now taking place in one or another form in hundreds of communities, mean for the future of artistic quality in America, will be discussed later. For the moment, it is important to note that the "democratization" of which we spoke earlier is more than a matter of breadth of audience. It involves the performers, the atmosphere, even the locale. More important, it involves the organization and control of culture.

To understand the nature of the partial democratization that is occurring, it is necessary to stand back for a moment and look at culture as an economic system. Once this is done, it becomes immediately apparent that the "culture system," in this or any other society, is composed of several interlocking elements.

First, there is the *creator* element. Here one groups playwrights, poets, novelists, composers, sculptors and so forth, creative, as distinct from performing, artists.

Second, there is the *disseminator* element—the institutions that communicate the work of the creator to the public. These institutions of dissemination include not only commercial publishing houses and galleries, but non-profit museums, symphony orchestras, theater companies and the like. In the performing arts, the process of communication sometimes alters the message itself. The violinist and the actor—agents of the disseminating institution—are themselves artists, affecting the lines produced for them by composer or dramatist. But this must not obscure the fact that dissemination is a central ingredient of the cultural process.

Thirdly, there is the *consumer,* the ticket purchaser, the art collector, the reader.

All three elements—creator, disseminator, consumer—stand in what engineers would call a "feed-back" relationship to one another. They all affect one another.

It is noteworthy that in almost all discussions of the relationship of culture to democracy, the focus has been on the creator or the consumer, and seldom on the disseminator. Walt Whitman declared that "to have great poets, there must be great audiences, too," thus emphasizing the two polar elements, but ignoring the fact that there must also be publishers with capital, courage, and taste. The same emphasis is to be found in the debate raised by the elitist charge that art and democracy are incompatible. This is understandable, since the expansion of consumption has been the single most dramatic feature of the cultural boom. But it diverts attention from an equally important and intriguing question: who controls the machinery of culture dissemination in America?

In the profit sector of the culture industry—the sector that includes book publishers, record manufacturers, broadcasters, private art galleries, and the like—many changes are taking place. Some of these, like the new interest that Wall Street has taken in publishing, affect control of the instruments of culture dissemination. But there is no single clear trend that cuts across all the lines, affecting control in each different field of activity. In contrast, among the non-profit institutions of culture dissemination, a single broad movement is discernible.

Today, wholly unpublicized and unnoticed, a political revolution is occurring in the boardrooms of non-profit cultural institutions—a fight for control over the means of dissemination. The lines of battle are seldom clearly drawn. The issues are frequently obscured by personality clashes. The groups drawn into the struggle vary from community to community. The differences often appear to be purely local. Yet if one cuts through the color, noise, and dust of battle, a significant pattern emerges. Control is being wrested away from an elite-oriented "old guard" representing entrenched wealth and position in the community. It is being captured by young activists representing the new comfort class.

To understand this pattern, it is essential to grasp one commanding fact: power over the non-profit cultural institution, whether a museum or orchestra, theater, or ballet is ordinarily exercised not by the audience, but by the patron. With few exceptions, such institutions operate on a deficit basis. Each year the difference between total cost and the income earned from the sale of tickets, goods, or services must be made up by voluntary contributions from patrons. Given enough patronage, in fact, it is theoretically conceivable for such institutions to exist almost independently of the consumer.

Ever since the Civil War and the development of our great industrial fortunes, the typical non-profit institution has depended on a few "angels" of tremendous wealth. The names of these patrons have come down to us carved in marble over the portals of the institutions they founded or nourished. These were men who with a flick of the fountain pen could endow a museum or underwrite an orchestra. Some were genuinely interested in the arts. For others culture was simply a means of attaining status. And in still others these motives were mixed with a conscious desire to shore up the privileges of class and wealth against the rise of democracy. Henry Lee Higginson, the financier who founded the Boston Symphony in 1881, expressed this attitude when, in writing to a relative, he warned of the necessity "to save ourselves and our families and our money from the mobs."

Merle Curti, who quotes this letter in *The Growth of American Thought*, tells us also that "when thirst for praise led newly rich men to dig into their pockets for the rising Metropolitan Museum in New York, they were cold-shouldered by the older aristocracy on the ground that they were not gentlemen."

The boards and membership organizations that are part of the formal structure of institutions like orchestras and museums have, ever since those days, been tense with internal politicking and jockeying for position and prestige. But as long as the distribution of wealth in America remained pyramidal in form, the individual large patron dominated these organizations, and, through them, controlled the policies of our institutions of dissemination.

What is happening now is a breakdown of this control. Because there are now more institutions clamoring for financial support, and because of progressive taxation, there are now relatively fewer authentic millionaires who can, or will, pick up that mighty fountain pen. In consequence, cultural institutions have had to seek financial support from the comfort class, the new rich, from businesses and other elements in the community, as well as from old-line wealth.

How far this broadening of the base of patronage has gone is made clear from recent testimony of the American Symphony Orchestra League before a Congressional committee discussing a proposed tax change that would have affected the treatment of small contributors. "In years gone by," the League declared, "the burden of contributions to symphony orchestras was carried by only a very few patrons. The economic shifts of the last fifty years have changed all of that. Today, symphony orchestras must seek relatively modest contributions from many people and business interests."

Mr. Higginson's Boston Symphony, the testimony pointed out, now depends upon "annual contributions from over 4,000 persons to help meet the annual operating costs of more than $2 million."

Altogether, the testimony continued, "nearly a third of a million individuals and business firms in this country contribute annually to the support of these orchestras. The very number of these contributions gives you a clue as to the nature of them. Over 85 per cent of the total number of contributions made to symphony orchestras are in amounts of less than $100. Of the 4,200 contributions made to the Boston Symphony last season 3,700 were in amounts of less than $100. Last year 2,000 of the 2,500 contributions made to the Philadelphia Orchestra were for less than $100. The pattern repeats itself in each orchestra—great or little known, in each city—large or small." The same change has occurred, it might be noted, in the support of museums and other non-profit cultural institutions as well.

Such a broad shift in the pattern of economic support of the arts could not be expected to occur without bringing in its wake changes in the internal political control of such institutions. And, in fact, it has been accompanied by a revolt of the comfort class. Representatives of the new patrons are demanding, and winning, seats on boards that control the institutions of cultural dissemination. They are bringing with them a wave of fresh energy, enthusiasm, and ideas.

This political revolt of the comfort class is well illustrated by what has happened in Detroit since the end of the war. Detroit, long a smoky industrial town immune to the blandishments of culture, and in fact almost a symbol of cultural aridity, has since the war undergone remarkable changes in economic and social structure. A city that until 1945 was more sharply polarized than most in its distribution of wealth, Detroit in the years since then has seen basic changes in the character of its industry. Although the city still produces 22 per cent of the automobile assemblies in the country, the auto industry has been busy decentralizing. Today, it may surprise outsiders to learn, only fourteen per cent of Detroit's work force is engaged in producing autos, parts, and equipment. Fully 57 per cent of the city's labor force is employed in non-manufacturing work—shipping, advertising, publishing, and other forms of service and white-collar activity. These facts help explain the new mood of the city. Says one observer, "There are scores of thousands of highly skilled, highly educated men working here. They have wives who are also college trained. These people require cultural quality in their city." These people, it needs hardly be added, are largely members of the comfort class, and the new mood referred to includes a great ferment in the arts. New cultural organizations and institutions have cropped up, old ones have been strengthened, until today Detroit can no longer be written off the cultural map as it once was. In the process, however, the nature of patronage and the control of its disseminator institutions have undergone drastic changes, too.

All through the 'forties the Detroit Symphony, for example, had been the bauble of a chemical millionaire named Reichhold who covered its deficits and called it, candidly, "my orchestra." When anyone complained about its programming or quality, he reacted with the hauteur of a medieval pope. "I like that kind of playing music," he is reputed to have said, "and it's the kind of music Detroit is going to get."

After a noisy dispute within the orchestra, Reichhold suddenly, in 1949, withdrew his support. The orchestra packed away its instruments, and Detroit became the biggest city in the country without a symphony.

Two years later, in the flush of the city's 250th anniversary celebration, a drive was launched to reconstitute the orchestra on a new, more democratic basis. The campaign was headed by a brisk, moon-faced gentleman, John B. Ford, head of Wyandotte Chemical. Unrelated to the automotive Fords but well connected, Ford was able within two weeks to raise a quarter of a million dollars for the new orchestra by proposing something that has since been named the Detroit Plan. Under this system, the individual angel like Reichhold is replaced by a group of corporations, each of which pledges the same amount of money per year —ten thousand dollars—and each of which gets one seat on the orchestra board. The Musicians' Union and a few foundations donate equivalent amounts and are also represented.

The base of patronage is broadened still further through annual campaigns for small contributions from other businesses and from the public. In all, the orchestra now receives contributions from about 3,000 different sources, individual and corporate. In 1958, an independent group called the Society of Contributors was started. This is composed of small donors who agree to give a fixed amount year after year without repeat solicitation. The organizer of this group was an Indiana-born estate attorney named Harold O. Love, who was promptly rewarded for his efforts with a seat on the board of the orchestra. "Love hit this place like a whirlwind. He's hell on wheels," a symphony staff member says. "He got others interested, too." Love brought in Dr. Alfred Thomas, Jr., a Negro lawyer, who tried to build support for the orchestra in the Negro middle-class community, and who became a member of the board. Love also attracted Alan E. Schwartz, a Jewish attorney, who soon rose to a place on the orchestra's executive committee. Efforts have been made to increase contributions from the Jewish community, too. (Cultural fund raisers, incidentally, are exquisitely sensitive to the economic and sociological make-up of their communities and keep close watch on shifts in neighborhood, retail trade patterns, and other indices that can help them spot untapped sources of patronage.)

A similar democratization has been evident in other institutions as well. It has not always been a smooth process, but it has brought a group of dynamic and hard-working personalities into the cultural life of the city. The most important of these is Larry Fleischman, a description of whose rise is worth a brief digression, inasmuch as it provides keen insights into the currents stirring the arts in Detroit.

Fleischman is an enterprising chap whose father owned a couple of carpet stores and a motel. Always interested in art and photography, he had begun to buy a few inexpensive paintings even before finishing college—to the chagrin of his family, who assured him that only millionaires collect art. By 1952 Fleischman was searching out the works of unknown American painters. This brought him into contact with Edgar P. Richardson, then director of the Detroit Institute of Arts.

From Richardson and from his own experience, Fleischman came to realize how little is known about America's art heritage. "You discover," he says indignantly, "that American art is downgraded. You discover there's no chair of American art history at any American university."

It wasn't until 1953, while researching the background of a painter named Quidor, that Fleischman came up with an idea for remedying this condition of less than blissful ignorance. With the encouragement of Richardson, Fleischman simply created, from scratch, something he called the Archives of American Art. Dipping into his pocket for $250 to get the ball rolling, he and Richardson went out to line up funds and support for his new idea. Richardson induced Mrs. Edsel Ford, a member of the Art Institute's board, to serve on the still-embryonic Archives board. Fleischman, on an impulse, picked up the phone and called Vincent Price, whom he did not know, and quickly persuaded him to sit on the board, too. Before long, the Archives had a formidable board of directors and modest operating budget. Richardson provided them with space in his museum.

Today the Archives, still based in Detroit, has an office in New York and researchers at work there and in Europe. Teams of scholars are combing the records of galleries, museums, and artists, microfilming for the Archives anything that bears on the history of American art. Other teams are out taping interviews with painters, and the Archives is quickly becoming known as a treasure-house of data for scholars and writers. The Archives has received a $250,000 grant from the Ford Foundation and, apart from this, has an annual budget of around $100,000 brought in through the vigorous and imaginative fund-raising activity at which Fleischman excels. Recently, for example, in what was undoubtedly one of the most unusual cultural fund-raising events ever, the Detroit Tooling Association sponsored an auction and sale of used machine tools and equipment for the benefit of the Archives. It raised $71,000.

The success of the Archives inevitably attracted attention to Fleischman. The USIA sent him to South America, Greece, Turkey, Israel, and Iceland to lecture on American art. Fleischman's next step into local prominence came in 1959 when he was invited to join the board of the Founders Society of the Detroit Institute of Arts. In the subtle hierarchy of social distinctions in the city, this board, a bastion of the Social Register set, probably ranks higher than that of any other cultural institution. The museum receives city funds for salaries and maintenance, but its money for buying art comes from contributions by members of the Founders Society. The Founders elect the trustees of the Institute, and dominate the tone and tempo of the Institute. In turn, the Founders were dominated for years by a small group of slumbering Grosse Pointers. Indeed, control of the Founders by this group was facilitated by a constitution and voting procedure that disenfranchised small contributors. No one who had contributed less than $1,000 was granted a vote. True, it did not all have to be donated at once, but the man who contributed only $100 a year would have had to wait a decade before he could make his voice heard. Thus in 1961, of 4,674 members only 257 were eligible to vote, and, of these, only 120 did. In reality, the Founders were so completely under the thumb of a small inside clique of old rich, that voting was no more than a formality anyway. Decisions were made around a dinner table in Grosse Pointe.

It was inevitable that the introduction of a man with Fleischman's drive would disturb the equilibrium. Not long after Fleischman took office, he came into conflict with the "old guard." Fleischman and Love, his friend and co-combatant, are careful to point out that even Grosse Pointe has a "young guard" which does not reflect the Toryism and do-nothingism, as they put it, of the old settlers.

One big battle shaped up in 1961. Fleischman, ever the activist, proposed an all-out effort to raise ten million dollars for a joint endowment of the museum and the Archives. "I had been on the board for a while and I was tired of seeing everything go down the drain because a lot of tired people said it couldn't be done. We talked and talked and nothing happened. It got so bad that at one board meeting I suggested we all resign because nobody wanted to solve the problems of the museum.

"That caused a tremendous reaction. It really stirred things up. I called for more planning, more action. I told them we needed more money for staff and salaries."

Out of this showdown came several decisions. Alvan Macauley of the National Bank of Detroit finished out his term as president of the Founders. But he did not run again, and he was replaced by Ralph T. McElvenny, president of Michigan Consolidated Gas. More important, Anne Ford, then still the wife of Henry Ford and a member of the board, agreed not only to back Fleischman's idea for a big joint drive, but to lead it publicly. Mrs. Ford was related by marriage to the leader of the Institute's "old guard," but for a variety of personal reasons frequently lined up with what might be called the "activists" on the board.

This was the way matters stood until one day when Richardson received a phone call from Mrs. Ford's doctor, who informed him that she was in no condition to undertake such an effort. To Fleischman's disgust, the board then dropped the whole plan rather than going out to find another prominent person to lead the drive. After this, Richardson, tired of wrestling with a skimpy budget, resigned to take another post in the East.

Since then Detroit has chosen a new, young Mayor, Jerome Cavanagh, who has, among other things, shown an interest in the troubles of the Institute. Cavanagh lost little time in replacing several long-time members of the Art Commission—the municipal body that channels public funds to the Institute. The Commission's members include some who are also members of the Founders board. It is a measure of Larry Fleischman's new influence in the city's cultural life that Cavanagh recently promised to appoint not only him but Harold Love to the Commission.

The rise to cultural power of a young, energetic comfort class in Detroit is only symptomatic of what is happening in scores of cities elsewhere, everywhere in slightly different form. (A staff member of the Louisville Symphony Orchestra, for example, in concurring with the above analysis, put the situation in his city in somewhat different terms. The new blood, he said, came from families that had moved to Louisville fairly recently—young executives and professional people who became important in the affairs of the symphony after "the tea party-D.A.R. set" had let things deteriorate there.) It helps to explain much of the bickering and back-door political maneuvering that makes board meetings of cultural institutions colorful and lively these days.

But this analogy with political revolution may be extended even further, for the rising new class has in fact brought with it an ideology, too. Marching under a banner of democracy rampant, it goes to battle full of evangelistic fervor. Its slogan is "action" and its philosophy is the exact opposite of art-for-elite ideology. It is based firmly on the notion that cultural institutions must carry culture to the masses rather than waiting for the masses to ask for it.

Thus, the revolt of the comfort class helps explain one of the most striking cultural trends of the past decade, the radical change of posture adopted by so many of our leading cultural institutions. Many have become almost as "sales-minded" as business. They are actively and consciously working to create new culture consumers.

The Metropolitan Opera Guild in New York recently staged special performances of an abridged *Cosi fan Tutte* at junior and senior high schools throughout the New York area. Symphonies everywhere have stepped up their special performances—pop concerts, suburban concerts, children's concerts. Small ensembles of symphony orchestra members are touring schools to show students what a brass group, a percussion group, or a string quartet look like and sound like.

The change in stance is most sharply evident in museums, once characterized by their austere reserve. Today museum collections are being transported out of the museum buildings to places where larger numbers of people can enjoy them. The Dallas Museum of Fine Arts, for example, maintains a rotating collection of paintings in the busy terminal at Love Airfield. The Boston Museum of Art circulates more than 60,000 color slides to art clubs, individuals and classes—about three times as many as ten years ago. The Virginia Museum of Fine Arts in Richmond has been a leader in finding new ways to build the culture audience. It not only opened its doors at night for those who cannot conveniently visit the museum during the day, it put the world's first "artmobile" on the road touring with a changing exhibition of paintings and sculpture. Such programs illustrate the fundamentally new spirit in which cultural institutions now approach their audience.

In Detroit the essential policy of the culture establishment was passive, if not restrictive. Dominated and attended by the white, Anglo-Saxon, Protestant, pre-automobile nobility of the city, the institutions were open to anyone who sought them out. But nobody bothered to hang out a welcome sign for Poles, Negroes, Jews, hillbillies, Catholics, Italians or anyone else. The Art Institute, a public facility, was administered like a private preserve. The concerts of the orchestra were a society event rather than a community event. The "old guard" was more than content to let matters rest that way.

Says one observer-participant about the Art Institute: "The Institute has never had a volunteer program. Volunteers to staff the membership desk, to supply flowers, and decorations, to run a coffee shop, to run a telephone squad. They don't want the people there. They don't want that kind of public involvement. All they had was a woman's committee that did nothing but pour tea. They wanted to keep it social."

Whether viewed as undemocratic or simply as lethargic, this policy was an affront to the cultural evangelists among whom, it should be emphasized, Love and Fleischman were only two. Thus the rising young guard has given the city's cultural efflorescence an air of being part Chautauqua, part crusade. Moreover, its philosophy has been widely adopted even by many who do not, by any leap of imagination, fit into any economic definition of the comfort class. Thus the sense of carrying the gospel to the unbaptized turns up in the lament of a librarian that so many of the city's workers are from the South and "have never had a book experience." But it is also present in the attitude of Mrs. George Romney, the Governor's wife, who in heading the opera drive one year, visited the meetings of ethnic groups to spur sales and commented: "We believe that culture belongs to all the people here, not like in Georgia, where it's just for society." (A good many of Atlanta's comfort class revolutionists would no doubt take exception to this remark.)

The missionary fervor is expressed in Detroit in discussions about switching the touring performances of the Metropolitan

Opera from the Masonic Temple, which has a glittering diamond horseshoe where all the Blue Book families vie for seats, to the Fox Theater, where social distinctions are less apparent in the seating arrangements. It crops up in Harold Love's repeated use of the verb "expose" when he speaks of "exposing new people to culture."

It manifests itself in flamboyant fashion in the good works of Harry Gregory Bradlin. A businessman who looks, as one friend puts it, "like a glorified headwaiter" and who drives a battered automobile, Bradlin corrals anyone he thinks might be interested in music, provides him with free tickets to the symphony, and wines and dines him at the London Chop House, one of the city's best restaurants. "Some people laugh at Bradlin," says his friend. "I've even heard them snicker at him while they're stuffing themselves at his expense. But he spends every cent he can to vaccinate people with the arts—thousands of dollars a year. What's wrong with that?"

The proselytizing passion for the arts turned up in quintessential form in a city-wide program begun a few years ago under the name "Detroit Adventure." Originated by Dr. William Birenbaum, then a vice president of Wayne University, the program brought together nineteen of the city's major cultural institutions for a series of joint programs. Detroit Adventure issued a common calendar of the arts. It held what it called "Conversations in the Arts"—discussions at libraries, in shopping centers, and in classrooms at which participants had a chance to meet working artists and discuss their work and ideas with them. The definition of art was broad enough to include such topics as city planning, and one discussion group flew around the city in a plane while city planner Charles Blessing pointed out to them the chief characteristics of the city and its problems. "Conversations" attracted enthusiastic members. One young man drove to Detroit from Perrysburg, Ohio, eighty miles away, several nights a week, to take part in them.

Once a year since its innovation in 1958, the Adventure program has culminated in a big city-wide "Conference" on a broad theme of cultural significance. At the 1960 Conference, Birenbaum flew in the poet Quasimodo, Carlo Levi the novelist, Agnes

De Mille, Sol Hurok, Robert Lowell and others for a series of discussions comparing the quality of life in urban Milan during the Renaissance with that in contemporary Detroit. Another program, called "Excursions in Music," sent chamber groups into the schools to perform for children, provoking among other things a flood of letters from six and seven year olds thanking the "very nice Orkschrro" (orchestra) for "onedrfal mewick." Birenbaum, who argued that in a democratic society art must involve a broad stratum of the public rather than merely a "white-tie-elite," has since left Detroit to become dean of New York's New School for Social Research. He was replaced by Hamilton Stillwell, an educator who is perhaps less of a crusader. "But," says Stillwell, "we are breaking our necks to get to the union members and lower-income groups. This was Bill Birenbaum's idea, and it's mine."

It is evident, then, that something more subtle than a partial democratization of the culture public is occurring. The rise to influence of a new kind of patron drawn from the comfort class exactly parallels the emergence of the new culture consumer. It brings with it a deliberate campaign to further extend and broaden the audience. It means, too, the unseating of "old guard" board members who identify themselves with the art-for-elite ideology, and their replacement by younger elements devoted to precisely the opposite. The "old guard" trustees and board members formed the political base of elitism within the culture system. That base is now being destroyed.

The events that have led to the rise of a mass public for the arts, the emergence of a new kind of individual patron, and the decline of elitist influence, are also tranforming the relationship between the culture industry and the rest of society. They are radically changing the links between art and the university, for example, and it is to these that we must now turn our attention.

6

Culture on
the Campus

EVER SINCE THE HEYDAY OF MENCKEN AND FITZGERALD THE AMERICAN campus has been pictured as a hotbed of insensibility. Its image in the 'twenties was compounded of two parts whiskey, one part raccoon coat, and five parts "boobism." Today that image is gone. A lab coat has replaced the fur coat. The rah-rah man is déclassé, and the campus exudes a new aura of super-studious scientism, of computers, reactors and mathematical witchcraft. Nevertheless, according to the critics, we are still producing boobs. The campus, they insist, is turning out "skilled barbarians" as innocent of culture as any flask-bearing philistine of the roaring 'twenties.

This generality is disputable. What is not disputable is that the American college and university, partly in response to such complaints, is now spending more time, money, and energy in "culturizing" its population than ever before in history. Almost unnoticed, the arts have moved in on higher education. A penetration has begun that is so enthusiastic and so widespread as to represent a basic change in the ecology of culture in America. It is changing the channels of distribution through which music, art, dance and theater reach their publics. It is creating a new class of campus culture managers. It is changing the position of the artist and the character of his art. It is changing both the curriculum and the climate of campus life.

Today colleges offer a wide array of arts courses, not merely in "appreciation" but in the applied creative arts as well. Even at scientific and technical schools, students are painting, acting, sculpting, confronting the complex problems of creation. Graduates with fine arts degrees are flowing off the campus by the thousands each year. Simultaneously, artists of national repute are coming to live and work on college or university campuses where, mingling with faculty and students, they introduce a droplet of creative temperament into the sometimes desiccated academic atmosphere. Thus we have the Budapest String Quartet at the University of Buffalo. We have painter Aaron Bohrod and novelist Elizabeth Bowen at Wisconsin. Names like Roy Harris crop up with increasing frequency in campus directories.

The campus cultural awakening shows itself also in a phenomenal rise in extra-curricular amateur arts activity. Students have been putting on concerts and plays at least since 1754, when a visitor to a small New Jersey college (since transmuted into Princeton) reported that "2 young gent. of the college acted *Tamerlane and Bajazet,* &c." But there has never been anything like the present profusion of student art exhibits, dramas, musical comedies, operas, dance recitals and concerts. The student with aesthetic inclinations is no longer a "long hair" pariah.

Even more concrete evidence of the new attitude toward the arts lies in the construction boom that is changing the face of the American campus. Colleges are building new dorms, classrooms, laboratories and libraries. But they are also pouring millions of dollars of capital funds into the creation of magnificent physical facilities for the study and enjoyment of the arts. Not long ago Dartmouth opened a $7.5 million cultural center complete with auditorium, theater, studios, galleries and rehearsal rooms. Harvard's $2 million Loeb Center includes a 600-seat theater and a special 100-seat experimental theater, and the school has just finished building a new Visual Arts Center—the first American building to be designed by Le Corbusier. Brandeis has put $660,000 into art studios. West Virginia University is constructing a "creative arts center" for opera, dance and concerts. Arizona State University in Tempe is putting up a 3,000-seat auditorium with classroom space for art, music, and theater. The striking building, designed by Frank Lloyd Wright, will cost $2.8 million. Smaller institutions, like the College of Idaho, which not long

ago opened a $600,000 concert hall, are also reverberating with
the clatter of cranes and jack hammers. Art museums are springing up on campuses, and it has been loosely estimated that by
1970 as many as 750 new college theaters will be built.

But the most spectacular and fascinating manifestation of the
campus cultural boom lies in the new role that has been quietly
assumed by the college—the role of local impresario. An impresario, in the words of one dictionary, is "the projector" of a
cultural enterprise. He is the man who puts up the money, hires
a hall, imports the talent, and stages the show. Today an estimated 500 colleges and universities have moved into the impresario business. They are buying, booking, and—in their own
genteel way—ballyhooing. They are hawking tickets, counting the
house, and turning a profit to help finance more, and still more,
cultural activity. This means that in certain cities local commercial impresarios are facing stiff new competition. As we shall see,
not all of them welcome it. But more important, it means that in
hundreds of communities too small to support a commercial
culture-entrepreneur an agency has been created the function of
which is to generate audience for the arts. In short, a new trans-
mission belt for the arts has been set up. One educator calls it "a
contemporary, sophisticated version of the old Chautauqua." But
it is more than that, and it is contributing to a revolutionary
decentralization of the arts in America.

Today, as a result, North Central College in Naperville, Illi-
nois, is staging concerts by Yehudi Menuhin and Risë Stevens.
The University of Kansas at Lawrence imports Joan Sutherland,
the Philadelphia Orchestra, and the Bach Aria Group. Isaac Stern
turns up at Fort Hays State College in Hays, Kansas, and Byron
Janis performs at Wartburg College in Iowa. In Augusta, the
Medical College of Georgia presents Rosalyn Tureck, and in
Loretto Heights College in Colorado, students attend recitals by
Giorgio Tozzi and Jean Casadesus.

Nor is all this touring talent musical. If Evgeny Evtushenko
failed to declaim his poetry at Princeton recently, it was Comrade
Khrushchev's fault, not that of the university which invited him.
For nowadays poets as well as musicians are putting on what
Variety would probably call "boff" acts. Robert Frost in his final

years never failed to fill a hall when he visited a campus, and John Ciardi does a thriving lecture business today.

Theater people, too, are beginning to swarm over the campus circuit. Players like Eli Wallach, Blanche Yurka, Walter Abel and Julie Haydon are materializing at schools like Millikin University and St. Cloud State College to deliver readings or to perform, often with student dramatic companies.

So active, in fact, has the college circuit become as a purchaser of talent that artists' representatives like Columbia Artists Management, Inc., or Herbert Barrett Management, Inc. look upon the campus as the fastest growing and best of all major markets. Columbia field salesmen told me that in many regions, including the East, the South, and the Near West, schools now account for more than 50 per cent of all sales. In the case of the Barrett firm, college sales have shot up to account for over 75 per cent of total volume.

Funneling talent into the campus circuit are several important agencies. Musical attractions are sent out by commercial representatives like Columbia, Barrett, or Sol Hurok. Lecture bureaus like Colston Leigh or Harry Walker in Boston arrange tours for poets like Ciardi. Theater people are sent out either by their own agents or under the aegis of a special section of the American National Theatre and Academy which has been very active in stimulating such tours. In addition to the above, there is a little-known but effective organization called the Arts Program of the Association of American Colleges. This group sends a regular stream of artists to about 350 colleges—mainly small, church-related institutions. In the 1963–64 season, for example, the Arts Program dispatched chamber music groups, a dance company, a mime, a small acting company, and a group that performs on ancient instruments like the virginal, the viola da gamba, the psaltery and the cromorne. Says Norwood Baker, the pleasant South Carolina lady who has been overseeing this program for years, "we differ from the commercial agents sending talent out in that our people must spend a minimum of two days on each campus, and not only perform, but be available for speaking, perhaps teaching a master class, and generally mixing with faculty and students." Demand for such visitors outruns the supply. Ever since about 1956 requests have increased year by year and, says Miss Baker, "we could have served 250 more colleges if we had more money for just plain administration." (The Arts Program is not a money-making affair; it is partly subsidized by foundation grants.)

No one knows precisely how much colleges and universities are now spending for such activities. But a glimpse at a few sample budgets suggests the scope of this new movement. The University of Michigan, for example, now spends $150,000 a year on artists' fees alone. Indiana University spends $85,000. U.C.L.A., Minnesota, Purdue—all these have large and well-financed "impresarial" programs. In Columbus, Ohio State University spends $60,000 a year to import talent.

Julius Bloom, who administers a cultural program for Rutgers University in New Jersey, explains, "My operation is not a big one. I don't have the plant, and I face competition from New York, which is near enough to attract an audience from Rutgers. Still, I have $50,000 a year to spend for artists. I dare say there are 15 schools with budgets over $50,000, and many, many in the $20,000 to $50,000 range." Says another college cultural manager, "I could name 20 schools in Ohio alone that spend over $20,000 a year on artists' fees."

These are sizable sums. Yet they represent only part of the total now being spent for non-classroom cultural activities. There are, in addition to artists' fees, such cost items as staff salaries, building expense or rent, publicity, advertising, insurance, travel, etc. Thus at Ohio State, for instance, the allocation for artists' fees represents less than 25 per cent of a cultural programming budget totaling approximately $250,000 a year. Nor is this the largest of such budgets.

The program at U.C.L.A. in 1961–62 offered 59 concerts; 40 film showings; 110 lectures; 151 performances of professional theater, and 89 performances of student theater, plus scores of art exhibits, dance recitals, and similar events. The student who wished to take advantage of all of them could have spent the equivalent of two hours or more per day, 365 days a year, attending or participating. This overall program rings up annual box office sales of approximately $500,000—despite the fact that many of the events are open to the public free of charge. To this sum, the university itself adds a small amount to help cover administrative cost. The result is that on this single university campus more than half-a-million dollars a year is spent for non-classroom arts activity.

Attendance figures are impressive, too. The U.C.L.A. program draws an aggregate attendance of 285,000 each season. At the University of Wisconsin theater attendance runs to about 200,000. At West Virginia University so many people flock to concerts that crowds begin lining up an hour ahead of time to be sure of snagging seats, and the story is much the same elsewhere.

Spearheading the move of colleges and universities into the business of culture are a group of men and women who comprise that new and as yet little known profession, campus cultural management. A great many schools still assign the chairman of the music department or the head of speech and drama to set up and run a "fine arts series." But at a number of institutions the job has grown too big for part-time or amateur executives, and a full-time impresario, often assisted by staff, is responsible for the coordination of arts activity. At U.C.L.A., for example, it takes 13 full-timers, including programmers, publicists, clerks and bookkeepers, to run the elaborate cultural machinery.

The profession is so new that no standard nomenclature has as yet emerged. Some campus impresarios go under the title "auditorium manager." Others call themselves "concert manager" or "director of cultural activities." Nevertheless, the profession already has its own national organization, the Association of College and University Concert Managers, its own annual convention, and a small newsletter.

It is worth taking a close look at the college cultural manager. It is particularly instructive to compare him with his off-campus counterpart, the commercial impresario. When this is done, the contrasts are striking, and nowhere more so than in Columbus, Ohio, home of both Ohio State and a genial gentleman named Herman Amend. Amend is a ruddy-faced, vigorous fellow with white wavy hair, horn-rimmed glasses, and a booming but mellifluous baritone. He wears a black suit, a white silk shirt, and a silk tie.

"I've presented the greatest here," Amend told me when I interviewed him in the listening booth of Columbus' main music store. "I studied music and I was in show business. I was a singer. Then I came back to Columbus and there was an opening here. There was a very successful impresario. He died and I stepped in. And in the past 30 years I've presented the best. Now I just put on one subscription series and a few extra spot attractions. I've brought in José Greco, Birgit Nilsson, Cliburn—that was the largest crowd we ever had—4,200 and a couple of thousand turned away! And we have the Royal Scots Greys, a bagpipe group."

Until a few years ago Mr. Amend was almost alone in importing good music, bagpipe groups, and other such amenities to Columbus. There was an organization that brought in chamber music groups, but since this appealed to a relatively small audience and had little commercial potential it did not conflict with Amend's activities. Now, however, Amend finds himself confronted with a member of the new class of campus impresarios, one Donald H. Horton. At 55, Don Horton is a tall, gentle-looking, modest man who wouldn't be caught dead in a silk shirt. He strides across the Ohio State campus in a snap-brim hat, a striped tie, and an Ivy League suit. He carries an attaché case. Except for the gold-rimmed glasses that give him a faintly old-fashioned look, he might be an executive with North American Aviation in Columbus. The physical dissimilarity with Amend is startling.

But the differences between the two men go deeper. Amend, like many of his counterparts in other cities, operates more or less out of his hat. He has no very large financial investment in his business. He is accountable to no one. Horton, on the other hand, is an organization man. He has a staff of eight. He is charged with running a $3 million auditorium. And he is responsible to a major state university.

When Mr. Amend wants to drum up trade for his bagpipe band, likely as not he will march into a local department store with a few of his kilted performers and manufacture a little impromptu hoopla. Mr. Horton, too, needs to publicize his wares. But his style is entirely different. (His office bookshelf sports a copy of Vance Packard's *The Hidden Persuaders,* and next to it, perhaps uneasy at the proximity, *Publicity for Prestige and Profit.*) Eschewing the colorful press agentry of the traditional "show biz" flack, Horton issues a stream of dignified, soft-sell press releases. And because he represents a major non-profit institution in the community, the local press gives these excellent display, more space perhaps than it would feel obliged to give to any commercial entrepreneur.

This illustrates still another difference between the new- and the old-style impresario. I would doubt that Mr. Amend ever felt the need to read a book about publicity. His talents as promoter are intuitive. He has a built-in flair for it. And his functions are shifting, ill-defined, "unstructured," to use the scholarly jargon. As he attunes one ear to public taste in Columbus, and another to the sales pitch of artists' managers, he plays his middleman's game strictly by ear. In contrast Horton is much more self-conscious; his role is spelled out for him. His responsibilities, for example, are outlined in three single-spaced typed pages of "job description" that state, in part:

> Supervises all Auditorium staff personnel . . . is ultimately responsible for all that goes on in the Auditorium as to the program presentation; housekeeping maintenance, ticket office operation and business operation. . . . Acts as official spokesman for Auditorium . . . meets artists and speakers at train or plane escorting to hotel. Arranges rehearsal time for artist. Arranges receptions or dinners. . . . Provides incidental entertainment of artist . . . instructs stage manager in proper lighting and staging . . . supervises conditions of heating and cooling, snow removal, cleanliness of grounds. . . .

And so on. Everything is explicit.

Under Horton's supervision O.S.U.'s 3,000-seat Mershon Auditorium presents eight major events a year as part of its Great Artists Series. For the 1962–63 season these were: recitals by Rudolf Serkin and Adele Addison; performances by the Robert Shaw Chorale, the New York City Opera Company, the National Ballet of Canada, the Symphony Orchestra of Hamburg, and the Orchestra San Pietro of Naples, a chamber ensemble. The pro-

gram was rounded out with an evening of excerpts from Shakespeare read by Helen Hayes and Maurice Evans.

In addition, there was also a second series including Robert Frost, Judith Anderson, Jose Limon, Carlos Montoya, the Texas Boys' Choir, a Greek folk music and dance group, and Earl Wrightson and Lois Hunt. Finally, there was a brief third series devoted to jazz and pop music—Brubeck, the Four Preps, *et al.*— plus a variety of single-shot attractions. In designing these programs, O.S.U. quite evidently attempts to balance them—to attract, to entertain, and to "uplift" its audiences.

Mr. Amend's contributions to Columbus' cultural life over the years need not be derogated, but as a commercial operator his first imperative is financial. Within the restrictions of the profit economy, his choice of programs may be good or bad, but they are his alone. The money invested is his. The chance to make a killing is his. The taste is his.

Mr. Horton's situation is utterly different. The money, obviously, is not his. There is no speculative drive: he cannot under any circumstances make a killing. Moreover, while he is expected to balance his books, he receives a variety of subventions from the university. These take the edge off his financial problems, making it possible to program, at least occasionally, something off-beat or esoteric. Finally, and most important, his programming is not a matter of personal choice. It is the result of consultation with an advisory committee consisting of the head of the school of music, the chairman of the speech department, a professor of English, an administrative dean, two students, and various other functionaries and faculty members.

The consequence of a system like this is an impresario cast in a completely new mold. Perhaps lamentably, the flamboyance and daring of the old-style impresario has been squeezed out. There is little room for individual caprice or color or flair in this rationalized, institutionalized setting. But the weaknesses so often associated with the old-style impresario have also been diminished or eliminated. Every vestige of the Barnum philosophy is dead.

Today in Columbus one may observe the ascendance of the campus impresario and the decline of the commercial entrepreneur. Mr. Horton, and not Mr. Amend, is now the principal culture importer in the city, and Mr. Amend, normally amiable, knows it. Says he with vehemence: "I'm hurting because the university is bringing in all that stuff. It's not only a matter of audience. For instance, I want to book *Tosca* by the Boris Goldovsky group, but they're after him, too.

"Horton's a fine fellow and a friend of mine. I like him. But if there was a need for more attractions in Columbus, we as promoters, would have brought them in. I say they're failing up there at Ohio State. They've got 30,000 students and 4,000 faculty, and still they have to sell tickets to the general public! It's fine what they're doing. But they should stay on campus."

After this rather spirited discharge, Amend sighs dramatically, "Aah, I'm losing the spirit to fight!"

O.S.U. officials, for their part, react indignantly to the charge that they are stunting private enterprise. "In a community of this size," says Dean Ronald B. Thompson, Horton's superior, "we have other groups who bring in cultural attractions. But it is only logical for a university to take the leadership and even subsidize cultural excellence. The fact is we have stimulated a community-wide demand for cultural services. We are broadening the public for the arts, not shrinking it. Business people have told me that again and again." By expanding the audience, he suggests, the university may even, in the long run, help Mr. Amend's business.

It would be too bad if, indeed, Mr. Amend lost the will to fight. Good, hot competition in the "culture business" is a refreshing novelty in most cities. Yet the historical fact is that the individual entrepreneur, the local impresario, began fading as a factor in the "culture market" even before the advent of the campus culture boom. In really small cities, an Amend cannot exist because the market is too small. In middle-sized cities like Columbus he remains for a long time the only source of live artistic talent. But when such a city begins to develop indigenous cultural institutions, like a symphony orchestra or a civic ballet, the need for the talent importer's services diminish. This may account for the fact that commercial impresarios, once the backbone of the musical and theatrical distribution system, have dwindled in number to a relative handful in the country. They survive today only in larger centers where the market is big enough to support both local cultural institutions and a talent "importer." If it is true that the rise of the college as cultural entrepreneur is hastening the demise of the commercial impresario in middle-sized cities, this must be weighed against two important advantages. First, the kind of non-profit operation it runs is better. It holds within it the potential for far better programming than any profit-pressed culture merchant could afford. Secondly, in hundreds of communities, the movement of the college into arts programming has not supplanted private enterprise; it has simply filled a vacuum. What, for example, would the cultural life of Bloomington, Indiana, be without the cultural programming of Indiana University?

Once the campus culture juggernaut began to roll, it was only a matter of time before its momentum would carry it beyond mere importation of talent and into the sphere of cultural *production* as well—professional production, that is, not merely student amateur work.

In October, 1962, in Ann Arbor, the University of Michigan invited 500 business, professional, and civic leaders to attend a performance of Sheridan's *School for Scandal*. It was a preview show, kicking off a 22-week season of theater mounted by a new resident company of paid, experienced professionals. The company, Association of Producing Artists, is composed of seasoned Broadway players like Rosemary Harris, Anne Meacham, Will Geer, and Cavada Humphrey. Under terms of a three-year contract with the Professional Theatre Program of the university, A.P.A. has played in Ann Arbor and has toured Michigan. In its first few months alone it accumulated a total attendance figure of 60,000.

Other universities established professional theater companies earlier. U.C.L.A., Baylor, and Princeton all have professional theater programs of one kind or another. But the Michigan program, involving the retention of a playwright-in-residence, a series of lectures by guest stars, fellowships to promising graduate students, art exhibits bearing on the theater, all in addition to straight play production, is one of the most ambitious. As such, it has attracted observers from universities all over the country. So, too, has the Tyrone Guthrie Theatre in Minneapolis, which opened in 1963 and is linked with the University of Minnesota. Between the Michigan program and Guthrie opening, fires have been lighted in other places.

Looking at this from the outside, one discerns a pattern applicable to the other artistic disciplines as well. It does not seem wild to predict that before long colleges and universities may begin to tinker with professional production of dance and opera. It has already been responsibly proposed that universities adopt professional orchestras during their off-seasons.

What is happening is an experiment in patronage. The arts have long been weak economically, compared with higher education. Moreover, colleges and universities are much further advanced in techniques of fund raising, in scientific management of their resources, in developing ties with industry, foundations, and other sources of capital. Thus we witness the arts seeking— and getting— help from a bigger, better organized sector of the non-profit economy.

What effect is all this having on the community, on the artist, and on the quality of the arts? The answer in all three categories is encouraging. For the campus and for its surrounding community, the upsurge of college-sponsored cultural activity means a widening of opportunity. There is a net increase in the number and variety of cultural experiences available to the public. This is not only of immediate value, but it is also an investment in the future: through encouraging student attendance and participation, the colleges are building an audience. This is of immense long-range significance to off-campus arts institutions.

Colleges also reach out beyond their own populations to build tomorrow's audiences. Thus San Francisco State College and many other schools put on high-caliber children's theater for kids in their communities. Princeton's McCarter Theatre also runs a young people's program under which high-schoolers come in busloads to see grown-up plays presented by professionals.

In addition, colleges affect the community by serving as resource pools for the local arts institutions. As university arts faculties expand, their members radiate into the community, find places for themselves in established local cultural institutions, or help to create new ones. In Columbus, the conductor of the symphony orchestra, the concertmaster, and the first cellist are all faculty members at Ohio State. In the appreciative words of one local lawyer I spoke to: "We couldn't have the orchestra we do, if it weren't for O.S.U. It brings musicians to the city who otherwise would pass us by." In Cheney, Washington, a suburb of Spokane, the chairman of the art department of Eastern Washington State College helped stage an art exhibit of local work. The exhibition was turned over to the Spokane public library, and card holders were permitted to borrow the paintings free of charge. Such cases illustrate the imaginative, complex, and useful relationships that are beginning to develop between the hitherto traditionally antagonistic "town" and "gown" communities.

Sometimes colleges, or their populations, take organized steps to bolster the local arts institutions. In Nashville the Inter-Fraternity Council of Vanderbilt University assists the Nashville Symphony with its regular fund-raising campaigns by sending freshmen out to canvass the community door-to-door. In Northhampton, Massachusetts, Smith College has cooperated with the local theater manager to attract touring Broadway road shows. It circularized parents of students urging them to buy subscription tickets to the theater for their children.

On a more reciprocal basis, the University of Cincinnati sends its graduate students of art to study art history at the local museum. In Washington, D.C., graduate drama students at George Washington University are accruing academic credits for work done with the Arena Stage, Washington's nationally-known professional resident theater. Such joint efforts enrich educational programs and at the same time help strengthen the local arts institution and root it more deeply in the community. We may well see more of such activties as more cities develop their own indigenous cultural institutions.

Colleges are also developing formal organizational ties with community arts groups, sometimes sparking joint community-wide action. For example in Detroit, Wayne State University, under the direction of its then vice president William Birenbaum, took the lead in creating the Detroit Adventure program previously described. In Winston-Salem, North Carolina, where local cultural groups are united in a loose federation, Wake Forest College is a member. The same is true in other cities.

Such developing links between the academic community and local cultural institutions may be mutually stimulating. They can help raise the level of taste and performance in both participants as they diffuse the arts through society. If the new campus interest in the arts has a salutary effect on the community, how does it affect the artist?

For the artist, the picture is complicated. There has, for example, been much criticism of the in-residence programs. This is not the place to rehearse all the arguments, but, in brief, it is contended that, no matter how fruitful a period of residence may be for the students and faculty, it is usually sterile for the artist —that artists find it difficult to create in the hierarchical, status-conscious atmosphere of the typical academic community. This is open to fair discussion, but much depends on the individual artist and the individual campus. Generalization in so subtle a matter is dangerous.

Similarly, it has been charged that as colleges and universities have expanded their courses in the fine arts, and especially as they have begun to provide professional training in the arts, they have lowered standards of excellence. Their professional standards, as compared with those of our better independent conservatories and art schools, are, it is said, abominable. W. McNeil Lowry, a vice president of the Ford Foundation and for seven years director of its program in the humanities and the arts, has charged that universities have "in the main" sacrificed professionalism and have "drifted along with the society in the perpetuation of the amateur and the imitator." Mr. Lowry, a man of considerable personal influence because of the largesse he is in a position to distribute for the Ford Foundation, may or may not have a point here. But one hesitates to agree with his advice to university deans that: "Under present conditions the best service you can perform for the potential artist is to throw him out."

In other important respects the university's interest in the arts has proved a blessing to many artists. In the performing arts it is

perceptibly widening the market for talent. Since college performances are by no means unremunerative, this is putting more
money into the pocket of the artist. As a rule, schools no longer
expect to get away with cut-rate prices. When performers of the
stature of a Roberta Peters, a Jan Peerce, or a Robert Merrill sing
at a campus, they command $3,000 to $3,500 per performance. A
recital by Serkin will cost a college impresario $3,500 to $4,000,
and a single concert by Cliburn may run to $7,000. Lesser lumi-
naries are are less well paid, of course, but rates equal those paid
anywhere else. Says actor Walter Abel, whose credits in both
Hollywood and the legitimate stage are extensive, "I go to a lot
of colleges and universities, and they often pay more than an
actor can make for equivalent work on Broadway. I make a lot of
money this way."

But this is only one of the reasons why artists, many of whom
do not need the money, are traveling the new "sophisticated
Chautauqua." For one thing, university dates permit them to
sharpen their skills and expand their repertoire. Actors get a
chance to play roles they otherwise might never perform. Says
Jean Guest, administrator of the American National Theatre and
Academy's Great Artists Program: "Recently Howard Morris
played Gogol's *The Inspector General* at Flint Junior College in
Michigan. This was a role he had talked about for a long time,
but never had a crack at. And Ed Begley—he's an Oscar winner
and is not exactly starving for work—called me up saying he
wanted a chance to do something different. I asked him if he
would like to play in *J.B.* He said, 'Who'd ever ask me to play
J.B.?' I said Otterbein College would. He went, and he came back
all charged up about it. He told me he not only taught something,
but learned something, too."

Abel, who has made many such forays, is even more enthusiastic. It is not only the opportunity to play different roles, but to
perform for audiences different from the well-manicured Broadway variety. "I went out to the Eastern New Mexico University
in Portales," he told me. "By God, we put on Giraudoux's *The
Enchanted*. And who was the audience? Students and the ranchers
of eastern New Mexico! It was exciting, I'll tell you."

At C. W. Post College on Long Island, Abel delivered readings from Plato and Thucydides. "I read Pericles' *Oration,* too, and the place was filled. Imagine that!" At M.I.T., which is supposedly turning out some of our best skilled barbarians, Abel gave a poetry reading at a graduate dinner. He read from Shakespeare and Edward Arlington Robinson. Afterward, he says, "they got so wrapped up in it that we flocked up to the professor's place. We drank beer and I read, more, and more, and more. The thing was supposed to be over at 8:30. I didn't get out until after midnight!"

What is perhaps most encouraging about the cultural awakening on campus is the fact that the audiences are not only different, they are, from an artist's point of view, good audiences. They are receptive to the new, the experimental, the complex and the esoteric. The University of Wisconsin polls its concert-goers and, to a degree, frames its programs to meet their interests. It recently summarized these interests as follows: "You have asked for new repertory, small instrumental groups, Bach, the guitar, unusual instruments, new artists, young talents, and as always, the great names." Edgar Kneedler, eastern sales manager of Columbia Artists Management, Inc., and a former musician himself, reports: "The colleges don't want hackneyed programs. More and more the unusual is requested, along with the best of the standard repertory. And they are wide open to the contemporary literature." This same finding is echoed by others, too. According to Norwood Baker, who has run the arts program of the Association of American Colleges for many years: "The audiences are more intelligent now than they were in the past. The musicians have their choice of programming. There is much more acceptance of contemporary work. The Dorian Quartet, for example, went out to South Carolina State College in Orangeburg. They played Hindemith, Piston, Barber and others like that and came back raving about the wonderful response they got."

This openness and searching is reflected in the number of premiere performances being given on campuses. At a recent arts festival sponsored by the University of Rhode Island, Charles Whittenberg's *Three Songs on Texts of Rainer Maria Rilke* received their first performance. The same festival offered the first American performance of *Happy Haven* by the British dramatist

John Arden. Similarly, composer Bernhard Heiden's opera *The Darkened City* received its first performance at Indiana. And premieres are accompanied by American debuts. The Leningrad Philharmonic, the Tokyo classical ballet, Komaki, the conductor of the Madrid Philharmonic, all made their initial American appearance in college auditoriums.

At the same time unusual work, new and old, is being given an airing it could never get on Broadway or in our major concert halls. East Carolina College has mounted *The Wages of Sin,* a play by U Nu, the former premier of Burma. At U.C.L.A. a recent concert of American chamber music featured quartets by Walter Piston and Roy Harris and one attributed to that versatile genius Benjamin Franklin. Little-known works like *The Fair at Sorochinsk* by Moussorgsky, *Der Glorreiche Augenblick* by Beethoven, or *The Bacchae* by Euripides are turning up with increasing frequency in campus programs.

The same questing spirit is found in other activities, too. The University of Michigan is considering a fascinating proposal by several faculty members to create a "Performance Arts Research Laboratory," that would probe into the architecture and technology of the arts. Other campuses are displaying an exhibition of plans, photographs, and text dealing with *The Ideal Theatre*. Yale has made a beautful color film on the technique of staging an art exhibit. Everywhere the movement is toward freshness and experiment.

This is not to suggest that everything is perfect. A much-publicized incident at the University of Mississippi saw the arrest of a faculty artist on grounds that he "did unlawfully desecrate a flag of the Confederacy." The plaintiff was a student. At just about the same time, Baylor University forced its professional theater to close down a run of O'Neill's *Long Day's Journey Into Night* because officials of the Baptist-affiliated university found its language "offensive." But in both cases the artists received broad support from the academic community, and both represent exceptions to the open-mindedness evident in most places. (San Francisco State College, in a series of art films, even went so far as to present *The Hard Swing,* "a subjective study of a strip

dancer," without arousing a snort from trustees or state legis-
lators.)

Indeed, if any broad criticism can be made, it is only that the
campus cultural awakening is so free and unchanneled that it
may not be achieving all that it conceivably might. Many musicians and managers, for example, still have not awakened to the
fact that they can put on better programs on the campus than
when they appear under the auspices of a commercial impresario.
Says one faculty member who until recently ran the cultural
program for his institution: "I would get absolutely disgusted—
especially with singers—because they would put in too much
popular material. They were always singing down." It is likely,
before long, that more artists will recognize and take advantage
of the new freedom that campus appearances offer them.

Moreover, the level of taste on campus—and ultimately in the
broad public—may be improved even further by a conscious
linkage of cultural programming with the academic life of the
school. At some institutions this is already done. Says one music
agent: "The fascinating thing about college and university audiences is that they often prepare for the concert. They listen in
advance to recordings of the work. They discuss the program." It
would be a pity if music and art were talked to death on the
campus. The important thing remains the performance, the
experience of listening or watching. But imaginative steps can be
taken to relate this experience to life and to learning. At Dartmouth, for example, students are offered a series devoted to
religion and the arts. Its planners hope that this relationship will
be explored not only on the stage and in the art gallery, but in
the classrooms as well. Here is a challenge to which university
cultural planning committees might well address themselves. Too
often their discussions revolve around mechanics, costs and similar
problems. Still new at the business of being impresarios, they are
spending too much time on these essentially secondary matters. It
might help if campus impresarios, and the committees that over-
see them, were placed under the authority of the president's
office, or of an academic dean, rather than, as often happens,
under "building and grounds," or "special services."

"Leave the big names to local enterprise," suggests Dean Birenbaum of the New School for Social Research, "Let someone else bring in the Isaac Sterns and the Robert Frosts. They're fine, but anyone can fill a hall with them. Unless there just is no one else to do it, the university should not bother with this. Instead, it should be the function of the university to be the 'cutting edge' —the promoter of the avant-garde, the innovational." Harold Taylor, former president of Sarah Lawrence, puts the sentiment in other words. "The university," he has said, "is the exact place for the exploration of the new." The campus is already moving rapidly toward the very vortex of imaginative experimentation in the arts. It can, however, advance even further in this direction— and it should.

On balance, one cannot assess the general tendency of culture in the U.S., or the impact of the cultural explosion, without taking into account the radically changed relationship between culture and higher education. The higher education industry has, as it were, undertaken to support the weaker and still underdeveloped culture industry. Those who have always seen a kinship between culture and education will be pleased, but not, perhaps, surprised. More startling, as we shall now see, is the changed relationship of culture and commerce in American society.

7

Culture, Incorporated

IT IS AN ARTICLE OF FAITH AMONG MANY CULTURE LOVERS AND artists that what is good for General Motors is *not* good for art. And Henry Ford did nothing to endear the American business system to artists when he asked Lord Duveen, "what would I want with the original pictures when the ones right here in these books are so beautiful?" Indeed, throughout American history the only thing lower than the businessman's reputation among artists has been the artist's reputation among businessmen. This mutual mistrust contributed to a sharp-edged alienation among artists which, at least according to some, is absolutely essential for their well-being. Today a rapprochement is under way between business and art in America, and it threatens to undo the cherished alienation of the artists as it changes the position of art in the American context.

Efforts to close the gap between business and art in America are not entirely new, as Russell Lynes, a perceptive and good humored commentator on American mores, has pointed out. As early as 1876 when the great Centennial Exposition opened in Philadelphia there were those who sought a marriage of art and industry. Most such early efforts had to do with industrial design, for it was recognized, at least since the days of Ruskin and William Morris, that the rise of the machine-made product would have a profound impact on aesthetics. It is only in the last generation, however, that design has become a truly important concern of industry. With affluence has come increased attention to the extra-functional characteristics of consumer goods. Today we see the work of the industrial designer in the beautiful curves and panels of the IBM Selectric typewriter, in the Ford Mustang, and in hundreds of other products. In architecture, too, business has begun to pay attention to how things look as well as how they function. To view the Whitaker Park cigarette factory of Reynolds Tobacco in Winston-Salem, and to look at older tobacco tobacco plants nearby, is to be struck with the contrast. The new automated plant may not be a work of lasting architectural glory, but it is visually pleasant. Its forerunners were not.

Moreover, while businessmen like Frick, Morgan, and Mellon were lavish art patrons half-a-century ago, the corporation, as distinct from the individual businessman, was sealed off from the whole world of the artist. It is only since the end of World War II, with the detonation of the cultural explosion, that we have begun to witness the development of complex, multi-level relationships between commerce and culture in America. Thus we find the American Export and Isbrandtsen Lines donating $135,-000 to the Metropolitan Opera to help underwrite the cost of a new production of *Aïda*. We find Olin Mathieson contributing to the Museum of Modern Art, Standard Oil of California donating money to a number of West Coast symphony orchestras, and Dow Chemical helping to finance a little theater in Texas.

A quick glance down any list of well-known American companies will reveal literally scores that, in one way or another, have become involved with artists or with cultural institutions: Johnson's Wax, Chase Manhattan, Shell Oil, Sara Lee Kitchens, not to speak of thousands of obscure small businesses which emulate the giants. In North Carolina a small gift shop turns over ten per cent of its profits on Christmas card sales to a local arts group, and in California a chain of apparel stores establishes a $5,000 annual prize for the best novel or collection of poems or stories by a young American writer.

Nor is involvement with the arts limited to cash donations. In lieu of money, many businesses nowadays contribute goods or services. The Boston Arts Festival, for example, has received free paint, trucking services, even structural iron from local companies. The Arts Council of Winston-Salem enjoys the assistance of Western Electric in working out job descriptions, pay scales, and other personnel policies for its employees. Elsewhere businessmen provide free meeting rooms or office space or free public relations service; they even "lend" executives to orchestras, museums, and other arts institutions to help during fund drives.

What is true of individual companies is also increasingly true of trade associations and other business organizations. Even chambers of commerce, those traditional bastions of phillistinism, are doing things of which Babbitt never dreamed. A survey of 147 chambers conducted by *Arts Management,* a newsletter for the executives of cultural institutions, found that nearly one out of every five chambers made direct financial contributions to local arts groups, and fully four out of five provided rent-free space, handled mailings, donated printing or other services to them. The Hartford, Connecticut, Chamber of Commerce even reported having a "Vice President for Cultural Resources."

Such organizations tend to be even more conservative and cautious than individual businesses. They tend to reflect, rather than determine, the attitudes of the companies affiliated with them. That these organizations have begun to inch toward the arts is a measure of the degree to which the arts have become respectable in business circles.

All such activities can be categorized as patronage. Through them business makes a gift of goods, services, or money to an artist or an arts institution. But patronage is only one of many links between the business community and the culture industry. Thus, in addition to serving as a patron, business is beginning to find it profitable to serve as entrepreneur in the arts.

The most interesting example of this second form of relationship is offered by Allied Stores Corporation, a sprawling complex of retail stores and shopping centers with annual sales of $770 million. Allied now finds itself in the business of producing legitimate theater. The corporation was the owner-operator of the Bergen Mall Shopping Center in Paramus, New Jersey, when an outside group approached it with the idea of mounting summer stock in the little theater located in the center. A lease was drawn, and for two summers Allied watched with growing interest as the musicals and plays attracted large numbers of enthusiastic suburbanites to Bergen Mall. In 1962 Allied decided that, instead of simply leasing the theater for the summer, it would go into the theatrical producing business itself on a year-round basis.

It remodeled and improved the theater building. It hired Robert Ludlum, a professional producer. It assigned him a budget and told him to assemble a staff. Today Allied's Playhouse on the Mall mounts eight performances a week of 18 or more productions spread over 11 months each year. Its presentations range from musicals and light farces to children's theater and Shakespeare.

The playhouse, according to Mr. A. F. Crowley, assistant real estate manager of Allied Stores, is now a profit-generating enterprise. The theater yields a return at least equal to the amount Allied would realize by leasing the property to a retailer. Moreover, it has brought with it a number of pleasantly profitable side-effects. First, because it lures big crowds, it has increased substantially the sales volume in the stores and restaurants nearest it, thus enhancing their profitability and real estate value. Second, says Mr. Crowley, the theater has helped attract to Bergen Mall an especially desirable type of customer. Since the theater-going suburbanite tends to be a cut above his non-theater-going neighbor in terms of education and affluence, he is as a rule a bigger spender, too. The experiment in Paramus has been so successful that the interest of other shopping center operators has been excited, and we may expect similar playhouses to crop up in other locations soon.

Allied's unusual decision to become an entrepreneur in the arts has its counterpart in the announcement by the Interpublic Group, the advertising agency, that it will operate a fine arts gallery, and in the decision of Sears, Roebuck & Co., to go into the business of selling original paintings. In a highly publicized move, Sears engaged Vincent Price, the Hollywood actor and art collector, to assemble a large collection of paintings for sale in its stores.

Whatever one may think of the level of taste reflected in the Sears collection, or of the admittedly commercial motives of the venture, no one can gainsay its economic success. According to George H. Struthers, the Sears vice president who originated the scheme, the show has been "a virtual sellout in almost every location." More important, it has been successful in attracting considerable middle-class traffic to stores in which the clientele had been predominantly low-income. This, indeed, was the real objective of the venture, and Sears public relations officials beam when they tell of the surgeon who came to buy an etching and purchased a pair of sneakers on the way out.

There have always been a few relatively small industries in the United States the primary function of which has been to sell culture or culture-related goods to the American consumer. The culture boom of recent years has been a blessing to them. Thus the musical instrument industry has watched happily as its sales climbed from $235 million in 1950 to $670 million in 1963. What is new and different today is the entry into this kind of business of companies whose primary function has little or nothing to do with the arts. What, for example, could be further afield from culture than the manufacture of medical supplies? Yet Johnson & Johnson, the *Wall Street Journal* informs us, "finds a lucrative market for scraps cut from plaster-impregnated bandages used for setting broken bones. Formerly the company paid to have the waste plaster carted away. Now, however, it sells the scrap to schools and art stores for sculpture work at up to $9.75 for 20 pounds." The Stanford Research Institute, in a study cited earlier, predicted that by 1970 the culture market will have grown to a startling $7 billion a year. Significantly, this $7 billion market-to-be is not entirely controlled by individual consumers. An important slice of it represents purchases to be made by cultural institutions. Thus business is also increasingly linked with the arts in the role of vendor to cultural institutions.

The tremendous proliferation of cultural activity around the nation has created, among other things, a great demand for new or improved physical facilities for the arts. Cities are engaged in a cultural construction boom unlike anything before in American history. Theaters, concert halls, museum wings, art centers are sprouting everywhere, and it is industry that is supplying the seats, the carpeting, the lights, the concrete, the steel girders, the air conditioning units, easels and acoustical tiles.

There is also a thriving multi-million-dollar business in the sale of insurance to museums, theaters, and other similar enterprises. A major moving company claims a "Fine Arts Division" that makes "exhibition tour arrangements." Companies are selling paper and printing, heating oil, food, paper cups, soft drinks, and hundreds of other items to the arts. There is even a burgeoning business in the sale of management surveys to institutions like symphony orchestras and civic groups planning art centers. Cultural institutions have always had to rely on business for certain goods and services, but they never before represented anything like a significant market, except for a few small specialized companies. Today for the first time, arts institutions have become a customer worth catering to.

Finally, business is not only serving as *patron, entrepreneur,* and *vendor,* but as *buyer,* purchasing the services of artists or of cultural institutions.

The most spectacular examples of this relationship between the world of business and the world of art lie in the interest in painting manifested recently by many companies. The $500,000 collection of contemporary art that adorns the walls of the Chase Manhattan Building in New York, the $750,000 collection of American art purchased by Johnson's Wax, the smaller collections bought by the Mead Corp., a Georgia paper manufacturer, all offer excellent examples. So enthusiastic has business become about collecting works of art that Ruder & Finn, a large public relations firm, boasts a department that does little else but arrange for client companies to sponsor art exhibits and buy paintings.*

Less well known is the tendency of business to buy musical services. Last fall when Basic-Witz Furniture Industries of Waynesboro, Virginia, wanted to commemorate its 75th anniversary, it commissioned composer Robert Evett to write a concerto for it, and then hired the National Symphony Orchestra to perform the work at a special concert, thus purchasing the services of both an individual artist and a musical institution. Similarly, the Manhattan Savings Bank, which employs a full-time "musical director" and sponsors noon-hour concerts in its lobby, purchases the services of the concert recitalists who perform for it. As time

---

* One reason for the enthusiasm lies in the rapid appreciation of the value of many company collections. The rising art market of recent years has made many a company comptroller chortle with delight.

goes by, business will increase its purchases from artists and cultural institutions.

The four relationships described above only begin to suggest the developing complexity of business links with the arts. For example, business might turn up in the role of moneylender, if an imaginative proposal made to the National Association of Music Merchants is ever acted upon. Addressing a meeting of this organization, E. B. Weiss, an advertising executive, asked, "Why shouldn't your total industry establish a revolving fund that would aid, within sound banking formulas, the financial needs of new cultural centers?" He pointed out that such a program offered "a unique opportunity to guide the expenditure of vast sums that will be directly applied to what you are selling—funds that do not come out of your own treasury. I know of no industry that so totally overlooks such a remarkable golden opportunity."

The industry is not, at this moment, rushing to take advantage of this particular golden opportunity. But the proposal suggests that what we have seen so far in the growth of intricate links between art and business may be only the beginning.

Taken together these newly important links add up to another basic change in the ecology of art in America. Why is it happening now? One reason is that the rise of the comfort class has created an entirely new kind of market-place in America. Business has responded not only by producing a higher proportion of luxuries and goods of marginal necessity than before, but by altering its merchandising techniques as well. For this vast new comfort class public the old advertising claim of low price has lost some of its potency, while the claim of quality has gained.

In consequence, we hear more and more talk among marketing executives about "the culture sell." What this means is not merely that culture itself can, in certain of its forms, be sold for a profit, but that it can be exploited to help move other products. For culture connotes quality, and Madison Avenue has found that it can, in public relations parlance, "upgrade the image" of a product by associating it with culture.

This associational linkage was consciously in the minds of the advertising men at Batten, Barton, Durstine & Osborn who arranged for Corning Glass Works to sponsor the telecast of the inaugural concert at Lincoln Center. It lies behind the use of DeKoonings and Baskins in the advertising of the Container Corporation of America. At one level, this is conducted with good taste. (Who can object when a bank uses an art gallery as a background for its advertising photography?) On another level, we have the kind of culture hucksterism symbolized by the article in *Drug News Weekly* that proclaims ungrammatically: "Chance to Cash In Seen On Current Pop Art Fad . . . Retailers! . . . There's gold in being bold!" In either case, one major motive behind the rapprochement is clearly and calculatedly commercial. Culture has public relations value today.

A second motivation has to do with employee relations. Industry relies to an ever-increasing extent upon highly educated technical, professional, and administrative personnel, and the entire work force must be better educated than in the past. These changes in the character of the labor force are reflected in the policies of many companies that encourage cultural activity among their employees. A paper company in Nekoosa, Wisconsin, and a bakery in Norwalk, Connecticut, sponsor art shows of works painted by their employees. General Motors distributes 600,000 booklets entitled *French Impressionism* and *Masterpieces from the Louvre,* while Bell Telephone Company in Newark, New Jersey, turns over an auditorium in which the Garden State Ballet can present dance-lecture demonstrations for the workers.

More important, as industry redistributes itself geographically across the face of the continent, it has come to consider the cultural ambience of a community a significant factor in plant location decisions. Highly educated employees do not like to live in culturally arid communities, and it is no accident that some companies in Cincinnati, for example, have sent descriptions of that city's cultural resources to workers they hope to recruit. This also explains why regions eager to lure industry are suddenly advertising cultural resources the way they once advertised cheap labor or low-cost power. A typical ad seeking to attract industry to the Middle South proclaims, "even small towns have theater groups, orchestras, art museums, concert and lecture series." The accompanying photo shows a pretty girl sculpting.

But, backing up all these corporate reasons is the often overlooked factor of personal interest. The idea is increasingly accepted nowadays that management must be responsible, not merely to the stockholder, but to the different publics of the corporation, including the consumer, the worker, the community. This notion, along with the growing divorce of ownership from control of industry, places the manager in the position of mediator among the sometimes conflicting demands of these different publics, and frees him, to a degree, to follow his own judgment and to indulge his own tastes. Since the modern business executive is himself, very often, a part of the affluent, well-educated comfort class, it should surprise no one if he shares some of its enthusiasms.

Thus one additional motive force behind the rapprochement is the businessman's own personal interest. This can sometimes be a very powerful factor. It was clearly the personal interest of Walter Paepcke that led the Container Corporation into its employment of first-rate contemporary artists for its advertising and impelled him to found the Aspen Festival. Similar, less-known examples could be cited again and again. However cynical one may be about business, it would be a mistake to underestimate the importance of the genuinely interested individual in propelling business toward its increasing involvement with the arts.

The rapprochement is thus fueled by a mixture of motives. Some businessmen are genuinely interested in the arts. Others merely want to make a buck. Some are interested *and* avaricious. Yet all important social developments spring from a variety of motives. Indeed, one might argue convincingly that all human actions—including the act of creating art—stem from mixed, or, as it were, impure motives. Once motives have been explored the more important question—that of effect—remains to be answered. What impact will the interlacing of business and art have on business itself, on cultural institutions, and, finally, on the artist?

Business will be touched and changed in many ways. The Stanford Research Institute study, apart from predicting sharply increased sales of various culture-related products, argues persuasively that business will become more conscious of aesthetics in general during the decade ahead. The emphasis on product design and attractive buildings will be strengthened. Moreover, it predicts, "Culture consciousness will influence the offerings and presentation style of all mass communications media as advertisers and the public demand increasingly high levels of artistic performance." Not only output, but production and organization will be influenced, the study asserts. Factories, it suggests, "might be rendered more attractive by areas with rotating cultural exhibits." Some firms, it continues, may go so far as to "develop an Arts Advisory Group" employing professional artists along with psychologists, sociologists, market researchers and other specialists, to guide the company in judging consumer taste, in redesigning products, and in advertising. The Stanford Research Institute report does not say so, but such groups might also ultimately be responsible for company policy affecting patronage, purchase of cultural services, or sales to the institutional cultural market as such.

Perhaps the most profound impact on the company will be made by the artist himself. Whether through the creation of such advisory groups employing professional artists, or through a great expansion of the purchase of service of outside artists and arts institutions, or through an extension of entrepreneurial activity in the arts, the business firm is going to come into increasingly intimate contact with the artistic personality. In the words of John Kenneth Galbraith, "the American businessman, having accommodated himself to the scientists in the course of accommodating himself to the twentieth century, must now come to terms with the artist. Artistic perception is as necessary to the modern manufacturer of consumer goods as engineering skill. Indeed, now more so."

For their part, cultural institutions will also be changed. Any increase in patronage funds from business, or sale of services to business, will help them economically. In addition, they are likely to seek and find new services to sell to business. Certain museums, for example, already offer specialized assistance to business. The Brooklyn Museum's Industrial Design Laboratory has been used by fashion companies, furniture makers, carpet manufacturers and others. We may find analogs of one kind or another developing in theater, music, and dance.

Another consequence of the rapprochement will be a significant increase in the local influence of cultural institutions. This will stem from their increasing importance as a customer for industry's goods. Arts groups frequently find themselves testifying before city councils, for example, on matters of zoning or civic beautification plans, or in an effort to obtain public funds for their projects. The fact that they may be in a position to award a million-dollar construction contract for a new arts center will not hurt them in their efforts to seek political support for their points of view. Building contractors, even building trades unions, have been known to bring their community influence to bear on behalf of a good customer or job provider. The indifference or hostility that cultural institutions have, on occasion, found among businessmen may well be replaced by a new respect. Money talks.

Because of this, there is peril as well as promise ahead for arts organizations. The new links with business could alter, in a negative way, the quality or content of the culture they provide for their communities. If, as a purchaser of services, business diverts the attention and energy of the cultural institution from its primary task, the cultural organization may find that it has sold its soul too easily. Similarly, if through its role as patron—that is, contributor—business demands an inappropriate *quo* for its *quid*, the cultural institution may find itself in deep trouble.

Exactly what business patrons may, or may not, expect for their money is a question that will receive increasing attention from the boards of museums, theaters, orchestras, opera companies and art centers. There is room for much debate over the proposal of Thomas Buechner, director of the Brooklyn Museum, who says, "I would recommend, and probably much to the horror of many colleagues, that large grants be accompanied by a request for representation on the board . . . at least during the period covered by the grant."

It can be assumed that companies will find increasing representation on cultural boards. This could have advantages. It is unfortunate but true that arts organizations are often miserably mis-managed. Increased business representation could bring with it sorely needed improvement. In the words of Devereux C. Josephs, former chairman of the New York Life Insurance Company and a member of several cultural boards, arts organizations can profitably borrow from business "many procedures which have been tested out in the pragmatic arena of our competitive society—accounting, budget-making, managerial responsibility, organizational structure, building maintenance. . . ."

But, should business turn into a powerful influence on behalf of artistic conservatism or of vulgar popularization, it may well be that the price for business patronage will have been too high. Cultural institutions in the past learned to accommodate themselves, through a combination of tactics, to the pressures of individual rich patrons. The pressures that emanate from the corporate patron will be no less demanding.

But the most subtle pressure of all will be reserved not for the cultural institution, but for the artist: the pressure of acceptance.

So deep has been the antagonism between culture and commerce in our country that artists and intellectuals are made nervous by the very mention of the two in the same breath. It is a fashionable critical cliché that any such rapprochement must, of necessity, bring with it a debasement of the artist. There is an uneasy feeling that the businessman, to the degree that he remains primarily interested in selling his goods, is "using" the artist. Of course he is. But is this necessarily evil?

The notion that "using" the artist is bad, in and of itself, implies a whole philosophy of art. It implies that art is self-justifying, and that when we make of the art work a means to an end we rob it of its integrity and value. Yet the history of culture abounds with examples of works of art produced and exploited for non-aesthetic reasons. Arnold Hauser reminds us that for the very earliest artists, the cave painters, art "had a thoroughly pragmatic function aimed entirely at direct economic objectives." The artist believed that his painting magically influenced his food supply. Painting was a kind of hunting-in-effigy.

In the sixteenth century the Catholic Church, then the single most important source of patronage, spelled out plainly in the Council of Trent that art, in its view, was not an end but a means. Indeed, it employed that very word in the explanation that "by means of the stories of the mysteries of our redemption portrayed in paintings and other representations the people are instructed and confirmed in the articles of faith." It would be difficult to maintain that the art produced for the Church (often by artists whose own religious sincerity was open to question) suffered because it was viewed as a means to a non-aesthetic end. And when the good Dutch burghers hired Rembrandt to paint their portraits, was this out of an intrinsic concern for art? Or was it out of the same considerably less elevated motive that nowadays sends the corporation president to have his photograph taken by Bachrach?

Because the artist is hired to produce a work intended to serve some non-aesthetic purpose does not necessarily mean that what he produces must be bad art. The relationship of the artist to the patron has always held peril (for patron as well as the artist). Whether such a relationship yields excellence or mediocrity depends primarily on the quality and integrity of the artist himself. For, at least in our society, the artist is under no compulsion to accept a commission that debases him. Every patron, consciously or otherwise, wants something in return for his generosity, though he may, in the interests of artistic freedom, refrain from pressuring the artist. It is up to the artist to strike his own deal in each situation. That is what artists have always done.

The fact is that vis-à-vis the business patron, the artist stands in perhaps a stronger position to assert his own will than he does vis-à-vis other kinds of patrons. The business community itself is complex and pluralistic. It embodies many different interests, levels of taste, and internal contradictions. Thus there is little likelihood that business patronage, as such, will push art in any single direction. When the Whitney Museum in 1960 mounted an exhibit composed of paintings and sculpture from company collections, one critic was moved to write, not without pleasant surprise, "what business buys turns out not to be categorically different from what the non-business buyers of American art have bought."

The hostility or cynicism with which many artists and intellectuals view the growing interpenetration of business and art can often be traced to an anachronous political liberalism that instinctively abhors business and all its works. Their objection is frequently expressed in terms of the artist's "sellout" to the blandishments of business. Implied in this point of view is the questionable premise that the artist's primary function is that of a social critic. If business lures the artist somehow into its sinister fold, will he then be able to discharge this function?

Frequently, the case is put in terms of alienation. If links between business and art proliferate, it is going to be harder and harder for the artist to remain alienated. Despite its pluralism, our society remains a business society, and to be alienated is to be, in one sense or another, opposed to business and the structure of values that surround it. It is easy to be opposed to the central institution of one's society when one is locked outside the system by neglect, indifference, or active hostility on the part of the men who make it run. It is much harder when one is invited within the gates and permitted to share its fruits.

We can now see ahead to the time when corporate payrolls will include at least a sprinkling of professional artists, musicians, dancers, perhaps even dramatists and composers—and not merely to produce overt advertising. More important, business money will become an increasingly vital part of the patronage that keeps our museums, orchestras, operas and theaters alive, and there will be an everyday interchange between the two worlds of art and business. In this situation it is going to be ever more difficult for the artist to remain irreconcilable.

This, according to some, is the greatest possible threat to the future of art in America. They see art as springing out of the tension between an artist and his society. Says educator Harold Taylor, "Alienation . . . is the source of one of (the artist's) greatest strengths." Poet Karl Shapiro insists that "there is scarcely a writer of any kind who is not at war with the society or Way of Life, or the Establishment. . . ." And Herbert Read declares that "the artist is an 'outsider' in a democratic community, and all our schemes for democratic patronage of the arts cannot disguise the fact." The artist's only salvation, he writes, is "withdrawal from the social contract."

Herbert Blau, co-director of the San Francisco Actor's Workshop, sharpens the attack. He charges that the artist in America today is already caught "in the Age of the Pay-Off . . ."; that he is in danger of being bought off by "the well-oiled, the Neiman-Marcus set and Cadillac crowd." Blau reminds us, "Matthew Josephson once wrote about Henry Clay Frick, sitting in a Renaissance chair under a Rembrandt, reading the *Saturday Evening Post*." The "strange new menace" of contemporary American life for the artist, Mr. Blau insists, is "the enormous danger of easy assimilation."

Apart from erring—it was a baldachino, not a Rembrandt, that poor Mr. Frick sat under, according to Mr. Josephson—Mr. Blau is overly exercised. The theory that art is impossible without alienation is widely held. But that doesn't make it true.

Assimilation does not necessarily spell doom for art. One need only glance again at the social history of art to realize that the theory implicit in such remarks is, actually, a relatively recent one, and that history overflows with examples of great artists who, at least so far as we, at this distance, can tell, appeared to be totally assimilated, wholly at one with their society. Alienation is not the *sine qua non* of art. As Rudolf and Margot Wittkower point out in their excellent study, *Born Under Saturn,* there are fashions in the posture that artists adopt toward their society. Alienation is merely one such posture that happens to be currently fashionable. It has its roots in the rise of romanticism; it has been given a boost, during our time, by the Marxist injunction that the artist must be a revolutionist (though only in non-communist societies); and it lingers on today. But leafing through history one can cite Rubens, Titian, Bernini, van Dyck, Velasquez or Reynolds as artists who would have smiled derisively at the theory that alienation is essential to art. In literature we would hardly characterize Chaucer or Samuel Johnson as "aliens" in their own societies.

This is not to argue that the artist must accept his society at face value, or that he must blindly accept the values of business. We need artists who are anti-establishment, perhaps even poisonously alienated. We need the Jack Levines who paint bitter caricatures of generals and politicians, and artists who satirize, expose, challenge or simply ignore business, businessmen, and all that business implies. But to insist that the artist "must" remain alienated is, logically, just as restrictive of his freedom as the demand that he become a yea-sayer to all he sees around him.

The artist needs freedom to rebel, to assent—or merely to shrug. Maintaining that freedom, like any other, requires vigilance and spunk. In the case of the artist or the arts institution it requires the courage to spurn a patron who attaches invidious strings to his patronage. But the brand of spunk needed is no different whether the patron happens to be a businessman, a corporation, or, for that matter, a university dean, a foundation bureaucrat, or a government agency employee. When has the artist not needed the courage of his convictions?

The rise of business interest in the arts not only is not, in itself, harmful; it may, in fact, be beneficial, since it increases both the sum total of economic support for the arts, and, more importantly, it increases the number of different sources to which art institutions and artists may turn for help. This is a fact of commanding importance. It *increases* the maneuverability of the artist. It puts him in a better bargaining position. Moreover, it might well be argued that business, by "using" art in one way or another, is giving it a much more important place in American life than hitherto accorded it. Those who bewail the divorce of art from life in industrial civilization, but at the same time insist that it remain totally isolated from the workaday pursuits of that civilization, including those of business, misunderstand the sociology of art. They want to have their cake and eat it.

What the rapprochement of business and art requires of the artist or the cultural institution like the orchestra or museum is a new awareness of their place in society, along with a consciously analytical attitude toward patronage. They must be prepared to scrutinize offers of support and to determine, in a rational and hard-headed way, whether the bargain implied in any patronage arrangement is advantageous or not. The artist, it goes without saying, should not lend himself to a deal that violates his own aesthetic values. He must be prepared to fight for them. But in this way he is no different from anyone else. The politician, the journalist, the professor, even the business executive, must also be willing to fight for his own professional integrity.

The artist is now going to be integrated into American society to a degree unprecedented in the past century. This must affect his work in some way. But art has never been produced in a social vacuum. It has always been under pressure. It is a mistake to assume that the pressure of acceptance will kill it. Art is more resilient that most of us imagine. And so is the artist. What is good for General Motors may conceivably be good for art.

8

The Organizational Revolution

WORLD ATLASES OFTEN CONTAIN MULTI-COLORED MAPS THAT DEPICT the distribution of the earth's natural resources—copper here, tungsten there, and oil in the sheikdom of Kuwait. If we could somehow create a "cultural resources" map of the United States as it was in the mid-'forties, and another showing the distribution of artists and cultural institutions in the mid-'sixties, striking differences would be immediately apparent.

If we were to place a blue dot on the map for every museum, theater, opera company, dance group or artist, we would find on the earlier map a heavy concentration of blue in a few major cities, principally in the East. There would be a light sprinkling of blue elsewhere. And there would be vast dun-colored stretches of desert in between. Today's map, by contrast, would still show heavy blue concentrations in our major cities, but the blue dots elsewhere would have multiplied miraculously, and the stretches of desert shrunk considerably. Decentralization has been at work. Although our best cultural institutions are still to be found in the great population centers, seeds of excellence have been scattered in many other places as well.

Scattered, however, is the word. For the blue dots, even today, form no sensible or systematic pattern on the map. They look as if they had, indeed, been scattered over the map by the random handful. Moreover, if we step back from the map and turn to the real world, instead, the impression of disorder is heightened. In one city we find several museums, but no theater; another will boast two theaters, but no dance company; a third has several of each of these, but no orchestra. In short, we are struck by the chaotic character of our cultural growth. And yet, beneath the surface a powerful counter-tendency toward order is operating. This impulse is one of the most important—and least understood —forces on the American cultural scene today. To understand it we must look at its several manifestations: at the emergence of arts councils, at the great cultural building boom, and at the rise of that startling new concept, the arts center. For these three, taken together, add up to a broad movement toward rationalization in the culture industry of the United States. They amount to nothing less than an organizational revolution in the arts.

Between 1945 and 1950 arts councils were formed in eight American cities. By 1955 their number had multiplied to 25. Today arts councils already exist in 125 communities from Jacksonville, Florida, to Tacoma, Washington, and new ones are forming all the time. An additional 35 councils have sprung up across the border in Canada.

An arts council is a loose federation that brings together the cultural institutions of a community for cooperative purposes. Typically, the arts institutions in a community are fiercely independent, each with its own devoted following, each competitive and suspicious of its neighbors. This rugged free enterprise has the advantages of being loose, free, and open, as well as colorful and lively. But it also has disadvantages, both artistic and economic. Thus it carries with it a tendency toward sectarianism and an instability that prevents maximum development of each institution's artistic potentials. It tends to limit the institution's effectiveness in attracting a wide audience or broad financial backing. The arts council is an attempt to overcome these disadvantages within the framework of voluntary cooperation.

In Albany, New York, for example, a council was born after a reporter from the *Knickerbocker News* found that he was supposed to cover three different cultural events all scheduled for different places at the same time. He called the three sponsoring groups together and complained. Such conflicts do more than inconvenience newspapermen; they cut the audience potential for each event. Recognizing this, the local arts leaders created a council, one of the continuing functions of which is to prevent scheduling conflicts. Elsewhere councils have been formed to solve other, more pressing problems, a need for a new auditorium, perhaps, or a chronic shortage of financial backing.

There is no "standard model" arts council. The movement is still too young and fluid. Some councils are no more than paper organizations; others are well-established by now, with a record achievement behind them. Just how the organization of an arts council can act as a cultural stimulant in a community is dramatized by the history of St. Paul, Minnesota.

St. Paul is right across the river from Minneapolis, and its citizens were often struck by a cultural anomaly. Minneapolis was the home of one of the nation's outstanding orchestras and a thriving art museum, as well as an academic community and many flourishing amateur arts groups. St. Paul, by contrast, was historically devoid of culture. Its great railroad magnates and merchants, unlike those across the river, showed little interest in becoming patrons of the arts. In the late 'forties St. Paul's cultural life, such as it was, centered around a group of rattletrap institutions, each fighting a lonely battle against extinction. There was an art gallery and school operated by a part-time director. There was a science museum crammed into a decrepit house. A little theater group presented an unending succession of thrillers and comedies. A nondescript opera society and a civic orchestra of little promise just about completed the picture. The only really going concern was the Schubert Club, which imported professional musical artists for concerts several times a year.

In 1949, with a grant from the Hill Family Foundation, the St. Paul Junior League engaged a research firm to survey the city's cultural resources. Its report, issued in 1950, painted an appropriately desolate picture, pointed out that one great need was for decent physical facilities for the arts groups, and urged that a central coordinating agency be created in the arts. The following year the orchestra, the opera, the science museum, the gallery-school, and the Schubert Club sat down together to do something about the situation.

For two years they met sporadically and struggled to solve the problem of physical accommodations. They needed exhibition space, classrooms, rehearsal facilities, and the like. And then a breakthrough came. Working closely with Frank Marzitelli, the city commissioner in charge of museums, libraries, and auditoriums, they managed to squeeze a $1.7 million appropriation proposal into an omnibus bond resolution placed before the voters in 1953. Passage of this resolution provided them, to their surprise and delight, with funds to build a downtown arts and science center that would eventually house their activities.

In 1954 the ad hoc committee dissolved and the St. Paul Council of Arts and Sciences was formally created. The council included not merely the original five groups, but also the local musicians' union and several civic organizations, including the Junior League, which had sponsored the original study and had been helpful right along. The council hired a full-time director. It named a commission to choose a site for the arts center. It engaged an architect. It began to publish a monthly arts calender and publicize the events of its constituents. It began to sponsor events of its own.

In 1957 its director resigned and Ralph Burgard, who had run an arts council in Winston-Salem, was brought in to take his place. A slender, bespectacled young man armed with enormous energy and joie de vivre, as well as a scintillating imagination, Burgard had been an advertising man until a bout of illness gave him time to rethink his life. He came to the conclusion that he did not wish to spend his life in advertising, and he eventually turned up as associate manager of a symphony orchestra in his home town of Buffalo, New York. From there he went to Winston-Salem and his first involvement with the still-new arts council movement. His arrival in St. Paul brought with it a burst of energy and activity in the city's cultural life.

In 1959, for example, the council, in cooperation with downtown business interests, presented a colorful and attention-getting arts festival on a downtown parking lot cleared for the purpose. In booths and on temporary stages there were art exhibits, puppet shows, folk dances, a comedy by Christopher Fry, operatic recitals and jazz performances. The Twin Cities brass ensemble, divided into two groups, and posted on rooftops facing each other across the parking lot, blew Gabrieli canzoni at each other. It was, recalls Burgard with tongue in cheek, "the world's first live outdoor stereophonic concert." Whatever it was, it was something new for St. Paul, and it attracted 10,000 spectators.

He also set the stage for the next major activity of the council. The arts council movement, in more than a dozen cities, including Fort Wayne, New Orleans, Cincinnati, St. Louis, and Winston-Salem, has pioneered a new and extremely promising technique of fund raising in the arts. Most cultural institutions regularly operate at a deficit. St. Paul's were no exception. To offset such losses each one would regularly conduct an independent and often competitive fund drive usually with amateurish enthusiasm but wholly unprofessional methods. A nuisance to the community, they were hardly worth the effort. These campaigns in 1958 netted the principal cultural institutions of St. Paul a total of only $43,000. The money came from 300 donors.

In 1959 the council launched its first pooled fund drive. Constituent groups agreed not to conduct rival campaigns, but to pitch into a common effort. They agreed to work out detailed budgets, to submit them to a hard-headed central budget agency for paring, to share the funds collected, and to prepare financial reports quarterly instead of annually. Such measures not only are good management, but they help persuade the community that the organizations are responsible. Moreover, by promising to eliminate the nuisance of rival campaigns, and by rallying a mass volunteer effort from the followings of all the member groups, the drive succeeded in gaining far wider public backing than all the independent drives combined could have achieved. When the effort was over, the arts council had collected $147,000—virtually $100,000 more than had ever been raised before. Each subsequent campaign has increased the total. By 1963 the sum collected had climbed to $212,000—nearly five times the 1958 total, and the number of contributors had risen from 300 to 3,500. Moreover, what all this meant could not be measured in terms of money alone.

The widely publicized annual campaign has the side effect of publicizing the work of the arts institutions. Thus gross attendance of arts council affiliates has doubled within a four-year period, rising to 300,000. Playing seasons have been lengthened.

Instead of offering three productions and nine performances a year, the opera now presents six productions and 33 performances —all given in a 2,700-seat auditorium. Even more spectacular has been the change in operations of Theatre St. Paul, a new drama company that joined the council in 1956. In a five-year period it went from six performances a year to 105.

Most important, the quality of artistic work has been substantially upgraded. A biennial exhibit organized by the gallery has been chosen by the American Federation of the Arts for national circulation. Theatre St. Paul is about to make the move from amateur to semi-professional status with plans to hire a nucleus of professional actors for the company. The opera has been enabled to import professional set designers and choreographers from New York to improve its performance standards.

This fall, after many intervening difficulties, the arts council will finally be able to move into its own new home—the arts and science center. It had to raise an additional $900,000 by private subscription to supplement the $1.7 million in public funds made available as a result of the bond issue. The new center occupies a square city block in downtown St. Paul. It will provide a 400-seat theater, a smaller recital and film hall, exhibition space for the science museum and art gallery, rehearsal space, offices and a rooftop lounge. For the first time in their history St. Paul's cultural institutions will have adequate physical accommodations.

St. Paul's need for better physical facilities for its cultural institutions was typical. The U.S. has long had—and still has—a shortage of first-class stages, concert halls, and other such facilities for the arts. Many cities, including some very large ones, are simply unable to book top-quality ballet or opera productions for want of adequate space and equipment. Today a determined effort is being made to remedy this deficiency. The wave of construction activity aimed at providing arts facilities on the American campus has already been noted. This trend has its off-campus counterpart. Together they comprise what has been called the cultural building boom.

In 1962 the newsletter *Arts Management* found culture-related construction activity in 69 of 147 cities surveyed. Its study suggested that the national building bill for such construction could well run as high as $375 million.

Another remarkable fact emerged from this survey. Thus, while theaters, concert halls, and museums were rising or being renovated in a great many cities, the single most frequently reported type of project was the multi-purpose arts center. Such centers, like the one in St. Paul, shelter a variety of cultural activities rather than a single artistic discipline. Winter Park, Florida, for example, a city of 17,000 near Orlando, was planning a theater-museum-concert hall combination. Peoria, Illinois, had engaged Victor Gruen Associates to design a $700,000 center. Other cities planning or building such multi-purpose centers included Laramie, Wyoming, Trenton, New Jersey, Hartford, Connecticut, and San Leandro, California. In Tacoma an arts council has remodeled a former jail into a small center for the arts, and in Rocky Mount, North Carolina, an abandoned railroad pumping station is being converted to similar purposes. Nor is the movement limited to small cities. Apart from the giant Lincoln Center project, about which we shall speak presently, centers are planned for Washington, D.C., Atlanta, and other major metropolitan areas.

This great wave of bricks-and-mortar activity has been made possible by the conjunction of two social needs. The first, of course, is the actual shortage of such facilities. The rise in cultural interest in the U.S. called public attention to this lack. At the same time, the nation has been growing increasingly concerned with the deterioration of its cities, after a decade in which the move to the suburbs reached the proportions of a historic migration. Thus many cities, left with rotting cores, have come to recognize that something must be done about urban renewal. What needs to be done amounts to a restructuring of the American city. William L. Slayton, Commissioner of the Urban Renewal Administration of the U.S. Housing and Home Finance Agency, not long ago told a convention of the American Symphony Orchestra League that, "A new city form—heavily dependent upon our cultural and educational institutions—is clearly in evolution."

Many urban redevelopment projects, Slayton said, are taking

this into account. The Lincoln Center project in New York and the new theater recently completed for the Arena Stage in Washington, D.C., were both part of broad-scale urban redevelopment projects involving not merely cultural facilities, but housing and other types of construction as well. In Milwaukee an urban renewal project will provide land for a concert hall. In Pittsburgh, the Lower Hill project calls for a concert auditorium, an art and industrial museum, and a theater. Many Americans think the federal urban renewal program is limited to supplying low-cost housing. This is a misconception, Slayton pointed out. For, to revitalize our cities, more than housing must be provided.

Thus the movement for urban redevelopment, often backed by downtown interests, and coming at a moment when cultural institutions were beginning to organize themselves into interdisciplinary arts councils, laid a basis for the building boom of which the multi-purpose arts center has become almost a national symbol. All this had a hidden effect on cultural institutions and arts councils. Building a new facility, or maintaining it after it is completed, brings with it an almost automatic increase in the amount of administrative work that needs to be done. Moreover, haphazard methods will not do. A higher level of management acumen is demanded. When the facility serves several different artistic disciplines, the problems of management and administration are escalated to an even higher level of complexity. All of this is exemplified by the case of Lincoln Center, the biggest and most important of the nation's cultural centers. No analysis of the organizational revolution and no account of the culture explosion can be complete without an examination of the colossus on Lincoln Square.

Lincoln Center is believed by many to be the prototype of the multi-purpose arts center. Other centers are often termed "junior Lincoln Centers" as if the New York project were the father and they the offspring. Yet the fact is that the idea for the multipurpose center did not originate in New York at all. Lincoln Center was born of a coincidence that did not occur until two years after the arts center idea had been discussed and even voted upon by the citizens of St. Paul.

The coincidence came about in 1955 when the board of the

Metropolitan Opera reluctantly decided the time had come to build new quarters for the Met. The beloved Metropolitan Opera House was simply no longer adequate. That same year New York's other great musical institution, the Philharmonic Orchestra, learned that its long-standing lease with Carnegie Hall would not be renewed after 1958. Carnegie, since rescued from the wreckers' ball, was scheduled for demolition. It was architect Wallace K. Harrison who brought the two institutions together with the suggestion that they solve their housing problems on a common site. Shortly before this, Robert Moses, then New York's slum clearance czar, had announced a large-scale urban redevelopment project centered around the Lincoln Square area.

The parts soon began to fall into place. A high-powered civic committee was put together, including such names as John D. Rockefeller, 3rd, Charles Spofford, and Devereux C. Josephs. It began meeting regularly at the Century Club to discuss the problems of the Met, the Philharmonic and, by that time, other cultural institutions as well. Before long the committee had hired a firm of consulting engineers. A feasibility study was made and the idea of building a single multi-purpose arts center began to take shape. On June 22, 1956, the Lincoln Center for the Performing Arts was incorporated as a non-profit organization.

Like an arts council, which it essentially is, Lincoln Center is a federation of cultural institutions. These include the Metropolitan Opera Association, the Philharmonic-Symphony Society of New York, the Juilliard School of Music, the New York Public Library, and two theatrical organizations that the Center itself has created: The Music Theatre of Lincoln Center and the Repertory Theatre of Lincoln Center. On behalf of these six institutions the Center will administer a 14-acre complex of six buildings. Two of these—Philharmonic Hall and the New York State Theatre—are completed as of this writing. The other four will be completed by 1967.

At the outset it was thought that the total project would cost a resounding $75 million—a sum larger than anyone had ever before considered raising for a single cultural enterprise in the United States. As it turned out, this was a monumental underestimation. By 1964 Lincoln Center was announcing that the cost of putting up its six buildings and of launching its operations would run to $160.7 million. Yet, by the time the new estimate was released, Lincoln Center had already collected the staggering sum of $140 million and no one doubted that the remaining funds would be nicely in hand when needed. The organizers of the project tapped foundations, corporations, individuals, the federal government, the State of New York, the City of New York, and even several foreign governments for contributions.

In its first season, with only one building in operation, Lincoln Center attracted an aggregate attendance of 725,000, and the Philharmonic Orchestra, first of the constituents to relocate at the Center, achieved its first completely sold-out season in the 121 years of its history. The Center staged concerts by other orchestras, too, the Boston, the Cleveland, the Philadelphia, the French National Orchestra and the Leningrad Orchestra. It mounted a successful festival of avant-garde films. It presented recitals by a glittering array of the world's finest musical artists. There were dance performanances, too, by Merce Cunningham, Jose Limon and others. There were chamber music concerts. And its presentation included New York or world premieres of works by Barber, Copland, Cowell, Harris, Hindemith, Piston, Poulenc, Shostakovitch, Milhaud and many other contemporary composers.

Nor is Lincoln Center merely a glorified landlord, leasing space to constituent institutions and visiting artists. It has served as a creative force as well by setting up a fund of $10 million to initiate special projects that no one of its affiliates could have undertaken by themselves. This fund has sponsored the program which has, in the Center's words, "brought performances by the Metropolitan Opera Studio, the New York Philharmonic, and young artists from the Juilliard School to more than a third of a million junior and senior high school students in the metropolitan area." It has allocated funds to help convert the Juilliard School from a music conservatory to an advanced training center for all the performing arts. It has provided the seed money necessary to create the repertory theater company. It will finance a series of summer art festivals beginning in 1966. These will bring together leading artists from all the performing disciplines and will present new works commissioned by the fund. It will also underwrite a special program under which performing arts teachers from all over the United States will be brought to the center for training.

Despite these achievements and plans, Lincoln Center has been embroiled in controversy since its inception. First, there were complaints about the choice of site. Next, there were those who believed it would be better not to concentrate all these facilities, but to disperse them throughout the city instead. There were charges that the Center's massed operations would somehow damage the New York City Center's excellent ballet and venturesome opera company. (This has not happened, and there is no evidence that it will.) There were critics who accused Lincoln Center of presiding over the murder of Carnegie Hall. (New York now has *both* Lincoln Center *and* Carnegie Hall, and *both* are thriving.) Later came complaints about the acoustics in Philharmonic Hall, and, still later, complaints about the works chosen by the repertory theater. There were complaints that tickets were too hard to get and too costly. There were complaints that the halls were too small and that no provisions had been made for standees. There were complaints about the sculpture in Philharmonic Hall and the parking problems outside. There were thoughtful, justified criticisms and snide, destructive ones.

Now it is true that any major project occasions controversy. Controversy is healthy. It proves somebody cares. But the controversy about Lincoln Center has been peculiarly plentiful, and it is important to recognize that one source of hostility is its very size. Lincoln Center is probably the single largest aggregation of buildings, artists, and managerial personnel ever assembled in one place in the name of culture. It is an irresistible target for irresponsible criticism.

And yet it also gives cause for legitimate concern. For Lincoln Center represents, in advanced form, the same tendency toward more elaborate and sophisticated organization that is symbolized also by the arts council movement, by the proliferation of national and regional arts associations and by the growing complexity of both art and its administration. There is a persistent myth that art is, by its very nature, simple. Nothing could be further from the truth, especially in the performing arts. Moreover, the processes involved in communicating art are becoming more specialized and refined all the time as new media open for the artist and as society grows more complex and interwoven.

How complex the job has already become is reflected in a few simple but dramatic figures. The Chicago Art Institute employs 400 people. The Museum of Modern Art in New York employs about 275. Some of the constituents of Lincoln Center make these figures look puny by comparison. Thus the Metropolitan Opera alone employs between 1,200 and 1,500 individuals during the course of a year, with about 900 employed in any given week during the season. These include prima donnas, musicians, carpenters, secretaries and spear carriers, plus a surprising variety of specialists from accountants to public relations men. All told, the six constituents of Lincoln Center will, when it is in full operation, employ approximately 2,000 people. And the Center itself, responsible for coordinating the program of its constituents and for supplying them with certain central services, will have a staff of 250. The Center alone deals with no fewer than nine different unions. It is involved with pension plans, fringe benefits, insurance, finance, auditing, booking, scheduling, real estate management, purchasing and a host of other specialized functions, not to speak of artistic direction.

To tidy up this complex super-entity, a table of organization has been drawn up that looks like something out of the Pentagon. There is a board of directors, a council made up of the chief professional officers of each of the constituents, and a so-called "cabinet" made up of the chief administrative officers of the Center itself, and it is often impossible to arrange an appointment with one of the Center's busy, conference-attending executives. Nor is Lincoln Center alone in possessing a complicated table of organization. In one such table prepared by Booz, Allen & Hamilton, the management consultants, for a proposed art center in St. Louis, the jumble of committees, panels, and councils makes even Lincoln Center look primitive by comparison. In short, bureaucracy has made its entrance in the culture industry.

Most cultural institutions, of course, are nowhere near as complex as Lincoln Center, or even its major constituents. Some are still simple and charmingly unprofessional in the way they manage their affairs. But even small institutions are increasingly caught up in a rising tide of paperwork. Indeed, helping their affiliates to cope with the growing volume of administrative detail is one of the most important services offered by the arts councils. Many provide central clerical services for their member groups. They purchase advertising, paper and printing, and similar items in bulk, thus cutting both cost and office work. They maintain central mailing lists and conduct centralized membership or ticket-selling campaigns. They provide central auditing, accounting, and even investment services.* Everywhere the pressures are toward growth and elaboration. Moreover, there are penalties for those who resist. It is not coincidental that when the Ford Foundation made its multi-million dollar grants to the dance field in 1963, the money went to the better-established and professionally-managed ballet companies, while the modern dance companies, which tend to be amateurishly chaotic in their management, received nothing. Other considerations entered into the Foundation's choice, of course, but a foundation cannot dish out its largesse recklessly. It must be persuaded of the financial responsibility of the recipient. The same is true of other kinds of institutional patrons. Moreover, fund raising in general has become infinitely more complex than it was in the era of the great individual patrons. Fund raisers today must make specialized appeals to different publics. They become more and more enmeshed with direct-mail promotions, statistical surveys, advertising, detailed presentations, and so on. Furthermore, while the rich patron of the past could afford to keep on an ineffective, but subservient, manager, the modern arts institution is looked upon increasingly as a public or quasi-public trust, and hence is held more closely accountable. It is expected to make efficient use of its limited resources.

But the pressures toward bureaucracy are not merely economic. Nor do they primarily arise from stupidity, venality, or power-hunger. They are a natural and unavoidable concomitant of growth in a bureaucratized environment. There is an internal pressure toward bureaucracy whenever an arts institution takes

---

* A few arts institutions, because they receive their funds more or less in a lump sum after a fund drive, invest in government securities and draw funds out as needed during the year.

on a new function. Museums used to be fancy storage bins. Today they are research centers, educational centers, and service agencies, as well as storehouses for the treasures of the past and present. Each new function they undertake requires additional skills and more highly refined coordination. Moreover, even the execution of old functions, like lighting or restoration of art works, is today more complex and scientific than in the past.

The changed posture of our institutions toward the public also contributes to the spread of bureaucracy. In the past, the museum may not have cared whether or not the public ever made use of its collections. Today it is busy trying to attract the public, employing and coordinating the skills of specialists to do so. The sleepy simple days are past.

Such pressures are inescapable. They can be resisted only at the cost of refusing to grow, refusing to service the needs of the community, refusing to set ever higher artistic standards. In the future the tasks of cultural institutions will be more cleanly defined. We shall see more division of labor. More rules and regulations will govern the hierarchy of authority. There will be more paperwork, and officials will look to the institution not merely for a job, but for a career.

Indeed, the organizational revolution is already reflected in the beginnings of a new profession—that of arts management. There are now several thousand persons employed in the United States as executives in the culture industry, and there is a distinct and urgent need for more. According to the Ford Foundation, "a shortage of competent administrators is inhibiting the development of artistic groups. . . . If competent management were assured, theatrical, operatic and musical organizations could rise to new levels of artistic performance," This new profession is developing a body of literature, of which *Arts Management* is an example. In 1963, at the behest of Alvin H. Reiss, editor of this publication, the nation's first college credit course in arts management was initiated at the New School for Social Research in New York. We may expect, as the years go by, to see a further crystalization of this new profession.

Not only is an influential new profession arising, but it comes at a moment when other forces within the institution are losing influence. The displacement of the individual donors of great wealth by a combination of small donors, businesses, foundations and others, has created a shift in the internal power balance within the institution. With the purse strings no longer so tightly gripped by a single fist, the manager is now freer than in the past to assert his own influence. This is directly comparable to the divorce of power from property in the corporation world.

Critics of bureaucracy point out its terrible defects, and we need not belabor the point that these defects are particularly dangerous to art. For the ideal bureaucrat is the opposite of the adventurer. He prefers safety and stability to innovation and experiment. He wants things comfortable and predictable. He is under pressure to produce measurable results. What all this may mean to art is too obvious to require exposition, and failure to spell it out should not be interpreted as insensitivity to these perils.

But there is another, frequently overlooked, edge to the blade. For the organizational revolution cuts two ways, and bureaucracy can bring tangible benefits as well as drawbacks. Firstly, there is, of course, efficiency. Many critics of Lincoln Center, in their resentment against bureaucracy, ask: "Why didn't they just take all that money and give it to artists? Who needs the ranks upon ranks of executives?"

This is the plaint of the little man who yearns for the simplicity of the past and is blind to the realities of the present. For the fact is that without grouping the various institutions into a single great center, there would simply never have been $160 million or even $75 million for that matter. The very act of combining these cultural institutions and conducting a common appeal to the public makes it possible to rally community backing that would otherwise be unavailable. No city or state government and few foundations or businesses would have been as generous to the Metropolitan Opera or to the Philharmonic as they were to a collective project that embodied in a single dramatic form several of the principal elements of New York's cultural life. Moreover, the very combination of resources made it possible to assemble the staff and skills needed to conduct fund raising on so massive a scale—and at a cost per dollar far below the cost of fund raising in a series of independent and perhaps competitive campaigns.

Bureaucracy was introduced so long ago into government and business that by now the evils of excess have set in. We tend to forget that in its early phases it is highly efficient. Its first virtue is that far from being wasteful, it tends to conserve resources and apply them rationally. Indeed, unless it were more efficient and economical, and unless it did open up new possibilities, it could never supplant the more primitive forms of organization that precede it.

Secondly, bureaucracy can bring with it continuity. The ephemeral character of so many theater groups, opera companies, orchestras and similar cultural institutions in the United States until now was not merely wasteful in an economic sense, it was appallingly destructive in an artistic sense. For it takes time, often many years, for an orchestra to develop to perfection, for a museum collection to grow, for an opera company to increase its polish and repertoire, for an institution to find its proper place in community life. The organizational revolution promises a longer life and a better chance for artistic development for many of our cultural institutions.

Thirdly, it makes possible a degree of planning that is impossible in a haphazardly managed enterprise or industry. The rise of higher organizational forms like arts councils or arts centers promises to make up for some of the weaknesses that come with scattering cultural institutions about at random like blue dots on a map. It is possible with the existence of Lincoln Center for its policy makers to look around them, to note that New York has lacked a high-quality repertory theater, and then to attempt to remedy that gap. A center or council is able to look beyond the needs of its existing constituents.

Finally, and perhaps most important, the bringing together of different artistic disciplines with the help of advanced organization techniques opens up whole new aesthetic vistas. The arts council and arts center provide a forum in which artists from different disciplines, hitherto confined to hermetic compartments, have an opportunity for day-to-day exchange of ideas and cross-fertilization of talents. They are encouraged to experiment with new fusions of music and theater or dance and the visual arts. It is not entirely accidental that artists are experimenting more today with inter-disciplinary forms. What may be beginning to take shape is a new unity of the arts in our society and a new conception of the meaning of the word culture.

None of this means that bureaucracy ceases to be a menace to art. But it does mean that the organizational revolution trails both promise and danger in its wake. It does no good to rail against bureaucracy. It is a feature of contemporary society that we must learn to live with and, more important, to exploit for our own ends.

This suggests that in the creation of new arts centers and arts councils continuing stress should be placed on the artistic autonomy of the constituent institutions. Their artistic decisions should not be centralized in the supra-organization. When the center or council undertakes to initiate artistic activities on its own, it should either allow them to be executed by its affiliates, without dictation from above, or it should create its own agency to do so in a way that will not affect the freedom of the affiliates to pursue their own artistic destinies. Most councils today are, in fact, sensitive to this question and hesitate even to offer artistic advice to their affiliates unless specifically asked to do so.

Next we must educate the whole new generation of artists, the increasingly powerful managers, and especially the new patrons and board members, to the inherent dangers of bureaucracy so that every decision that increases bureaucracy may be weighed rationally before it is adopted. Moreover, a whole new attitude should be inculcated toward our arts councils and centers. We should encourage their development, but we must view them opportunistically. The time will come, sooner or later, when the process of bureaucratization will advance to excess and begin to standardize our cultural production. We must be prepared for this eventuality. At that point we may, figuratively speaking, have to tear down the centers and councils we are now building and reorganize the culture industry in ways as yet unimagined. This should not dismay us, for the process of growth, decay, and regeneration in society is unending.

Finally, what the organizational revolution implies is that, at the very same time that we do all we can to encourage the development of councils, centers, and efficient management, we must also take pains to nurture those cultural institutions that are too young, too daring, too experimental, or just plain too bullheaded to join in cooperative ventures. In each city, as time passes, we shall develop a core of established institutions, probably linked with one another. These institutions may tend toward the "safe"—which is not altogether evil. It is perfectly legitimate and necessary for a nation to have a body of cultural institutions that are conservative, for it is through these that gains are consolidated and a tradition built. But around this core will grow smaller, less solid institutions. For these, life will be increasingly difficult, unless we realize that they may be quite as important, in the long run, to the health of our culture as the core institutions are today.

In short, the matter of judicious timing is critical. Today and for the forseeable future we must regard the organizational revolution as being, on balance, a healthy, stimulating, and positive force. Tomorrow we may have to re-evaluate it.

PART THREE

Art and Money

9

The Wages of Art

IN 1960 TWO INQUISITIVE SOCIAL SCIENTISTS NAMED BEARDSLEE AND
O'Dowd burrowed into the psyches of 1,200 college students in an
effort to learn what young Americans think about a number of
occupations and professions. Among the careers studied was that
of "artist." The students, all from liberal arts colleges, were
asked to rank the artist on a series of scales. The end result was
a word picture of the mental image conjured up at the mention
of the word "artist."

The artist, God help him, turned out to be, according to these
youngsters, an "intuitive, rash, changeable, excitable, and attention demanding" fellow, while being at the same time "deep,
interesting and colorful." His "outstanding individualism and
radicalism" went hand in hand with "irresponsibility and un-
willingness to contribute to society in a disciplined way. . . .
Neither wealth nor status nor any other marks of the rich full life
are associated with the artist," a summary of the findings reported.

In short, nobody in his right mind would want to pursue the
muse professionally.

The study did not define "artist" and it left many questions
up in the air. But, had a pair of probing sociologists conducted
the same kind of survey 25 or 50 years ago, one suspects their
findings would have been little different. For it is obvious that
the college students were still picturing the artist in terms of an
old romantic stereotype. This represents a cultural lag. The fact
is that *la vie bohême,* as a pattern of life for the American artist,

is dead or dying. America still has a good many painters, sculptors, and composers who live in lofts, those modern-day equivalents of the garrets of old. But this is hardly typical. Except in Greenwich Village, where rents are high and romanticism rife, it is safe to say that most artists nowadays can be found in comfortable suburbs or in lower- or middle-income housing developments. A resident of the art gallery district of Madison Avenue can watch from his windows as the artists arrive to deliver paintings to their galleries. They drive late-model station wagons. It is surely some kind of portent that a Fifth Avenue Volkswagen dealer a while back conducted a special promotion aimed at selling Microbuses to artists at $2,290 apiece.

As we shall see, there are reasons to be optimistic about the economic future of the artist in America. Still and all, it would be premature to assume that his problems are solved. They are not. It is a disconcerting fact that the culture explosion, which has led to the birth of so many new galleries, stages, and concert halls and has enormously broadened the market for cultural goods and services, has been slow to translate itself into a satisfactory economic return for the artist. To understand this seeming contradiction, it is helpful to explore the economic facts of life as they operate in the life of the musical artist.

In eighteenth-century Russian newspapers, according to musicologist Nicolas Slonimsky, readers could commonly find advertisements like this one:

> Musician for sale, age 26, 6 feet 2 inches tall, plays double-bass and clarinet, sings bass; he is a leech, can let blood with lancet, knows barbering, applies clysters.

Since those days, civilization has progressed. Medicine, marching ever onward from great moment to great moment, has done away with the lancet and the leech, and musical artists are not exactly bought and sold on the open market any more. Nevertheless, many of them still seem to think of themselves as serfs.

Strikes and labor troubles have rocked some of the nation's most important musical institutions in the past few years. Significantly, in many of these conflicts the players themselves, rather than their union officials, have led the protests. Rank-and-file committees, often led by younger musicians, are springing up, not only to challenge orchestra management, but to attack the American Federation of Musicians for being too conservative. A new mood of militancy is apparent.

What is ironic about all this, of course, is that it occurs in the midst of rising concert attendance figures and increasing record sales. Irony or no, the creative cadre of American music is, with only a handful of exceptions, still suffering from a peculiar economic malnutrition.

The most restive and also the most powerfully organized segment of the classical music "labor force" right now is composed of the orchestral musicians of the nation. The American Federation of Musicians estimates that of its 277,400 members, only about 12,500 perform classical music professionally. Among these are 3,250 members of 26 major orchestras in the U.S. and Canada and 1,000 members of opera and ballet pit orchestras. These are the hard core of the serious orchestral players in the nation. In addition, there are about 6,500 classical musicians employed irregularly by the nation's secondary orchestras.

In 1961 the A.F.M. conducted a sweeping survey of the economic conditions of these musicians. Among the classics of revolutionary literature, the resultant document fits somewhere between Jack London's *The People of the Abyss* and Maxim Gorky's *The Lower Depths.* Not only was it full of the most depressing statistics, but the penciled comments of the respondents shed an appropriately gloomy light on the life of the orchestral player.

The survey limited itself to members of major orchestras only, who are better paid than most. Despite this, it found that the average man's earnings from symphony performances were less than $4,000 a year. And, in an era of high-flying fringe benefits, only ten orchestras among the top 26 had any kind of pension fund. Only four offered their players hospitalization benefits. Many musicians are not even eligible for unemployment benefits during their out-of-work periods.

But the overriding complaint of the symphony player, overshadowing even wages as an issue, is the brevity of the playing season. When the Philadelphia Orchestra not long ago signed a contract guaranteeing its players 48 weeks of work per year plus a four-week vacation and minimum income of $12,400, it made musical history. This contract is a portent of the future. But, as of the time of the A.F.M. survey, only nine of the top 26 orchestras were able to employ their men for as many as 30 weeks of the year. The average season length was 27 weeks, and among the smaller orchestras it was even shorter.

Since the stomachs of all these musicians function, with varying degrees of efficiency, for all 52 weeks of the year, it is not surprising that many are driven to fill out their incomes through other jobs. None of the musicians surveyed claimed to know barbering or to be handy with lancet or clyster, but they did do just about everything else. Says Herman Kenin, president of the A.F.M.: "We have among our members at least one pari-mutuel official, a proofreader, a Fuller Brush man, an exterminator, a mental health therapist, an ice cream vendor, a butcher, a bank teller and a bartender, not to speak of an aerial surveyor, a forest guide and a pea picker." Not only does moonlighting take time away from practice and distract the musician, but it usually creates a case of quivering schizophrenia in him. The individual responses of the musicians to the union survey reflect this, along with a snake pit full of other fears, resentments, frustrations and angers. "All I can say," wrote one man, "is that I think it is a shame—music and housepainting—quite a combination for a God-given gift of music talent. But believe me, if it wasn't for painting, I, my wife and child could not make it. However, I LOVE MUSIC!"

"I have worked very hard," scrawled another, "to keep my professional standards at a high level. I have spent lots of money to become a musician and have spent lots of money on a good instrument. It hurts me down deep to know that I can't make a steady income through the whole year. I really don't want anything for free. I want work. . . ." Another, a man with 46 years of playing experience, lamented: "I have never made $5,000 in any one year. I should make at least that."

One musician summed it all up this way: "We need an annual income which will at least equal that of a common unskilled laborer. As it is, we are forced to live like cultural Okies."

What sharpens the bitterness of the pit player is the ever-present contrast that his conductor presents. In the majors, where the spirit of rebellion runs highest these days, conductors' salaries begin at about $16,000 and whoosh rapidly upwards. Men like Bernstein or Ormandy can earn $50,000 a year or more in salary alone, and most name conductors fatten their pay envelope by putting in guest appearances with other orchestras, by appearing now and then on the air and, more often, by collecting record royalties.

When to this difference in standards of living the conductor adds pressure for discipline and a studied coolness toward the problems of his men, as some do, the steam generated can be explosive. Striking members of the Philadelphia once demanded a look at the orchestra's books, in part because they wanted to find out just how much Eugene Ormandy was receiving. (They never did.) At least one conductor manages to make matters worse by regularly exhorting his men to forget money and think only of art—while his wife flaunts a new Parisian wardrobe each season. To the man in the second violinist's chair, the conductor often looks like Croesus, and it was no surprise that when one martinet-maestro took off by plane for a guest appearance somewhere, his string section met to pray for his plane to crash. The only demurrer came from one member who said it was unfair "to do that to all those other innocent people on board."

The conductor of a major orchestra can probably earn an income 10 to 25 times more than the orchestral violinist makes at the peak of his career. This is a wide spread, but in the concert business (as distinct from the orchestral world), extremes of wealth and poverty are even more starkly dramatic. Few if any conductors see the kind of paycheck a concert recitalist earns when—and, of course, if—he ever really "arrives."

There are in the U.S. today roughly five hundred men and women who earn their living as professional concert recitalists. Of this number, probably no more than five per cent, at a guess, earn as much as a leading conductor. But within that tiny circle of concert luminaries are men and women who earn $250,000 a year or more and others who could, if their accountants would let them. Many concert artists, responding to the law of diminishing after-tax returns, quickly earn $100,000 or $150,000 and then call it quits for the year.

Perhaps the highest-paid individual performers in America today are pianists—Rubinstein and Cliburn, both of whom can command $6,000 or more a performance, although Cliburn frequently prefers to play for a percentage of the box office gross rather than a flat fee. Among violinists, with Heifetz relatively inactive, Isaac Stern, Nathan Milstein, and Zino Francescatti are the top earners, all of them reputedly clearing the six-figure mark, but none of them orbiting in the rarified Rubinstein-Cliburn belt. Some opera stars do all right, too. Today Callas and Tebaldi could each probably equal the earnings of a Rubinstein, if they chose, and Leontyne Price, who rocketed into the top rank only recently, is already among the high earners. Some male opera stars, like Richard Tucker, are also in this class.

But the concert business has a less glamorous, less talked-about underside. Many concert artists, including "names" like Heifetz, who don't need to, belong to a union—the American Guild of Musical Artists. A.G.M.A. has helped improve the lot of opera singers, choristers, and dancers. But because the recitalist is a self-employed professional rather than an employee, he is less inclined toward group action. Moreover, for a recitalist to admit he is having economic difficulty is to suffer a blow to his ego. For these reasons, the public hears less about the plight of the concert artist than about that of orchestral players.

Nevertheless, the problems of the recitalist start early. In the past generation the United States has developed a gigantic educational machine for the training of professional musicians. This machine, having been set in motion, is now overproducing. For the number of careers open to concert performers is still small and the competition for recital careers is heartbreakingly keen.

The candidate for one of these careers must make a huge investment in advanced training and in a fine instrument. Once having achieved the level of professional competence, he must find a manager. Without one, it is simply impossible to function as a professional. Managers are besieged, belabored, bedeviled by young hopefuls.

The usual gambit is for the aspirant to hire Carnegie Hall,

Town Hall, or a more modest auditorium for a so-called New York debut. This may cost from $1,000 up, and its sole object is to lure a handful of critics, who would much rather be elsewhere, into the hall. If the performer wins merely enthusiastic praise in the morning papers, the debut will probably have been a failure. For the praise must be absolutely rhapsodic before a manager will read past the first line or two of a review. If the critic has been positively ecstatic, there is a chance that a manager will audition the newcomer and also then a slim chance that he will take him on. (Some small managers need to be encouraged to do so with a "sweetener" of $1,000 or $2,000.)

Today two managements—Columbia Artists Management, Inc., and Sol Hurok—tower over the concert business, collecting and distributing perhaps 75 per cent of all professional recitalists' fees. About a dozen other companies, of which the largest are Herbert Barrett Management and National Concert and Artists Corporation, account for the rest. The function of the manager is, of course, to "sell" his artists to concert-sponsoring individuals or groups—universities, local impresarios, local good music societies, companies—and to receive a commission for this service. Columbia and National also control a chain of so-called organized audiences. These are local associations, set up with the help of subsidiaries of Columbia and National specifically for the purpose of sponsoring a series of concerts. Members of the associations pay "dues" which are, in effect, the price of admission to a concert series. Columbia, through a subsidiary called Community Concerts, Inc., helps administer and service such groups in 720 towns. National, now owned by the Summy-Birchard Company of Evanston, Illinois, has ready-made audiences in almost 100 cities through its subsidiary, Civic Concerts, Inc. Community towns "buy" most of their talent from Columbia; Civic towns from National. Other managers charge that their artists are excluded from the organized audience circuits.

When an artist is finally accepted by a manager, his name is put on the list of performers whose talents are touted by the manager's field salesmen. These salesmen scour the country to find bookings for their artists. The newcomer's fee at the start will be about $450 per concert if he is on the Columbia list. Other managers may start their beginners at even lower fees. On the face of it, $450 sounds like a lot of money for one evening's work. But appearances are deceptive, as Zvi Zeitlin, a violinist in Columbia's higher ranks, points out. Zeitlin, a sturdy, dark-haired Israeli artist, started his professional career abroad at the early age of sixteen. In 1951 he settled in the U.S. and since 1953 has been concertizing for a living. A mature artist today at forty, he is no longer among the ranks of the beginners, and his fee is in the middle scale. But he and his Canadian wife Marianne talk passionately about the difficulties that confront the young recitalist today.

"Take that fee of $450," says Zeitlin. "Any time you play before an organized audience, there is a standard fee—a 'differential' you must pay to Community or Civic to help them cover the cost of organizing these local associations. Without these organized audiences, performers would be in really desperate shape. They have done a lot for music. But that 'differential' runs to about one-third, or $150, which leaves you with only $300. Then you pay another 15 per cent to your manager. This is $45 and it leaves $255. Out of this," says Zeitlin, "if you are a violinist like me, you'll have to pay for an accompanist—maybe $75 more. If you are a pianist and you don't need an accompanist, you often have to pay the cost of renting or shipping a first-rate piano."

There are other expenses, too. "Every artist," explains Zeitlin, "pays for his own advertising and promotional material—leaflets, posters and the like. Then he has to pay travel expenses, hotel rent for both himself and his accompanist, plus food for himself. He has to pay for formal clothes, plus cleaning bills. Living on the road is no picnic. It's expensive. Actually," says Zeitlin, "it's not unusual for the $450 artist to finish up with only $50 or $75 net per concert." Off the organized-audience circuit, which is the bread and butter of most low- and middle-fee recitalists, the artist pays no "differential," but his manager's fee is 20 per cent instead of 15, and as a rule he has, in the initial stages, fewer bookings.

Zeitlin's fee schedule today is considerably above the beginner's level, but, he goes on, even at $750 or $1,000 a concert, an artist's take-home pay after all expenses may be shockingly slim. "After a while," Zeitlin says, "an artist takes stock, and if he can't bring his net for a concert to a few hundred at least, he just quits." According to manager Herbert Barrett, "The artist is left with about 40 or 50 per cent of his gross income. To make even $150 a week, he needs 14 concerts a year at $1,000 each. If he doesn't have that he is in for trouble."

Obviously, one solution to this is to boost his fee, and most artists feel that they suffer a loss of face in the business if they don't do that periodically. But by jacking up his fee, the artist pushes himself into that no-man's-land of music, the so-called middle-fee bracket.

The low-fee artist may not be able to make a living, but there is at least a place for him in the musical scheme of things. The performer who manages to hoist himself into the next fee range finds himself about as popular as a streptococcus at a convention of contraltos. This is so because people who plan a concert series all too often invoke a musical version of the principle of the excluded middle. They spend half their budget on a single big-name performer for one concert. This is the Roberta Peters, the Rudolf Serkin or the Francescatti whose name in the promotional literature will, they hope, sell tickets for the entire series. They then divide the tattered remains of the budget by the number of remaining concerts, and they come up with just enough to hire low-fee artists for the evenings that are left.

This helps explain why the artist often finds it hard to increase the number of concerts he gives a year. Calculating roughly, if 500 professional recitalists need 14 concerts per year at the $1,000 level, a total of 7,000 $1,000 recitals are needed to support the active professionals alone. If the average price per concert is lower than $1,000—as in reality it is—the number of "dates" necessary rises still further. Today, even with the rapid expansion of musical interest, there are not yet enough such bookings to go around.

As a result, says Marks Levine, the dean of the concert management business, "a tragically large percentage" of the nation's five hundred artists "hardly are able to make a living."

The third significant creative group in the classical music economy are the composers, the least organized, least vocal, and least affluent of all. Nobody knows exactly how many serious composers there are in the U.S. today or, for that matter, how to define a "serious composer." But the American Music Center, an organization the purpose of which is to help the serious contemporary composer, recently ran a survey of its own. It sent questionnaires to 1,171 composers and drew replies from 430. One man reported earning $103,824.83 in 1960. Fifteen others earned between $5,000 and $41,750, but some 400 revealed that they had earned under $5,000 a year from their musical labors, and most of these were far, far under that figure. The survey is open to many technical and definitional objections. But no one quibbles with the overall portrait of poverty that it paints.

The high earners made most of their incomes from composing for Hollywood, Broadway, and television rather than from the composition of classical music in the strict sense. Of the rest, almost all either worked as teachers or held some kind of job for a livelihood. The returns, like those of the musicians, were full of the most distressing comments. One composer, a man of fifty with a fairly distinguished catalog of works to his credit, wrote: "I hope you will include in your tally the 25 years of spiritual and physical agony, and I ask you this in the hope that it may help to prevent some young American from throwing away his life."

To understand these figures, it is helpful to study the sources of income open to the composer who sticks to classical music. First, he may receive a "commission"—i.e., a flat fee in payment for a work written for an orchestra, foundation or other sponsor. Second, he receives a performance fee from the ensemble playing his work before a live audience. Third, he receives a royalty on the printed scores of his music. Fourth, he receives a performance fee from broadcasters who play his music. And last, he receives record royalties on his works. With all these channels of payment, he should be drowning in money. The truth is, he hardly gets his big toe damp.

Commissions, which are eagerly sought after for their honorary value, run from $50 to $5,000. But most of the time they do not even cover the costs the composer himself must pay for having his notes copied and duplicated. (Just having the instrumental parts of a 15-minute orchestral work copied may cost the composer from $300 to $500. A full-length symphony would be much more.) The royalty that the composer collects from a symphony or quartet for the right to play his work is so small it is practically subliminal—perhaps as little as $25. This obviously can add up to significant income only if the work is performed repeatedly. A high earner like Menotti, whose operas have become popular with local opera-producing companies, and whose *Amahl and the Night Visitors* has become a Christmas standard, is the exception to the rule that performance royalties are microscopic.

Even more insignificant, however, is the income from the royalties on the sale of scores. Sales of these are so small for serious works that many composers never even bother asking a publisher to print them.

Broadcasting, one might think, should be a major source of income for the serious composer. It isn't. To collect royalties for works of theirs that are broadcast, composers belong to one of two performing-rights organizations—the American Society of Composers, Authors and Publishers or Broadcast Music, Inc. ASCAP and BMI charge radio and TV stations a fee for the right to broadcast the music of any composer listed in their catalog. They then monitor the airwaves, keep a log showing which compositions are played, and distribute their income, minus expenses, to their member-composers. These distributions are theoretically based on the frequency with which each man's work is performed.

This theory works out in practice for the pop composer, whose compositions are played so frequently that it is possible for ASCAP or BMI to monitor a sampling of stations and statistically project overall usage from that base. Contemporary classical works, however, are so infrequently broadcast that the monitoring samples pick up hardly enough data on which to base a projection. In the end, although each society goes through a different rigmarole, each winds up paying its composers what amounts to a flat annual retainer rather than royalty payments. Indeed, these organizations basically exist to serve pop composers. BMI and ASCAP need serious composers the way Bach needed twenty children. It reduces itself to the fact that an annual retainer of

$3,000 is considered fat pickings for a serious composer. A few make more; most make under $1,000 a year from broadcast music.

This leaves one other possible channel of income—record royalties. A contemporary composer receives ¼ cent per minute of his music per record sold. This princely sum he must split 50–50 with his publisher. This means that on the sale of 1,000 LP records, each with, say, a full 40-minute symphonic work, the writer of the music gets $50. For Aaron Copland, who has more than two dozen works in the Schwann catalog and whose *Billy the Kid* and *Rodeo* sell several thousand copies a year, record income is worth calculating. But a typical contemporary record by an American composer may sell only a few hundred copies. As one composer recently said, "If every now and then $1.19 comes in in royalties, you figure your uncle is active in Chicago."

In 1963 culture consumers purchased 17.5 million classical records. If, of these, fully ten per cent were by contemporary composers (an unrealistically generous estimate) then, at the ¼ cent per minute rate, they would have received only $87,500 in royalties. To put it even more graphically, this means that, of the $76.4 million spent on those 17.5 million records, living composers and their publishers received a maximum of one eighth of one per cent.

This Cook's Tour of the money regions of music suggests that the great rise in audience for the arts has not yet been transmuted into financial benefit for the artist, and the same is true in the other artistic disciplines. Indeed, orchestra musicians are regarded as economic royalists by many stage actors. Actors' Equity, the theatrical union, claims approximately 13,000 members. According to testimony before a Senate subcommittee, however, Broadway shows cast only 2,061 parts in one recent season. Thus, including even the bittiest of bit parts, Broadway provided roles for fewer than one in six Equity members. In all, of Equity's 13,000 enrollment, only 6,920 appeared on the professional stage at all during the 1957–58 season. Of these, 55 per cent worked for fewer than 10 weeks.

How much do the lucky ones earn? Leaving aside "stars," the Broadway minimum for a professional actor is $112.50 before taxes. On off-Broadway the minimum is only $45 per week, and in summer stock it is $65 per week for dramatic shows, $75 for musicals. These are paid during the actual run of a show; during the rehearsal period before the show opens, minimums are substantially lower.

The same kind of dismal statistics are available on employment among dancers, choral singers, and other performing artists, and the situation is at least equally bleak for painters, sculptors, poets, novelists and other categories of creative or performing artists.

Clearly, whatever reservations there may be about the precision of the data or the terms of definition, the economics of artistry leave much to be desired. In all the arts a tiny handful make an excellent living, and a mass of practitioners do not. This, however, does not conflict with what was said earlier about station wagons and suburban homes. The paradox is resolved by the existence of ample supplementary employment. The U.S. economy has been prosperous enough in recent years so that thousands of artists have sought and found alternate employment in the schools, in the mass media, and elsewhere. Few, if any, artists are starving. What is wrong is that they are not able to maintain a comfortable level of income from art alone.

Why should this be true? How is it that the country can experience a cultural boom without at the same time providing decent economic conditions for its artistic work force? Part of the answer lies in supply and demand. National employment statistics on the arts are far too crude to make possible refined economic analyses, but a recent Census Bureau report indicates that, except for the theater, the 1950–1960 decade saw an increase in the number of artists in all fields. The figures, unfortunately, lump practicing artists along with teachers, and no one, not even the Census Bureau, has yet come up with a universally acceptable definition of "artist." But granted these difficulties, the figures seem to support one another. Thus it was found that musicians and music teachers rose in number from 162,000 in 1950 to 198,000 in 1960, a gain of 22 per cent, as against a gain of only 18.5 per cent in the nation's overall population. Dancers and dancing teachers multiplied at a faster rate, from 17,000 in 1950 to 22,000—a growth of 26 per cent. Artists and art teachers proliferated even more rapidly. Their numbers swelled by 30 per cent from 81,000 to 105,000. And the figure for literary artists jumped from 16,000 to 29,000, a leap of nearly 77 per cent. Only among actors was there a decline. Here the census men reported a drop from 18,000 to 13,000 during the decade. Granting all the shortcomings of such statistics, the number of artists in America does appear to be increasing.

It is quite possible, therefore, that the increase in consumption of culture in our country has been accompanied by an even greater increase in the number of artists. The number of concert dates to be played, the dance recitals to be given, the number of art shows may all have increased. But a society that consumes a lot in the way of cultural goods and services also produces a good many artists. Jerome Robbins, the choreographer, has said that when he was casting the musical *West Side Story* in the late 'fifties he found it nearly impossible to find enough first-class dancers under the age of twenty. Only a few years later, when he was casting the movie version, he found a good many competent dancers among sixteen-year-olds. Even within a few years the supply of talent in this field had changed perceptibly. This expansion of the labor supply would at least partly explain why, despite all that has been said earlier, so many professional artists have benefited little from the great increase in public demand.

Moreover, if this is in fact the case, it may be time to take a hard look at the whole process by which our society trains professional musicians, dancers, painters, and actors. If the professional schools are turning out many more young hopefuls than the artistic labor market can possibly absorb, it may be sensible to concentrate on quality of training rather than quantity. This is not to say that the labor market in the arts should ever be in balance. It is healthy for the supply always to exceed the demand by some margin. This enforces a competition that is conducive to excellence. In a society as rich as ours, as long as there are other jobs to absorb those who do not quite reach the first ranks artistically, the benefits of competition probably outweigh the disadvantages of imbalance in the labor market. Nevertheless, we might at this stage encourage fewer young Americans to become professional artists and do more to educate those who do elect this career. The fact is that, particularly in theater and dance, the level of artistic training in this country is less than satisfactory.

If we had more reliable data on such matters, it might be possible to regulate gently, within crude outer limits, the balance of supply and demand by adjusting the number of scholarships and other incentives upward or downward. The result could be to stabilize the artistic labor market at a level of optimum competition and to help our professional artists benefit from the culture explosion. There is precedent for this in the way we have stimulated an increase in science and engineering education in recent years. Given the state of our knowledge, however, and the political and social realities, such refined planning is not merely unlikely, but perhaps even undesirable. It remains an alternative open to us; other developments, however, may make it unnecessary to move in this direction. For there are already signs of a break in the logjam. Whether the relative labor imbalance grows better or worse, there will certainly be an absolute increase in the number of paying jobs for artists. Even Actors' Equity, which for years has been issuing justifiably bleak reports about theatrical employment, now has begun to see hope in the future. According to the actor Ralph Bellamy, Equity's outgoing president, the rise of professional theater outside New York will increase overall theater employment. In Chapter Seven I alluded to the likelihood that business might become an important employer of artists in the future. A more immediate likelihood is that novel schemes will be hatched to bring the artist and his market together in profitable way. Exactly such a scheme was designed recently to help stimulate serious drama in the U.S. Called American Playwrights Theatre, it links together nearly one hundred and twenty college and community theaters, each of which agrees to stage one of the two plays released for production each year by the central organization. In effect, the program creates a circuit of stages for new works and makes it possible for a serious dramatist to earn well over $10,000 in a single academic year without a New York production.

Such an imaginative venture was impossible in this country until the culture explosion brought about a proliferation of theaters and audiences. The boom made it possible. We may confidently predict that a great many other, equally imaginative, arrangements will be worked out, not merely in theater but in all of the arts, in the years to come. For example, it is not impossible for a group of painters or sculptors to put together a first-class exhibit and syndicate it to galleries and museums around the country, with the understanding that a small admission price will be charged the public. The artists could share in royalties from these proceeds, just as the playwrights do. There is money enough and audience enough to make such a scheme practical. But whether this particular arrangement is adopted or a wide variety of others are developed, ways will be found in the coming period for the artist to take advantage of the great increase in culture consumption.

In the meantime, however, the wages of art remain slender, indeed, and such optimism about the future should not obstruct our search for immediate ways to ameliorate the artist's continuing poverty in the midst of prosperity. Imbalance in labor supply, as a matter of fact, is only one element in the picture. As we shall see next, the problem of the artist is only part of a much larger and more complex problem.

10

The Culture Industry

SOMETIME THIS YEAR IT IS LIKELY THAT MOST READERS OF THIS BOOK will be approached, through the mails or in person, by someone pleading for a financial contribution to a needy cultural institution. The plea may take the form of a mimeographed letter begging for a few dollars for a hard-pressed civic opera. Or it may be presented by a suburban matron who knocks at your door and urges you to help the museum build its necessary new wing. Should you be a person of means, your name will become the subject of heated discussion by a committee whose task it is to dissect your sources of income, weigh your contributions to other local charities, estimate your stock market losses and your tax bracket, and finally to rate your so-called "giving potential." Once this is determined, a person of approximately your own social and economic standing in the community will be delegated to wheedle you into making a substantial gift to the orchestra's annual fund drive, to live up, in other words, to that potential. You will be asked to become a patron of the arts.

Your visitor will gently point out to you that he, himself, has already made a sizable contribution. He will call attention to the fact that a business rival of yours has given $500. (Can you do less?) He will paint the need in desperate terms. The musicians, underpaid and grumbling, demand that the season be lengthened beyond its present twenty-two weeks. The conductor, who has done such a fine job and has been such a social asset to the city, may depart for greener pastures. There is danger that those wonderful concerts for underprivileged children will have to be discontinued. The very life of the orchestra is at stake.

Before you have fully absorbed this grim news you will learn that even more than music is involved. For, as every good fund raiser knows, the "case" presented to a potential donor must always relate the specific requirements of the institution to the broader needs of the community. Thus you will be reminded that the loss of the orchestra would be a dreadful blow to the campaign for the revitalization of the downtown neighborhood in which its hall is located. The city's pride and its attractiveness to new industry would also be undermined. In brief, your failure to contribute would be both anti-cultural and anti-social.

In the end, your innate generosity and your love of music will triumph, especially if your caller (not accidentally) turns out to be the principal customer of your small business. Before he pumps your hand in gratitude, he will carefully pocket the check you have signed with the pen he proffered at the moment of truth.

This, of course, is only one of the hundreds of ingenious methods by which money is raised to help finance culture in the United States. You or your wife may be invited to a tea party, a rummage sale, a fancy ball, a benefit performance or a banquet, at which your fears for the future of art will be aroused, your sympathy sought, and your wallet slenderized. Col. Samuel Rosenbaum, a member of the board of the Philadelphia Orchestra and no novice at such matters, has said: "Give me six women, a bag of cookies and a box of tea, and you will have a symphony orchestra." That there are other pathways to culture the good Colonel has also made clear by his explanation of one of the fundamental differences between musical life in Europe and musical life in America. In Europe, he has suggested, if a musician and a rich lady are placed in intimate proximity, the result may well be a baby. In the U.S., the result is more likely to be an orchestra.

This calls attention to one of the more curious paradoxes of the culture explosion. If it is true, as this book has contended, that a great expansion has occurred in culture consumption, if Americans are, indeed, spending more than ever before for painting and sculpture, music, drama, and dance, why does an air of crisis seem to hang over so many of our cultural institutions?

Unless we have a clear picture of the economic condition of our cultural institutions we shall never be able to assess the impact of the culture boom, for, as we have emphasized, art and money, the quality of one and the quantity of the other, are intimately connected. And yet, oddly enough, most informed Americans, even most artists and critics, have only the blurriest impression of the true state of the artistic economy. Those who are devotees of one artistic discipline are usually horrendously ignorant about the problems of the others. And professional economists, to whom we should be able to turn for help, have until recently been marvelously uninterested in the whole subject.* One searches their journals and texts fruitlessly for any discussion of the culture industry. It is almost as if it did not exist.

The culture industry, which as a matter of fact does exist, and which, as we have seen, involves literally billions of dollars, is composed of thousands of organizations, associations, clubs and companies that offer the public a wide variety of art-related end-products. For the sake of shorthand we have throughout this book used the term "institution" to include all of these, whether they are profit-making businesses or non-profit organizations, whether they are professional or amateur, whether they are large or small. For the term, as we employ it, refers not to size, motivation, or quality of product, but merely to function. An enterprise is a cultural institution, in this sense, if it finances and coordinates the production and/or distribution of cultural goods or services.

If we look at the cultural institutions in our society, we are struck by their almost dazzling variety. But we also quickly note that they fall into two distinct groups—a profit sector and a non-profit sector. The latter (with which this book is primarily concerned) consists of orchestras, museums, ballet companies,

---

* This attitude is just now beginning to shift. J. K. Galbraith has talked about producing a book on the relationship of economics to art, and the Twentieth Century Fund has made a grant to a Princeton economist, William J. Baumol, to undertake the collection and analysis of basic economic data on the arts. Within the next few years the economics of the arts may begin to emerge as a new sub-specialty in the profession.

operas, arts centers and all their offshoots and variants. Different as these are from one another, they all end each year with red ink in their ledgers, then resort to that sophisticated form of mendicancy known as fund raising to bring in enough money to balance their books. This means that they must be subsidized, either publicly or privately. In short, they rely on patrons and patronage.

Subsidies and fund drives are so integral a part of the American cultural scene that we often tend to forget the existence of a whole range of institutions that manage to get along quite nicely without them. Book publishers, record manufacturers, art reproduction printers, good music broadcasters, concert management agencies—all these meet the definition of a cultural institution. Yet most of these require no subsidies to stay alive. Not all of them actually turn a profit. But the very fact that they are organized as commercial enterprises indicates that they operate in a field in which profit, if not universal, is at least potentially attainable. Taken together, these institutions form the profit sector of the culture industry.

Certain difficulties in classification arise. The American theater, for example, is divided between the two sectors. The Broadway and off-Broadway theater, musical arenas, summer stock companies and the like, mainly fall into the profit category. But the professional resident theaters now springing up around the nation, and the sprawling amateur theater movement, both, by and large, fall into the non-profit sector. Some book publishing functions are carried out by university presses, which are, in effect, subsidized non-profit operations. There are a few small non-profit record companies and broadcasters. But the overall cleavage in the industry exists, and unless we understand it we cannot gain a clear picture of the economic condition of the arts in America today.

For, when we compare these two broad sectors, we cannot help but notice a strange fact. The culture explosion, with its accompanying boom in consumer spending for art-related goods and services, has affected each sector in a different way. It has, for example, brought rosy prosperity to many of the institutions in the profit sector.

Commercial book publishing provides a case in point. All

during World War II, despite shortages of paper and other inconveniences, the American book publishing industry flourished. Shortly after World War II, the industry began a sharp downward spiral. By 1947 industry spokesmen were speaking grimly of "the crisis in book publishing," and a 1949 report on the industry begins by assuring readers that "It is not true that the American book publishing industry is chronically sicker than other industries."

During the early 1950's, however, as the culture boom began, matters improved. Then came the "paperback revolution" and the spurt in college enrollments, and since then publishers have been the happy beneficiaries of a seemingly inexhaustible public hunger for their products. By 1963 overall sales volume had climbed to more than $1.6 billion—more than three times the post-war record. To be sure, much of this gain was in textbooks. But there were increases, too, in other categories. Sales of adult hardcover trade books—among which are to be found new novels, poetry, belles lettres, and books about music, art, theater and dance—rose 62 per cent between 1952 and 1960. The really spectacular change came in the quality paperback category. Here sales leaped 788 per cent, and the paperback bookshop, with its thousands of titles spread before the browser's bewildered eye, became a pleasant and profitable part of the American literary picture.

By 1962 Richard Schickel, writing in *Show* magazine, could report: "More titles are being published than ever before (nearly 20,000 this year), and profits in some areas are healthier than anyone ever dreamed they could be. The industry has been attracting . . . large chunks of Wall Street money, the kind that is customarily reserved for plunges into new and growing industries like electronics and copying machines." Indeed, during the late 'fifties so much enthusiasm was generated among investors that publishing stocks were pushed to inflated heights. It took what Wall Street euphemistically calls a "correction" to bring them down to realistic levels again. Nevertheless, the basic prosperity of the industry continued to make headlines. In late 1963 *Forbes* magazine could report: "The 19 largest (publishers) . . . boasted on average a profit margin of 5.8 per cent, a return on stockholders' equity of 13.7 per cent. It was a performance that put book publishing among the half dozen most profitable industries in the U.S. economy." This profit was spread over a great many types of publishing operation, but even the trade book houses, traditionally the most hard pressed, were registering an average after-tax profit of between three and four per cent.

The culture explosion had a similar impact on the record manufacturing industry. Of all the branches of the culture industry's profit sector none is further advanced along modern capitalist lines than record manufacture. It employs highly developed merchandising methods, mass advertising, and supermarket distribution. It is relatively concentrated. Two companies dominate the market for classical records. This market has grown phenomenally during the years of the culture expansion. This period was marked by the introduction of the long-playing record and superior high-fidelity equipment. By 1957 Americans were spending $54.5 million a year for classical recordings, and sales were climbing irregularly upwards. In 1963 the sum spent for classical music records reached $76.4 million. An incredibly rich and diverse selection of recordings, many of them musically superb, were made available to the public. A typical issue of the Schwann catalog lists approximately 25,000 records, mainly classical, beginning with the *Sonata in C for Two Violins and Continuo* by Evaristo Felice Dall' Abaco, ending with sonatas for violin, viola, and piano by Eric Zeisl, and embracing hundreds of works by the great masters in between.

Nor were the record makers in business for their health alone. The two major companies, RCA Victor and Columbia Records, both subsidiaries of larger corporations, bury their classical music profit figures in their parental financial statements. But both have done well on their classical operations. There is reason to believe, for example, that Columbia has averaged a net profit of roughly five per cent on sales of classical records. This is lower than the overall return of 5.7 per cent after taxes for its parent, the Columbia Broadcasting System. But it is higher than the 4.2 per cent median profit realized in 1962 by the 500 largest industrial corporations on *Fortune*'s much quoted list.

It would be too glib to state that all culture-related commercial enterprises did as well as the publishers and record companies. On a smaller scale, some of the hundreds of privately owned art galleries that sprang up during recent years to take advantage of the passion for possession were undercapitalized or badly located and have had, in consequence, a hard time of it. Similarly, not all of the FM radio stations that cropped up in recent years to serve the public's craving for classical music have moved into the black as yet. Each branch of the culture industry faced its own peculiar problems. But overall, the growth of the arts audience in America has been a financial blessing for many of the commercial entrepreneurs serving the culture market.

Unfortunately, this has not proved to be the case in the nonprofit sector. Here, instead of rising profits and sweetly purring investors, we find rising deficits and perplexed patrons.

Take the dolorous example of our orchestral economy. Our 1,250 symphony orchestras range from the Boston Symphony and the New York Philharmonic down to purely amateur aggregations that collect periodically to produce a little friendly cacophony. Musically, the two ends of the scale are worlds apart. Economically, they have much in common. Both lose money. Many orchestra managers and musicians are offended by such blunt terminology. They disapprove of words like "loss" or "deficit," arguing that they belong in a counting-house, not in a cultural institution. Be that as it may, whatever terms are selected, the fact is that orchestras spend more than they earn. Economically speaking, they are going into the hole.

In all, it costs about $30 million a year to operate these 1,250 orchestras. But they earn only $16 million from the sale of tickets, recording royalties, program advertising and other items. The remaining $14 million is subsidy income collected from patrons, and the amount of subsidy needed is rising.

This is true even of our best and strongest orchestras. The New York Philharmonic, for example, sold every seat for every concert during its 1962–1963 season. Yet it managed to earn only $1,300,000 at the box office, as against a total cost of roughly $2 million. It earned an additional $400,000 or so from broadcast fees and recording royalties, but it had to ask its patrons to make up a loss of approximately $300,000. In 1953–1954, only nine seasons ago, the deficit was $125,000, less than half as large as it is today.

Actually, as other orchestras go, the Philharmonic's deficit is relatively low in percentage terms. The peculiar situation in which American symphonies find themselves after a period of hectic cultural growth in the nation was summed up succinctly in a statement issued by the American Symphony Orchestra League in 1961: "Whereas ten years ago, the major orchestras were, on the average, earning about 61 per cent of their total costs of operation, the present average is 53 per cent in spite of more sold out concerts than at any previous time in the history of the orchestras."*

This pattern is repeated in the field of opera. Americans spend more than $10 million annually (how much more is hard to determine) for opera tickets, of which a very substantial portion goes to a single institution—the Metropolitan Opera. So established is the Met that it regularly sells 97 per cent of all available seats, and charges prices up to $13.00. Altogether it requires about $8 million to run the Met, and even with its high prices and commanding position in the United States it manages to earn only about $5.9 million at the box office. Other forms of earned income—broadcast fees, for example—bring in about $700,000. But the 1962–63 deficit ran to nearly $1.4 million. This compares with a deficit of only $219,000 ten years earlier.

On a reduced scale, the situation elsewhere is the same. The Chicago Lyric Opera opened its doors for the first time in 1954. By the end of that first season it had accumulated a deficit of $70,000. Today, despite virtual sell-outs at its performances, its annual deficit is $450,000, representing roughly 40 per cent

---

* The League defines a "major" orchestra as one having a budget of $250,000 or more per year. There are 26 orchestras in this category. There are another 27 orchestras in the "metropolitan" category—i.e., with budgets of $100,000 to $250,000 per year. There are, in addition, more than 900 "community" orchestras with budgets under $100,000, plus about 275 college or university orchestras. The smaller the scale of the orchestra, the larger its deficit relative to its annual budget. Thus in the metropolitan classification and among the larger community orchestras, earned income averages only about 49 per cent. When one reaches down into the smaller community orchestras it averages only 33 per cent.

of the cost of operation. There are, all told, 30 to 40 professional opera companies in the United States, plus about 430 struggling amateur companies and 240 university-sponsored producing groups. The sum total of patronage required to keep them all functioning rises each year.

Rising deficits, intensifying the need for subsidy, exist in the other performing arts as well. Until not long ago the professional theater in the United States was almost synonymous with the commercial theater in New York. The years since the beginning of the culture explosion have seen the unexpected rise of a group of professional resident acting companies outside New York. These include the Arena Stage in Washington, D.C., the San Francisco Actor's Workshop, the Mummers Theatre in Oklahoma City, the Fred Miller Theatre in Milwaukee and similar companies in Louisville, Houston, Dallas, Seattle and other cities. New ones continue to crop up at a rapid rate.

Most of these are non-profit institutions, and they take their theater seriously, eschewing musical comedy and the star system. Their programmatic leanings are exemplified by the announcement by the Fred Miller Theatre that it would choose the seven plays for its 1964–65 season from among the works of the following writers: Albee, Ionesco, Shakespeare, Shaw, Chekhov, Wilder, Williams, Wilde, Noel Coward and T. S. Eliot. Their financial condition is exemplified by the case of the Seattle Repertory Theatre which recently launched its first season and ran up a loss of $180,000. Not all the professional resident companies lose quite such large sums, but it takes more and more subsidy to keep their stages lit.

Of all the performing arts disciplines, the dance—ballet, modern, and ethnic—is in the most precarious position. Recent large grants by the Ford Foundation have given an important economic shot in the arm to the ballet, but other fields of dance received none of this largesse. Moreover, the need for such subsidy merely underscores the inability of the dance to pay its way at the box office. Those who organize dance companies know in advance that they can expect patronage needs to increase, rather than decline, as time goes by. In Washington, D.C., for example, the newly formed National Ballet, a professional company, ran up a deficit of more than $80,000 in its first season. It fully anticipates that by 1968 its deficit will have climbed to the neighborhood of $200,000.

The problems of museums are quite different from those of the performing arts, but the economic end results are similar. Of the more than 5,000 museums of all types in the United States, almost all are hard-pressed for money, staff and space. It is ironic that the rise of public interest in painting and the proliferation of private collectors has inflated the art market, forcing museums to compete with private buyers and pay higher prices for the works they wish to acquire. This has produced a snowball effect, driving up other costs as well. The critic Aline Saarinen has pointed out that the cost of special exhibitions "is becoming a frightful burden, not only because of rising costs of packing, shipping, etc., but because the booming art market has raised insurance costs to astronomic heights."

At the same time, the gift of works of art to museums, encouraged by the tax laws, has been an artistic boon but a real estate headache for the recipients. The Museum of Modern Art in New York reported in 1960 that, out of a collection of 18,510 items including drawings, posters, photographs and other special materials, fewer than 300 could be properly exhibited at any given time. The remaining 98 per cent of the collection was stored away in areas that were either "inconveniently accessible" or entirely inaccessible. The bulk of the collection sat in a warehouse six blocks from the museum, and some precious items were stored in a vault in the country twenty miles away.

Since then the museum has conducted a successful drive to raise $25 million for a new building. The space pressure has eased, but the economic problems remain. It requires about $2.4 million annually to operate the museum, one of the finest in the world. Of this, however, less than $900,000—37.5 per cent—is earned through admission fees, the sale of some 800,000 publications each year, film rentals, and other sources. More than $1.5 million remains to be raised through donations and from the sale of memberships which are, in many respects, disguised contributions, although the museum classifies them as earned income. Nor is the record of this museum poor. It is, in fact, excellent. Its earned income from paid admissions is extremely high by museum standards. Indeed, a study of 52 art museums conducted by the American Association of Museums showed that their average income from paid admissions runs to only 2.6 per cent of their budgets. They earn another 2.5 per cent from sales of one kind or another. The remaining 94.9 per cent of their incomes represents memberships and patronage, the need for which is universally rising.

In short, while the profit sector of the culture industry has managed to prosper economically, the non-profit sector has gotten into the curious position of earning more each year but needing more and more subsidy nevertheless. The years of cultural expansion in the United States, far from lessening the need for patronage, have increased it.

There are those who take a kind of perverse delight in reading of the plight of the non-profit arts institutions. Persuaded that the United States is fast going to pot, that its culture is doomed to mediocrity, and that the future holds nothing but trouble, they view the rising deficits as unshakable proof that Americans are boors or boobs, and that our cultural institutions are heading toward collapse.

It would be irresponsible to play down the financial difficulties faced by these institutions. Any suggestion that the situation is less pressing than it really is serves them ill. In a real sense, our museums and ballet companies, our theaters and orchestras and operas are bulwarks against much that is cheapening, dehumanizing, and life-stunting in modern industrial society. If, as we have contended, it is true that this country faces an unprecedented challenge to prove that democracy and culture are compatible, we doom ourselves to failure if we ignore these difficulties.

And yet, we do them even more harm if we misinterpret their troubles. For the strange and heartening fact is that despite the constant upward creep of deficit, we almost never hear of a symphony forced to dissolve. Instead we hear that orchestras are lengthening their seasons. For every museum that has been compelled to padlock its doors for lack of patronage in the past decade, twenty have sprung up to take its place. Theaters, operas, and dance companies plead for subsidy income and send out armies of volunteer money collectors, but at the same time they increase the number of performances they offer the public. The truth is that although we Americans go about financing our culture in ways that are splendidly haphazard, we are, in fact, financing it better than ever before. We find, to put it simply, that what our non-profit cultural institutions are suffering from is not a degenerative disease, but the exquisite pains of growth.

This chapter has described the two sectors of the culture industry and described the peculiar plight of the non-profit arts institutions. We now must trace the roots of that plight. Why, in a period of booming public interest in the arts, is each step forward accompanied by an ever-more-acute need for subsidy?

11

The High Cost of Culture

WE HAVE SEEN THE DEFICITS SURGING UPWARD. WE HAVE HEARD THE
spiel of the fund raiser and the rattle of the tin cup. What we
have not heard is a sensible explanation of why these deficits are
rising, and why they will rise in the future. A hardheaded businessman, asked to contribute to a cultural fund drive, would be
justified in asking why we can generate profits in one part of our
culture industry while in the other we need constant and increasing infusions of subsidy.

It is astonishing how infrequently such questions are asked—
even by hardheaded businessmen. It is even more astonishing
how our non-profit institutions have been able to go on raising
larger and larger sums without answering it. For if a skeptical
businessman did pose this question to an artist or a culture
executive, they would have a tendency to brush it aside. The
chances are excellent that the questioner would be rewarded with
a condescending smile. There would then be trotted out the bland
(and not wholly accurate) assertion that orchestras and museums
and operas and dance companies have always, under all circumstances, required patronage. He would be reminded of the
Medicis, the Archbishop of Salzburg, the Mellons.

This, of course, is a non-answer. It is well intentioned. But it is
inadequate. Even if it were true, it would not explain why the
non-profit institutions in the United States should continue to
need subsidy today in the midst of the greatest boom in culture
consumption that history has known. We need a better answer
than that. Let us try to frame one.

Patronage, of course, is more than a matter of money. It has a direct bearing on the quality of the art produced. First, patronage frees the recipient from the pressure of the box office. This means a freedom to soar beyond the immediate limits of popular taste. In an institution, the higher the percentage of patronage income as against income earned at the ticket window, the freer it is to present program material that is experimental, esoteric, long forgotten or out of favor, perhaps even offensive to the public. This freedom is essential to the continuing development of art. In short, patronage makes it possible for the artist or the institution to lead, rather than merely reflect, public taste.

The second virtue of patronage is that it frees the artist from the tyranny of his peers, "the tribunal of his rivals," as d'Alembert shrewdly called it. Even artists who despise the public, or pretend to, often quail at the thought of offending their peers and rivals. Who wants to be thought a fool by his colleagues? Moreover, a conspiracy of rivals, conscious or unconscious, can sometimes choke off an artist's access to the public. The willingness of a patron to support a counter-movement, or a lone voice in opposition, when the public would not, has more than once made a profound contribution to culture. One may disagree totally with Huntington Hartford's taste. Yet his willingness to subsidize a museum to display the work of painters or schools of painting that are currently unpopular among artists could conceivably turn out to be a major service to art. Only the passage of time will tell.

Thus patronage can be a liberating force, freeing or stimulating the artist or institution to ever higher levels of performance. This means that even if there were no other reasons for it, patronage would be important.

There are, however, other reasons for it, too. One of these is social as well as aesthetic. For patronage ensures the artist a more varied, more democratic audience than he might have in its absence. If everyone who wanted to enjoy a concert or ballet recital or an opera performance or a stroll through a museum had to pay his pro-rated share of the true cost of production, large segments of the population would simply be barred from the pleasures of contact with art. And the artist would be barred from contact with them. Millions of dollars of the subsidy poured into our non-profit arts institutions in the past decade have gone to underwrite low-price concerts for children, public concerts in parks and outdoor shells, free performances of Shakespeare or Mozart, free art exhibits and similar services. If everyone paid the full cost of his orchestra ticket, the price would have to be almost exactly double what it is today, and large numbers of people, including many students, would be locked out. A ticket of admission to the Museum of Modern Art today costs $1.00 or less. If the Museum last year had had to exist without patronage income, it would have had to boost its average admission price to at least $2.05.* Take away subsidy income from the Metropolitan Opera and the top price for a single seat in the orchestra might be forced up to about $16.00. Even at our present level of affluence, that is a bit steep. Thus, by artificially supporting lower prices, patronage broadens the audience. In addition, it helps build audiences for the future. The children attending free ballet performances today may become lifelong devotees of the dance who will buy tickets later on when they are adults.

Let us assume, however, that our inquisitive businessman is not impressed by such arguments. What, he may well ask, is the economic case for patronage, as distinct from the social or aesthetic?

If he put this question to the Metropolitan's Mr. Bing, he would no doubt be told that high cost lies behind the need for subsidy. He would be reminded that it takes a tremendous amount of money to produce culture. It would be called to his attention that while it takes only nineteen railroad cars to move the so-called "greatest show on earth," the Ringling Brothers and Barnum and Bailey Circus, it requires fully forty railroad cars to transport the people and paraphernalia of the Metropolitan when it tours. He will be told that Act Two, Scene Two of *Aïda*, in which Radames and the Egyptian army return from trouncing the Ethiopians, requires a small army to perform. Someone once took the trouble of tallying up the number of people involved in mounting that famous scene. The score: 96 choristers; 92 orchestra members; 71 stage hands; 60 extras; 36 ballet dancers; a stage band of 21; 8 soloists; 4 assistant conductors; 4 stage man-

* Or $2.69 if membership income is counted as unearned, and hence part of the subsidy revenue.

agers; 4 wardrobe mistresses and 4 wardrobe men; 2 make-up men; and 1 conductor; not to speak of assorted wig specialists, a prompter and the administrative staff—more than 400 people all told.

Now it is true that costs are rising. Wages of all these people, plus the actual costs of props, sets, lighting, exhibition fixtures, transportation, building maintenance, insurance, advertising, etc. —all these are indubitably climbing. The cost argument cannot lightly be laid aside.

Still, even this argument will not entirely satisfy our tough-minded businessman. He knows that his costs, too, have risen without preventing him from making a profit. What is more, the relative sums involved do not overly impress him. For while the $8 million it takes to operate the Met is, in absolute terms, a great deal of money, it is small when compared with the $10 million or more that many medium-sized businesses will spend merely to launch a new product on the market. What our businessman will insist on knowing is how these costs relate to production, to prices, and to the size of the market.

Pursuing his inquiry he will find that almost universally the non-profit institutions of culture, as noted earlier, have been sharply increasing their production. The National Ballet of Washington, which as we have seen lost more than $80,000 in its first season and foresees a deficit of nearly $200,000 several years hence, also foresees increasing its production from 17 public performances a season to 72. In a decade, the Chicago Lyric Opera has doubled the number of its performances. In St. Paul we observed that the theater company has increased the number of its performances each season from six to 105 in a five-year period alone. The seasons of orchestras and other institutions are stretching longer each year, the number of performances is multiplying. Indeed, it is almost safe to assume that wherever an institution's deficit has risen in the past decade that increase has reflected an increase in production. Moreover, there is evidence that not only quantity but quality has risen in many places. There has been a remarkable general improvement in the collections of our museums and in their standards of exhibition. Many major performing arts institutions have been tuning themselves up, augmenting a string section here, investing in better sets or costumes there, hiring first-rate soloists more frequently, and offering the consumer more in the sense of physical comfort as well: wider seats and aisles, air conditioned halls, carpeting, and so on.

This being the case, our inquiring businessman would no doubt ask, "Have they been raising their prices commensurately?" Some have, certainly. But we lack comprehensive data on pricing in the non-profit sector as a whole, and the fact that deficits have been climbing would appear to indicate that prices have not in fact kept pace with costs.

And so we begin to close in on the heart of the matter. For our persistent businessman knows that price cannot be discussed without also discussing the buyer. We must turn once more to the culture consumer. Laying aside all questions of aesthetics or altruism, all questions of democracy and social class in the audience, stripping the matter down to cold, hard economics, we must ask: If it is true that there has been a great growth in the culture public, if the estimate of 30 million to 45 million in the culture public is anywhere near correct, and if, as this book has suggested, this public is part of America's "comfort class," why can't it support the institutions in the non-profit sector on a pay-as-you-go basis instead of relying on patrons to underwrite knock-down prices?

The answer is that, although we have used the term culture public, it is really more accurate to speak of a great many overlapping culture publics. For the audience for the arts today is fractured and fragmented. There is, for example, one substantial slice of the overall culture public that spends none of its money in the non-profit sector at all. All of its expenditures for culture are channeled into the profit sector. This group consists of those millions of Americans who satisfy all their cultural wants by buying books or records, or listening to fine music on the radio, and who never set foot in a concert hall, a museum, or other non-profit cultural institutions. Because of this, the market served by the non-profit sector is smaller than the culture public as a whole.

Next, among those Americans who do consume the services of the non-profit sector, there are dozens of subdivisions along interest lines. There is a chamber music public that cannot be flogged into attending a symphony concert. There is a public for contemporary painting that has no interest in the great masters. There is a public for painting of all periods, only some of whose members are even remotely interested in sculpture. There are balletomanes who are icily indifferent to modern dance. There is a public for musical comedy that will not under any circumstances attend the theater of Albee or Ionesco. It is one of the great virtues of our culture that it offers rich diversity. The more variety there is, the better. But this means that the number of potential buyers in each artistic discipline is limited.

That is not all. Unlike the books or records or art reproductions turned out by the profit sector, the products of the non-profit sector are not easily or inexpensively shipped. Wrapping up a book and mailing it somewhere is one thing; transporting the hundred men of a symphony orchestra and paying their expenses on the road is another. This is a crucial economic factor. For these high distribution costs usually make it necessary that the products of the non-profit sector—mainly live performances—be produced at or near where the audience is.

The fact that these arts institutions are restricted to serving local markets is of paramount economic importance. We have already subtracted a large slice of the overall culture public from the non-profit market; we have already divided what remained by the number of basic interest groups. We must now further subdivide these along geographical lines into from 1,000 to 2,000 local publics for each of the artistic disciplines represented in the non-profit sector.

When we have completed this super-fine fractionalization we are left with relatively small markets for each individual non-profit institution. In each of these miniature markets some consumers are able to pay the true cost of culture production; others are neither able nor willing to pay the true cost, but are willing to pay a smaller amount or to consume the products given away free. The result: those who are devoted to a particular institution within each community, and who are able to afford it, must provide a subsidy to assure its continued existence.

We may predict that some few orchestras, dance groups, operas, and resident theaters, operating in unusually favorable local economic environments, will be able to improve their economic condition in the future. As their publics grow in numbers and in spending power, they may be able to raise prices to the point at which they inch into the black or even begin to turn a profit. Some non-profit institutions are within reaching distance of this condition now. Indeed, looking far enough into the future we are likely to see some commercial entrepreneurs enter fields now reserved solely for the non-profit institutions. Most of the companies they establish will be touring operations at the start. Later they may settle in some of the larger cities.

But this trend will be severely limited by the operations of an iron law not previously mentioned. We might term this the Law of the Inefficiency of Art, and it is so fundamental, it explains so much about the difference between the two sectors of our culture industry, and it is so little understood, that it merits close examination. Because of this law the need for subsidy will probably rise sharply in the aggregate as the years go by, rather than diminish. For this law guarantees that the cost of certain cultural services (chiefly live performances) will not merely rise, but climb upward at a rate faster than the cost of other goods and services in our society. Until we grasp this fact, we miss the essential significance of patronage today.

To understand the law we must begin with the end-product created by each sector. In the non-profit sector the end-product is most frequently a live performance—a concert, a recital, a play. If, for purposes of economic analysis, we consider a live performance to be a commodity, we are immediately struck by the fact that, unlike most commodities offered for sale in our society, this commodity is not standardized. It is not machine made. It is a handcrafted item.

Economically speaking, the production of this commodity is out of step with the times. In terms of the method of production, it is a throwback to an earlier stage of society when all goods were handcrafted, when the skill of the artisan was all-important and the contribution of the machine minor or non-existent. Because of this anachronous quality, the production of a single performance of a play or concert or ballet is *relatively* costly. Art, in this sense, is inherently inefficient in today's world.

The spread of automated production throughout the rest of society lowers the real cost of other goods and services. This means that the relative cost of the handcrafted product rises. Automation will no doubt bring with it new artistic forms—electronic music is merely the first tentative suggestion of what the future may have in store. But we will without question also want to conserve the art forms of the past, and these "conventional" forms —live concerts, live theater, live dance recitals—these are not automatable through any presently available technology. The cost of any individual performance or art work relative to the cost of other goods in society will thus be forced upward.

Contrast the output of the non-profit performing arts institutions with that of the record manufacturer. He, too, sells what appears to be a performance. But it is not. It is a replica of a performance, a mass-produced embodiment of a performance. While the original performance is a handcrafted one-of-a-kind item, the record company captures this product, modifies it, and congeals it in a mass-producible form. The book publisher, in effect, does the same. The original manuscript of the poem or novel represents the author's work of art, the individual, the prototype. The book in which it is subsequently embodied is a mass-produced replica of the original. Its form of production is fully in keeping with the level of technology in the surrounding society. As production techniques become more advanced, the publisher is able to take advantage of their economies. The performing arts institution cannot, and the relative cost of its services is forced to rise at a faster rate than that for most other products of our society.

The workings of the Law of the Inefficiency of Art are reflected in the profit segments of the American theater—Broadway, off-Broadway, the road companies and musical arenas. Fighting to offset the pressure of the Law, they have moved into a form of production that represents a transition between true handcraft production and true mass production. An orchestra, for example, presents a concert of Bach tonight, Beethoven tomorrow, and Brahms the following night. At best, it repeats the same program four or five times. The profit-making segments of the theater, on the other hand, all present exact repeats of the same program night after night.

They are engaged in what might be called "quasi-mass-production." The first-night performance of a play is the culmination of weeks, months, sometimes even years of work. This one evening of culmination may be considered the true art product of the theater. But the producer on Broadway operates on the assumption that his play or musical will receive not merely one, but dozens, perhaps even hundreds, of repeat performances. So he turns the original art work into a living replica, a stamped out, quasi-mass-produced product presented to the audience again and again until there are no further ticket-buyers.

These successive performances, of course, vary slightly from night to night. There are human differences. But they are essentially stampings or prints of the original, and the actors, like assembly-line workers, grow weary and bored with their repetitive functions. As this boredom grows, the meaningful variations diminish until, by the end of a long run, the performances are so like one another that they are almost machine-made copies. In this sense the economics of Broadway, off-Broadway, and the other profit-making theater companies resemble those of a commercial enterprise engaged in mass production, and because of this the theatrical entrepreneur reaps part of the advantage of mass production—a declining unit cost of production.* If we take the total cost of presenting a show for one year, lumping together production expense (i.e., cost before opening night) and operating expense (cost of the first and all successive performances), the cost

---

* This, incidentally, explains why the drama critics in New York are so much more powerful than the music critics. One or two bad reviews by major New York theater critics can drive a play off the boards in 24 or 48 hours. A bad review of a concert by the New York Philharmonic will not put the orchestra out of business. For one thing, the orchestra sells seats by subscription, so that many of its listeners have paid in advance for the whole season. But beyond this, the concert-goer knows that even if Alan Rich of the *Herald Tribune* charged the orchestra with being slack when it played Beethoven last night, it might be superb in its performance of Brahms tomorrow. In contrast, if Walter Kerr of the *Tribune* says that the script of a new play was thin and its staging poor, the audience knows that these defects will be built into each subsequent stamping of the play.

per performance decreases as the number of performances increases. But he is able to go only so far. The manufacturer engaged in true mass production can and does go further. He not only is able to amortize his tooling-up costs and administrative expense over the production run, but the very fact that he is turning out great quantities of a product makes possible economies in purchasing and shortcuts in the actual physical process of production. These are beyond the theatrical entrepreneur. He still needs one actor to play Polonius and another for Hamlet, and both must be present all the time that the script requires them. There are no shortcuts.

The advantages of quasi-mass-production place Broadway and off-Broadway in the profit sector—but only marginally. They remain unstable and highly risky. Their prices, unsupported by the artificial prop of patronage, have been driven up sharply in recent years. And the pressure will become worse over the long run. It is not that the production of art is becoming any less efficient than it ever was, but that its level of efficiency is falling further and further behind that of the economy as a whole. Indeed, in this very difference lies much of the attractiveness and appeal of art. It is not a shiny, standardized, predictable product of the machine. But therein also lies the explanation for rising costs. Some day, if automation makes us all Croesus-rich, this may not matter. We may be able to pay our pro-rated share of the true cost of production of live art. Until that utopian day, however, the pressure of cost is likely to increase the pressure for patronage.

It is this long-range prognosis that makes it so important for us to consider, more consciously and rationally than ever before, how we are going to go about providing the needed subsidy.

12

The New Patrons

PATRON—THE VERY WORD CONNOTES EXCELLENCE, ELEGANCE AND tradition. The names of the great patrons march down the halls of art history. Pericles, who built the Parthenon, opened the theaters to the poor, initiated competitions for singers and harp players, and whose investment in the arts is still, in the words of one historian, providing dividends for the hotel-keepers of Athens. Maecenas, who subsidized Horace and Virgil. The House of Han, patron of poets in the China of 200 B.C. Cosimo de Medici and Lorenzo the Magnificent, patrons of Michelangelo, Donatello, Brunelleschi, and Luca della Robbia. Prince Esterhazy, whose court found room for Haydn. Even minor kings and princelings have ensured themselves a measure of lasting fame through their patronage of the arts. Who would recall Ludwig II of Bavaria, but for his patronage of Wagner?

The legacy of art produced with the help of patrons is so rich that a myth has grown up around it. This myth, often propagated by the cultural elitists, holds that the patrons of yesteryear were more sophisticated, more educated, and more decent than those of today. A typical expression of this point of view, chosen at random from among many such statements that appear in books on music and art, tells us that "The old patron *liked* art rather than *used* it. Sometimes he loved it. . . . Patron and artist were quite often friends and worked together; the one proposing, the other executing."

This idyllic picture, with its pejorative implications about our own era, is fine as far as it goes. But it goes only halfway towards truth. For while Dürer could write to his patron, Pirckheimer, "you stink so of whores that I can smell it over here," and manage to get away with it, not all patron-artists relationship were quite so easy and affable. Michelangelo's agonies with his succession of papal patrons, Rembrandt's troubles with the officers he immortalized in the *Night Watch*—these need no recounting. And Johnson's definition of a patron as "commonly a wretch who supports with insolence, and is paid with flattery," has the sting of truth. One might fill volumes with the difficulties caused artists by patrons who were blind, bullheaded, and boorish.

The reason the myth lives on, of course, is that patrons have their cake and eat it. Their triumphs live; their blunders, by and large, are forgotten. Patrons who were stupid enough or uncultivated enough to support the mediocrities of their period fade into richly deserved obscurity. Only those who guessed right are remembered. The history of patronage is thus biased and selective. There is no reason to believe that the patrons of the past were superior to our own. They were, however, very different. During its lengthy history patronage has shifted its base many times. In Athens, Pericles' projects were financed from public funds. Maecenas was a private individual. During the Middle Ages and the Renaissance the Church was the pre-eminent patron. Later on royalty assumed the responsibility. With the republican revolutions that swept clean the thrones of Europe, there came once more a shift toward the use of public funds. Indeed, a survey conducted a quarter of a century ago with the help of U.S. consulates around the world came to the conclusion that "Since the beginning of the twentieth century, state support of art may be said to have become universal, having been adopted by practically all countries in which some system of government patronage had not previously existed." The survey found evidence of official state patronage all over the world, from Sweden to Siam.

In matters of patronage, however, the United States has always been different. We have never had a feudal aristocracy or a monarchy to assume financial responsibility for the arts. We have no tradition of ecclesiastic patronage, and, in fact, during the colonial period, when for a few years the Church exercised State power, it was actively hostile to art.

Furthermore, for a variety of reasons too well known to require restatement, we have always mistrusted the federal government, particularly when it comes to matters touching upon personal conviction or taste. Even our brief fling with federal support through the arts project of the Works Progress Administration in the late 1930's was, it must be remembered, a desperate economic measure designed to provide employment, rather than a conscious program to encourage art.

Instead, art patronage in the United States fell, originally, to individuals. Russell Lynes, in *The Tastemakers,* tells the story of Luman Reed, the retired New York grocer, who in the 1830's became "the ideal and unique art patron of his day," buying paintings from contemporary American artists, opening a gallery, and counting among his friends not only painters like Thomas Cole, Asher Durand, and William Sidney Mount, but also writers like Washington Irving, James Fenimore Cooper, and William Cullen Bryant. In the same period there was Thomas Jefferson Bryan, an eccentric Philadelphian with inherited wealth, whose dream was to collect paintings that might form the core of a national museum. He opened a gallery and hung it with the works of Dürer, Mantegna, and Velasquez. There was James Jackson Jarves, too, son of the founder of a successful glass company, who spent a lifetime collecting art with the hope of creating a national gallery.

But such men were merely forerunners. The fortunes created by the Civil War and the explosive growth of industry in the next three-quarters of a century spawned a new class of tycoon-patron, rich, sometimes vulgar and ostentatious, often more concerned with status than art, but sometimes shrewd and often generous. In San Francisco William C. Ralston, the shipping and railroad magnate, subsidized the theater. In the East, Harriman bought great quantities of American art to decorate his estate. John Pierpont Morgan's claim to connoisseurship has often been disputed, but even he proved discerning at times. Strolling through the exhibition of French paintings at the Chicago World's Fair of 1893, Morgan snorted disdainfully. It looked, he said, as if the art had been selected by a committee of chambermaids. He was right. It did. Morgan paid so lavishly for paintings, he paid such high prices and encouraged, by example, so many other rich men to don the mantle of patronage, that a wave of consternation rolled through the London art market when he died in 1913.

Even today the tycoon-patrons—from Higginson and Havemeyer to Hearst, from Frick to Corcoran, from Mellon to Rockefeller and Guggenheim—remain rooted in the history of American culture. There was hugger-muggery, wheeling and dealing, tax avoidance and not a little snobbery mixed with less base motives during the era dominated by the tycoon-patron, but this historic personage did, after all is said, leave behind something that had not existed before, a few great collections, a few great musical institutions, libraries and historical restorations.

Striding colossus-like through the world of art in America, the tycoon-patron may not have known it at the time, but he was a doomed man. Income tax and other hideous plagues were soon to strike him down. In 1929, the year of Black Thursday, 513 individuals took home paychecks of $1 million or more clear—after taxes. Their aggregate income was more than $1.1 billion. By 1955 their ranks had been decimated. There were only 276 true "millionaires." Their combined income equaled only $600 million. The dollar was worth only about half of what it had been a generation earlier and—horror of horrors—this $600 million represented income *before* taxes.

Today the individual patron of great wealth is still to be found here and there, an oddity in the art world. There is Lincoln Kirstein, the Boston department store heir who has pumped millions into the New York City Ballet. There is Lucia Chase of carpet and watch wealth, who has done the same for the Ballet Theatre. There is the indestructible Miss Ima Hogg, 81 years old, lady bountiful for the Houston Symphony and the Houston Museum of Fine Arts. There is Mrs. Norman "Buffie" Chandler, who, in the not wholly inaccurate words of *Time* magazine, "has established a near-dictatorship of culture in Southern California." And there still is an occasional Vanderbilt who can give Lincoln Center $750,000 at a clip. But such "philanthropoids" are lumbering relics of a vanished past.

The past is never as simple as history paints it. The tycoon-patron was never the *sole* source of patronage support for the arts in America. But for a long time he was the dominant source.

Today the individual patron remains an important source of patronage, but, as indicated in Chapter Five, he is no longer likely to be a great robber baron or merchant prince, taking out time from his titanic financial adventures, his steam yacht cruises or his summers at Newport, to devote a few fleeting hours to art. He is not likely, as were some of the tycoon-patrons, to purchase a pair of opera glasses for $75,000, to engage an orchestra to serenade a new-born infant, or to transport a whole theater troupe from New York to Chicago merely to entertain a few friends. Typically, he is instead a $40,000-a-year executive, a $30,000-a-year physician, or a $15,000-a-year engineer whose wife teaches sculpture at the nearby college. Moreover, the money and time he devotes to his favorite orchestra, or museum, or resident theater, is likely to mean more to him than it did to the tycoon-patron.

The individual patron of today, more than likely a member of the comfort class, cuts a less flamboyant swath than the tycoon-patron of old, but he does not walk alone. He has partners in patronage. Today, apart from contributions from individuals, subsidies are channeled into the non-profit institutions of art from five basically different directions: from businesses; from foundations; from universities; from other types of organizations; and from city, county, and state governments. To understand what alternatives we, as a nation, have in meeting the problem of rising deficits in the non-profit sector of the culture industry, it is helpful to see how the situation is changing with respect to each of these sources of patronage.

We have described in an earlier chapter the newly emergent relationships springing up between business and the arts in America. Patronage is merely one of these relationships, but it is of increasing significance. It is encouraged by the fact that corporate philanthropic contributions are deductible from federal taxes, so long as they do not exceed five per cent of pre-tax net income in the company. Although corporations by 1963 were, by conservative estimate, giving away $536 million a year for a wide variety of purposes, they were not nearly within reach of the five per cent limit. Indeed, total corporate philanthropy represents only about a fifth of the allowable amount. There is, thus, substantial room for increase on a percentage basis. In absolute terms the amount is moving upward.

Equally important are the changes in the distribution of these funds. The sum given to the arts or to art-related causes is still minute by comparison with the amounts given to health and welfare. But what appears to be a long-range shift is occurring. The National Industrial Conference Board, which issues periodic studies of corporate giving, reported in 1963 that, "For the first time since the Board has been conducting these surveys, gifts to education exceed those to health and welfare. Company funds allotted to civic and cultural causes also figured more prominently." Contributions in this category still only account for 5.3 per cent of the total, but that represents almost a doubling of the percentage three short years earlier. In short, the outlook for increased patronage of the arts by business would appear to be optimistic.

A similar tendency is observable in the fast-growing field of foundation philanthropy. Foundations, one of the more curious fruits of the tree of affluence, give away money for an astonishing variety of purposes ranging from the preservation of the prairie chicken to support of nursing schools in Taiwan. Somewhere between the two fall the arts and humanities. By 1963 foundations were issuing grants at an estimated rate of $820 million a year, up $10 million from the 1960 level. Like corporations, they give relatively little to cultural causes. But this relatively little amounted to a tidy $40 million in 1963. Not all of this went to non-profit arts institutions; some of it went to individual artists or to scholars for humanistic studies of one kind or another. Nevertheless, here, as in the field of business patronage, the amount allocated for cultural purposes was distinctly on the rise both absolutely and relatively.

The changed relationship between universities and the arts was the subject of an earlier chapter. In this connection, as we saw, universities are beginning to "adopt" certain professional theaters, chamber music groups, and individual artists. The chief way in which universities funnel money into the arts is through their subsidization of the hundreds of on-campus amateur orchestras, opera producing units, theaters and dance groups that they operate as part of their educational program. At the same time, an intricate tracery of ties between colleges and off-campus cultural institutions is also beginning to crop up. As a rule these do not yet involve grants of money from the university. But the possibility is not to be discounted that in the future the university will begin to emerge as a direct patron—a money-giver—to independent non-profit arts institutions, as well as to professional artists or groups under its own sponsorship.

Still another source of subsidy funds for the arts is the private or voluntary organization. Americans, as de Tocqueville observed very early in the game, are notorious joiners. Today we find interest in the arts reflected in fraternal organizations, community service clubs, churches and labor unions, and there are small but intriguing evidences that these may become a regular source of patronage funds in the future. The role of the Junior League in helping to subsidize arts councils has already been noted. The role of churches and trade unions as patrons is less well known. Many churches underwrite amateur theatrical or musical groups of their own. Synagogues buy a quantity of sculpture and art. Both, to an increasing degree, employ imaginative architecture in their building programs. Only infrequently do they make outright grants to non-profit cultural institutions. Labor unions, on the other hand, buy little in the way of art and sculpture (although there is a statue in front of the Bauhaus-modern headquarters of the auto workers' union in Detroit, and a large mosaic mural in the headquarters of the AFL-CIO in Washington). They are, however, beginning to make direct grants to non-profit arts institutions. The $10,000 contributed each year to the Detroit Symphony by the musicians' union local in that city, and the contributions of the International Brotherhood of Electrical Workers to Lincoln Center, are merely two examples. Not long ago the Retail Clerks International Association contributed $1,080 to the Washington Civic Opera Association. The AFL-CIO has contributed $5,000 to Joseph Papp's New York Shakespeare Festival, and additional small donations were given by ladies' garment workers' unions, milliners, and drugstore and hospital worker locals.

The aggregate sums still are tiny, but the two-day conference on the constructive uses of leisure sponsored in 1963 by the AFL-CIO reflects a growing sensitivity to the problems that the shorter work week will bring in its wake for union members. If labor ever manages to organize large numbers of professional and technical workers, or white-collar employees, its interest in the arts is likely to increase. Indeed, part of the problem in organizing such workers lies in the old fashioned "blue-collar" image of the labor movement. It should surprise nobody if certain unions begin to purchase abstract art, to participate in cultural events, and to increase patronage contributions as part of a conscious effort to update and upgrade their image.

Unions, churches, and community organizations are all, in effect, private organizations serving specialized slices of the public. Subsidies from cities, counties, and states, on the other hand, are made in the name of the entire public. As the tycoon-patrons of old died, they frequently left their collections of painting and sculpture to the cities in which they had lived, on condition that the municipalities erect a museum to house them, sometimes with the added stipulation that the museum bear their name. Thus by the 1870's and even earlier American cities had fallen into the practice of subsidizing art museums. By the end of World War I there were 119 art museums in the U.S., and some two dozen of them received municipal or state money. Today probably 25 per cent of all art museum revenues come from municipal sources.

It was not until the end of World War II and the coming of the cultural boom that cities also began to provide widespread patronage for performing arts institutions. Orchestras, generally, were the first of these to receive municipal aid, and even today more city subsidy goes to orchestras than to opera groups, ballet companies, or theaters. But the tendency is toward a broadening conception of municipal responsibility for the arts. In many cities municipal patronage is earmarked for special school performances or outdoor public concerts. But this is not true everywhere. The city of Waterloo, Iowa, for example, with a population of about 70,000, channels its patronage through a recreation commission that for a time underwrote half the salary of a professional conductor for the symphony. New York provides virtually rent-free space for the New York City Opera. City money is helping to finance many of the arts centers rising around the country.

In most cities, patronage funds come out of the general treasury. Not so in San Francisco, which has placed a three per cent tax on hotel room occupancy. This tax raises approximately $1 million annually for use in attracting tourists, a purpose toward which the arts clearly contribute. Of this sum, more than $200,000 is set aside for direct subsidies to non-profit arts institutions. The San Francisco Symphony Orchestra and the San Francisco Ballet each receive $80,000. Smaller sums go to the Spring Opera, a chamber music society, a theater, and several small ballet and modern dance groups.

As long as culture consumption was regarded as an elite activity of interest to only a narrow constituency, public authorities understandably felt unjustified in allocating city funds for art patronage. The massive expansion of the culture audience has made it possible for an enlightened city council or mayor to provide subsidy without being accused of coddling an already overprivileged special interest group. It is no accident that more cities are now giving more dollars to the arts than ever before. A rough and ready kind of democracy is at work.

American counties have been slow to emulate the city, but a few make significant contributions. The largest county patronage program is that of the Los Angeles County Music Commission which supplements a rather extensive program of municipal art patronage by the City of Los Angeles. The county commission divides $190,000 between the Los Angeles Philharmonic and the Hollywood Bowl Association, a music-sponsoring organization. It distributes another $230,000 in small donations to dozens of non-profit musical institutions from instrumental ensembles to choral groups. It is probable that more counties will undertake limited programs of patronage in the years to come, but they are likely to remain small in aggregate.

States, on the other hand, may become quite important. States have been making contributions to the support of arts institutions at least since 1936 when the Virginia Museum of Fine Arts was created as a state-owned and state-operated enterprise. The museum now receives upwards of $300,000 a year of state funds.

It has set up a network of regional affiliates to which it circulates exhibitions; it operates a theater, as well as an "artmobile." North Carolina, immediately to the south, also appropriates state funds to subsidize the arts. It allocates approximately $75,000 to support the North Carolina Symphony, a touring group, and makes small contributions to the Brevard Music Center, a theater, a museum in Raleigh, and a number of historical pageants that are performed during the summer. Recently, during the administration of Governor Terry Sanford, who took the unusual step of appointing a novelist, John Ehle, his full-time advisor on the arts and education, the state appropriated funds to create a school for the training of performing artists. When it opens in Winston-Salem, it will be the first such institution financed by public funds outside of New York City.

A few other states—Kentucky, for example—have also experimented with art patronage on a limited scale. It remained for New York, however, to establish the first large-scale state arts program. Created by act of legislature in 1960, the New York State Council on the Arts has become an important and energetic patron. By 1963 it had a budget in excess of $560,000 and, under imaginative direction by John MacFadyen, the state was pioneering new patronage techniques.*

Originally, the Council offered what were, in effect, grants to certain well-known professional performing arts groups to help them underwrite the cost of tours to some of the state's smaller communities. Later, instead of offering aid to the touring groups, it channeled money directly to local arts organizations. In turn, these chose the touring companies they wished to invite, and used Council money to help pay the costs. This broadened the choice among touring groups and shifted initiative to the community. Under this system, the town of Auburn (pop. 35,000) was enabled to hear the Cincinnati Symphony; Corning (pop. 17,000) played host to the American Ballet Company; Jose Greco turned up in Alfred, New York (pop. 2,800); and the medium-sized cities Syracuse and Troy presented performances of the San Francisco Ballet and the Boston Pops.

The Council also made special funds available for education

---

* MacFadyen, an architect by profession, resigned in April 1964, to return to the drawing board.

programs of various kinds. The Buffalo Philharmonic, under its distinguished composer-conductor Lukas Foss, held training clinics for members of smaller and weaker orchestras. The Council helped a group of struggling local opera companies create a regional organization through which they might share sets, costumes, music, and the like. It encouraged the establishment of arts councils in many communities.

In addition, the Council set up what is, in effect, a technical assistance program in the arts—the first one of its kind in the United States. Under this arrangement a local arts institution needing specialized outside consultation, but unable to afford it, can apply to the Council for help. The Council finds the right expert, pays him, and dispatches him to the scene. Through this program small museums have been able to import professional experts to help them improve exhibition and restoration techniques; small theaters have had the help of professionals in staging and lighting; arts groups involved in building programs have received assistance from architects; arts councils have consulted with a professional public relations executive on how to improve their communication with their communities; and specialized seminars and training sessions of various kinds have been organized in cities all over the state.

All of this has been accomplished with a minimum of red tape by a small and hard-working staff housed in modest offices on the shabby end of 57th Street in Manhattan. The program has attracted attention all over the United States and has been, in part, responsible for the rash of arts agencies established by other states in recent years. By March, 1964, at least 24 states claimed to have arts councils or commissions. Most of these were still in their formative stages; almost all were paper organizations. But there are signs that the techniques developed in New York may before long be emulated elsewhere. California has voted $50,000 for initial surveys and planning work, and it is likely to become the second state with a comprehensive program of arts patronage conducted by an agency set up for the purpose.

Seldom, if ever, in history have the arts of a nation drawn patronage simultaneously from so many diverse sources. Individuals, corporations, foundations, universities, voluntary organizations and city, county, and state governments are all, in

178 THE CULTURE CONSUMERS

their different ways, channeling funds into the non-profit sector of the culture industry. This pluralism of patronage contrasts sharply with the patterns of the past when a single source—king, Church, tycoon—dominated the economics of art and the artist. Indeed, this system, conforming exactly to the outlines of our open society, comes close to being an American invention.

Viewed from outside, this invention looks more like a Rube Goldberg contraption than a piece of sleek cybernetic instrumentation. It rattles and clanks as it grinds out money for the arts. Yet the outward look is deceptive, for the system has many hidden virtues.

The first of these is practical. Pluralism of patronage avoids the trap of placing the artist in total debt to a single sponsor. Dependence upon a single tycoon-patron meant sudden death for the Detroit Symphony in the late 1940's. Today the Detroit Symphony receives patronage from a bloc of individuals, from corporations, from voluntary organizations, and from the municipality, and it would take much more than individual caprice to kill it.

Nor is caprice the only danger inherent in reliance on a single source. A dip in the fortunes of individual patrons, in the profits of a corporation, in the membership dues of a union, or the tax receipts of a city, can cripple the arts institution dependent upon any one of these. By the same token, diversifying the base of patronage cushions the institution against the ordinary fluctuations of the business cycle. A recession is still usually accompanied by a falling off of contributions, but the more diverse the sources of patronage, the less severe the impact is likely to be. While many museums or operas, dance companies or orchestras are unquestionably unstable today because of erratic financing under the present system, the non-profit sector as a whole is probably more stable and secure than it would otherwise be.

A second, more important advantage is that plural patronage helps root the arts institution in the community. Through this system the tastes and interests not merely of individuals, but of organizations representing broad publics, are communicated to the arts institution, and the institution is encouraged to serve the needs of society. Much of the municipal money channeled to our symphony orchestras, for example, is earmarked for the specific purpose of providing free concerts for school children. This imposes certain limits on the orchestra's choice of music for those specific concerts, but it also cements the orchestra to the community. By directing the arts institution toward objectives outside itself, plural patronage provides links between art and society. Such links are healthy. They give culture social relevance. They give the arts institution an organic place and purpose in society.

The more varied the sources of patronage, the more varied the purposes for which subsidies will be earmarked. The Art Institute of Chicago, for example, receives money from a corporation on the stipulation that it offer a prize "for the best sculpture produced by oxy-acetylene welding and cutting." In itself, this very narrow purpose may seem unimportant. But it is clearly important to the patron, a division of the Union Carbide Corporation, and the more such purposes are served by art, the more deeply embedded in society and the more vitally indispensable it becomes. Our system of plural patronage assures that art will serve a wide variety of social purposes.

Finally, and most important, plural patronage makes possible a higher degree of freedom for the artist than any conceivable system of single-source patronage. It is exactly comparable to the self-employed professional who, because he works for many bosses, is his own boss in the end. As in American society as a whole, the centers of power and decision are widely dispersed in a system of plural patronage. This openness encourages a great variety and richness in production. It enhances the likelihood of support for artistic ventures of the greatest possible diversity. This does not, of course, mean that all such ventures do find the financial support that they need. But failing to attract patronage in one quarter, the artist or arts institution has the option of seeking it elsewhere.

The vulnerability of the artist under a system of single-source patronage was dramatically revealed not long ago when one of the nation's fine professional ballet companies, the Robert

Joffrey Ballet, was simply forced out of existence because the Rebekah Harkness Foundation, which had been subsidizing it, deliberately cut the props out from under it. The Foundation demanded that the company be reorganized under a new name—the Harkness Ballet. Joffrey, its brilliant young director, stalked out charging that he had been offered the position of artistic director with the re-organized company "but with only vague assurances about who would exercise final authority over the company's artistic policies." He took his case to the press with these questions: "Should a foundation that has supported a ballet company and its policies suddenly require that the company change these policies and be named for the foundation? Should the foundation's officers have the right to decide matters that are strictly artistic, including the choice of choreographers, composers and designers?" The questions were rhetorical. Whatever the foundation's complaints against Mr. Joffrey—and it, of course, has its own side of the story—the incident merely demonstrated the volatility of single-source patronage. Had Joffrey had a variety of patrons, his company would no doubt be alive today. Indeed, the existence of so many other potential sources of subsidy make it highly likely that, like the phoenix, it will rise from its own ashes before long.

The fact that subsidy in our society comes from so many different sources creates interesting possibilities. The existence of plural patronage makes it possible to adjust the "mix" of patronage funds in various ways. Let us for a moment ignore the difficulties in adjusting the mix. There are difficulties, though they are not insuperable. Let us just imagine that some magic hand could regulate the taps from which the various streams of subsidy flow. If this were the case, it would be theoretically possible to structure the flow of funds to achieve different ends. For example, assuming that certain aesthetic pressures accompany each gift (a roughly accurate assumption), it is possible, by controlling the mix, to create a situation in which the pressures from the various sources cancel one another out, leaving the artistic director responsible to no one but himself, thus creating a situation of maximum freedom from external pressure. This is not possible where subsidy flows from a single tap.

Nor is this potential entirely theoretical. For even today, even without a "magic hand," many an astute museum curator, many an artistic director in an orchestra, opera, dance company or theater, makes use of the conflicting interests of his patrons to create a position of power for himself. As mediator between them, and as the man who knows most about the day-to-day operations of the institution, he is frequently in a position to direct the interplay of pressures for his own artistic ends. When the money comes from a single source, he has little power. The more different sources there are, the weaker any individual pressure is. The greater is the potential influence of the artist.

What the United States has developed, therefore, is a system of patronage that is broadly based, flexible, and that gives the artist or the arts institution great freedom. Yet the fact that deficits are rising in the non-profit sector has led many to question the long-range workability of this system. Wouldn't it be more efficient and sensible, they ask, to bring the federal government into the patronage partnership? Shouldn't the federal government, as well as state and local government, show its concern for the future of art in America by systematically supporting the arts as so many other national governments do?

This question will be asked with increasing frequency as the deficits continue to creep upward, pushed along by the inexorable pressure of the Law of the Inefficiency of Art. We shall attempt to answer it in the chapter that follows.

13
Art and Politics

AT 2:00 P.M., OCTOBER 17, 1963, THREE AGENTS OF THE UNITED States Internal Revenue Service climbed a flight of stairs in a grimy building at Fourteenth Street and Sixth Avenue in New York City. At the top of the stairs they entered a tiny lobby. This opened into a small auditorium, at one end of which they saw a stage barricaded with barbed wire—part of a theatrical set. Like a trio of Keystone Kops walking innocently into a custard-pie ambush, they were totally unprepared for the events of the next few days—an ironic confrontation of bohemian and bureaucrat.

This shabby 150-seat playhouse occupying a second-floor loft was the home of the Living Theatre, an avant-garde drama company run by Julian Beck and his wife, Judith Malina. The Living Theatre, then seventeen years old, had won an international reputation for staging such unsettling contemporary plays as *The Connection* by Jack Gelber and *The Brig* by Kenneth W. Brown. It was a force in American theater.

Unfortunately, whatever else it was, it was also stone broke. The Living Theatre owed its landlord more than $4,000 in back rent, and it was $28,000 behind in its tax payments. Most of this represented money withheld from the paychecks of the cast, but never turned over to Uncle Sam. The Becks worked a 12- to 14-hour day and never earned more than $40.50 per week. Their actors worked for a pittance. But the cost of innovation and rebellion runs high. The Becks, committed to both and faced by continual losses, simply dipped into the tax money to keep their theater alive.

This system of deficit financing may have much to commend it; but it is frowned upon by the federal government. Over a period of many months, therefore, Internal Revenue agents reportedly met with Beck 22 times and held 55 telephone conversations, the gist of which can be easily imagined. Now the United States government had apparently reached the far end of its patience. The three agents standing at the head of the stairs had been sent to padlock the premises and confiscate whatever physical assets might be sold for tax money.

Julian Beck and Judith Malina, however, advancing to meet the invaders, had no intention of being driven out of business by so mundane a consideration as back taxes. They and their cast decided to fight back in the only way they knew. They proceeded to turn the T-men into unwilling actors in an improvised *opera buffa.*

Someone began by hanging a battle banner from the Living Theater's office window. It charged: "U.S. government stops art!" Soon a crowd of friends and supporters of the drama company, drawn by news of the approaching showdown, began to mill about on the sidewalk beneath the playhouse windows. Reporters and television crews began to arrive in swarms. Police and revenue agents cordoned off the building. The Becks thereupon announced that they had ten beds inside, and that the cast planned a sit-in. Friends on the street below passed food and supplies up to them in a wastebasket lowered from the windows. Pickets carried signs proclaiming the principle: "Art Before Taxes."

By the next morning the picket line had dwindled to three lonely stalwarts, but inside, the actors were still entrenched behind their barricades chanting "Help save Living Theatre!" Desultory warfare continued all day Friday and on into the night, the obstinate actors refusing to leave, the revenue agents, befuddled but square-jawed, determined to do their duty. Then, sometime before dawn on Saturday morning, the Becks decided to stage one more performance of *The Brig.* They passed the word by telephone to the outside world.

The tax men by now had managed to lock off the auditorium itself from the offices and other rooms, but Beck discovered two unsealed fire doors. That evening, with a cry of "To the theater!"

he led his forces through these doors into the auditorium, reporters and television cameramen scurrying along behind. The revenue agents, resorting to technological warfare, pulled a fuse and plunged the room into darkness. Against this, the Becks were helpless. But they found support in an unexpected quarter: the television crews made such a protest that the tax men restored the lights.

Outside more than a hundred partisans and playgoers had gathered. Police insisted that they keep moving. Beck yelled counter-advice to them from his window. Three actors from another off-Broadway theater company arrived with a ladder, set it against the building, and climbed through a second-story window to reinforce the beleaguered Beckites. Police captured the ladder. The crowd booed happily. Someone found that it was possible to outflank the police and enter the blockaded theater by going to a nearby building and crossing over the rooftops. A detachment of the crowd immediately did so. Others, offered a lift into the theater via the lowered-rope-and-wastebasket route, eyed the slender rope and discreetly declined.

At 9:45 the Living Theatre staged *The Brig* before an audience of about 25. The I.R.S. men, invited to watch, chose not to. During an intermission a collection was taken up for the Living Theatre. It netted a grand total of $16.50. At the end of the play the audience applauded the cast. The cast stood up to applaud the audience. The tax men asked everyone to leave.

Now, however, to the horror of the revenue agents, part of the audience decided to join the sit-in. This was the final indignity. The last rampart of bureaucratic tolerance had been breached. The T-Men issued an ultimatum: clear out or be arrested. Nothing could have delighted the crowd more. By 1:30 A.M. 23 arrests had been made. The battle was over. The Living Theatre—symbol of the conflict between cash and culture—was dead, slain by the federal government.

Art, however, is as tough as an alleycat, and has many more lives. The entire imbroglio was pleasantly reminiscent of Montmartre three-quarters of a century ago. But there was a touch of the affluent society about it, too. Before the weekend was out, a real estate operator and theater owner had offered the Becks free use of another, better theater. Within a few weeks a new company had been organized by the Becks, and *The Brig* was back on the boards again, played by the same cast under the same direction. All prisoners of war had been released by the police the day after the pinch. Only the Becks stood trial—and not for tax evasion, but for impeding federal officers in the exercise of their duty.

What the Living Theatre did, of course, by financing operations out of money that legally belonged to the federal government, was to force the federal government to subsidize art. Today, as deficits continue to rise not merely among struggling avant-garde theater groups but among large, well-established and quite conservative non-profit arts institutions, more and more Americans are beginning to think that federal subsidy may be the only solution to the economic ills of the arts.

The "federal aid to the arts" controversy, rattling around in the rear of the national consciousness for a generation or more, threatens to become distractingly noisy. Charges, prophecies, and laments rend the night. The air is filled with the smell of frankincense and myth.

Mythologists are to be found hard at work on both sides of the argument and at every cocktail party at which the issue arises. Lack of facts has never seriously hindered a controversy, of course, but here the absence of reliable and comprehensive data is chemically compounded with an absence of judgment. Thus on the one side we hear accusations that plans for federal aid to the arts would have "disastrous results" because they coincide with a Moscow plot to promote "the ugly, futuristic, and arrant in art, literature, the drama, music, the practice of crude orientalism, modernism, and degenerate perversion." On the other, we hear critic Kenneth Tynan tell a crowd of wealthy art patrons, assembled to raise money for the Manhattan School of Music, that the state should "hold the theaters, concert halls, newspapers and film studios in trust for the artists." Considering his protests on civil liberties grounds when the Senate Internal Security Subcommittee hailed him down to testify about a television program he had made, it is refreshing to see how unshaken his faith in centralized authority remains. Nobody has since stormed the barricades to deliver the means of artistic production over to the tender mercies of the state, but there are others who hold the equally innocent notion that it is the federal government's job to foster innovation in art. Author Lawrence Lipton, for example, has unburdened himself of the view that the federal government should give to "the creative talent at the growing edge of the arts as much money as it can spare from the conduct of the cold war and preparation for nuclear genocide, and give it without strings." He does not propose a litmus test by which the federal government can determine just whose talent stands "at the growing edge of the arts" and whose talent has already been mossed over.

Most Americans would hesitate to go quite as far as Mr. Tynan or Mr. Lipton toward inviting the federal government into partnership with art; at the same time, not many actually believe that proposals for federal assistance to the arts are part of a grand conspiracy to foster modernism and perversion in culture. The simple truth is that most Americans are confused and uncertain about what is right. Not so, the myth-makers. They may be confused; they are never uncertain.

Myth number one, widely held, is that the federal government does nothing for the arts. This idea is usually launched in cocktail party conversation by the dark-haired case worker wearing Scandinavian jewelry and a black jersey outfit with last year's hemline. She is just back from a charter flight to Europe, and America, she tells us in tones of cynical certainty, has never looked worse.

We may leave aside the obvious, but often overlooked, point that any government may aid the arts more by preserving peace, by ensuring economic prosperity, political freedom and general welfare than through any specific program engineered for the purpose. We may also ignore the fact that through copyright legislation the federal government helps protect creative artists such as composers, authors, dramatists and poets. But we should not overlook some of the less obvious ways in which the federal government has helped foster the arts. Peter Pollack, former director of the American Federation of Arts, referring to Congressional removal of the tariff barrier on the import of works of art, has declared "The passage of this one bill alone can be credited with having made possible the collection of priceless treasures which are now to be seen in the nation's museums."

Moreover, the federal government is itself in a limited way a purchaser of artistic goods and services. It buys paintings to hang in its buildings. It hires Edward Durell Stone to design an embassy. It employs artists and sculptors to design statues, murals, medals and postage stamps. More directly, under the cultural exchange program of the Department of State, it exports American ballet companies, orchestras, theatrical troupes, dance companies and individual creative and performing artists to the far reaches of the earth. Violinists like Ruggiero Ricci and Isaac Stern play in Iceland; Hal Holbrook impersonates Mark Twain in Zagreb; Jose Limon dances in Brazil and Uruguay. All such government programs, whatever their motives or deficiencies, provide work and a small amount of income for artists.

But the single most important economic contribution made by the federal government is through the tax system. Other governments give direct financial subsidies to the arts; our government, instead, chooses to give tax incentives to private individuals, businesses, and others who contribute funds for cultural purposes. This is patronage via the back door, and it should by no means be dismissed as insignificant.

Treasury officials, noting the various deductions available to patrons, say that on the average, for every dollar contributed to a cultural cause in the U.S., the donor receives an estimated fifty cents back in tax savings. If this estimate is correct, it means that the federal government puts up at least $5,000,000 every year for the support of our symphony orchestras; it puts up roughly $700,000 toward the deficit of the Metropolitan Opera; and so on down the line among all our non-profit theaters, museums, dance companies and the like.

The American Association of Fund-Raising Counsel, Inc., has estimated that Americans gave away a total of $10,025,000,000 to philanthropic enterprises in 1963. Of this, approximately $300 million went to what are described as civic or cultural causes. The Association attempts no finer breakdown, but if we assume that as much as two-thirds of that goes toward non-cultural activities, it still leaves roughly $100 million a year contributed specifically for cultural causes. The Treasury Department estimate would indicate that the federal contribution is, therefore, $50 million. This is hardly a massive sum. Lest it be underestimated, however, it is worth noting that it is more than eight times greater than the amount of public funds distributed by the much-publicized Arts Council of Great Britain for a population roughly one-quarter the size of ours. In fact, it may come as a shock to some Americans who favor a program of direct federal subsidies to the arts that this back-door contribution is probably more than England, Austria, West Germany and Italy combined contribute to the arts out of their national budgets.

Nor does the larger American contribution merely reflect a larger population. It is greater in per capita terms as well. The figures are admittedly rough, but a 1961 report on government subsidy to the arts in Europe prepared by Henry Lee Munson indicates that the across-the-board contributions of these four countries work out to between 21 and 22 cents per capita. The U.S. contribution—indirect though it is—works out to more than 25 cents per capita. The figures are not intended to make Americans smug. We can easily afford much more and it doesn't really matter whether we give more or less than some other country. But it is simply not true that the federal government makes no contribution to the arts. Its contribution is mainly indirect; it is hard to calculate; it is largely invisible. But the arts could not get by without it.

A second myth beclouding the controversy over federal aid is the idea that art is so mysterious and fragile a wonder that no government can possible understand or help it. This myth is normally the property of the soulful young fellow in a bleeding Madras shirt who sprawls in the wing-chair eating avocado canapes. He is, of course, not merely opposed to federal aid to the arts, but also to organization men, to foundations, to space research and all-digit dialing. His point of view was expressed more than a century ago when Courbet scorned the Cross of the Legion of Honor with the comment: "The state is not competent in artistic matters." It is echoed today by Larry Rivers, the painter, who says: "The government taking a role in art is like a gorilla threading a needle. It is at first cute, then clumsy, and most of all impossible."

Of course, it is not impossible at all. The state may be incompetent at producing art, but it need not be incompetent at creating social arrangements that foster art. Art is neither as romantically detached from society as the remarks of Courbet and Rivers presuppose, nor is government quite as bumbling or sinister. Intelligent and imaginative men can devise intelligent and imaginative government policies to help cultivate the arts. The fact that nearly every civilized nation in the world does make grants to the arts—and that artists are not anywhere in revolt against the system of state subsidy as such—would dispose of this myth once and for all if myths, like Kleenex, were disposable.

Myth number three holds that it is both inefficient and demeaning for the arts to have to run fund drives to raise money. This notion is offered by the crew-cut mathematician who is efficiently getting loaded on neat scotch as the cocktail party swirls around him. He insists on being introduced to everyone as "Dr." and, unconsciously flicking a piece of lint from the sleeve of the man standing next to him, he explains that a single monthly subsidy check from Washington could eliminate all the annual folderol of committees, volunteers, and fund raisers. It does not occur to him that, as any orchestra manager or museum fund raiser will tell you, for all its creaking inefficiency, the process of soliciting money from the general public has certain peculiar advantages. It stirs wide community interest in the arts institution and its services. It develops a cadre of people in the community who care deeply about its fate, who participate in its government, and who take pride in its quality.

Similarly, when our man grumbles that it is downright disgraceful for a ballet company or theater to have to don the tatters and eye-patch of a beggar and rattle a tin cup for money, he needs to be asked whether it is also *infra dig* for Princeton or Harvard to solicit their old grads for donations. The present method of financing in the non-profit sector of the culture industry is odd, no doubt, but, like the inefficient system called representative democracy, it has virtues worth preserving.

It is precisely here that myth number four fits in, for this one holds that federal subsidy to the arts would dry up all the sources of private patronage. This non-fact is tossed into the cocktail party conversation between mouthfuls of cottage cheese by the local Republican precinct captain, a heavy-set lady with incipient jowls, who is herself a member of the women's committee of the local orchestra. In an authoritative tone she quotes testimony before a Senate subcommittee by Douglas Richards, manager of the Phoenix, Arizona, Symphony, to the effect that "volunteer support might eventually cease entirely and the fine arts would then find themselves in the undesirable position of having to depend entirely upon federal tax dollars to replace the revenue lost from volunteer support."

This prophecy is ill-founded. Federal subsidy has not had the effect of reducing private patronage in any other field, and it is unlikely to do so in the arts, should federal subsidies ever materialize. In 1947 the U.S. government made its first subsidy grant for hospital construction under the Hill-Burton Act. Since then it has approved grants to more than 6,000 hospital construction projects. These totalled $1.4 billion and were matched by $3.6 billion in non-federal expenditures in the same projects. This can be interpreted to mean that every dollar of federal subsidy encouraged the contribution of about $2.57 in non-federal money. What the absence of this incentive has cost the arts is impossible to determine.

No organization in America stands to lose more from a decline in private philanthropy than the American Association of Fund-Raising Counsel, whose members run the major fund drives for hospitals, universities, and other non-profit institutions. If there were any evidence to support the notion that private giving declines when the federal government steps into a field, the American Association of Fund-Raising Counsel would be the first to object. Significantly, the professional fund raisers have come to quite the opposite conclusion. According to Eldredge Hiller, executive director of this trade association, "Our experience so far with federal subsidy is excellent. When Uncle Sam puts money into a field he doesn't necessarily drive out other donors. Very often he jogs loose private money that would have been otherwise unavailable. He gives the private donor an incentive to give. Hill-Burton has been a wonderful demonstration of this fact."

By now, fortunately, the cocktail party is over and the hostess, with a tired smile, is gently herding everyone toward the door. The bar has been devastated; the remaining canapes look like they belong in a morgue; the cigarette burn in the end table will never be repaired. Yet the conversation has hardly come to grips with the main issues in the federal aid controversy. It has so far only skirted the periphery.

The most sober and sensible attack on the concept of federal aid to the arts has been made by Russell Lynes, who dubs himself a friend of both art and government. While others oppose federal subsidies to the arts on the same grounds that they oppose any extension of big government, Lynes argues from another tack. "I am not worried about creeping socialism in the arts," he says, "but about creeping mediocrity. The less the arts have to do with our political processes, I believe, the healthier they will be." At best, he argues, a program of federal subsidies will create an arts bureaucracy in government which will make decisions by committee vote and contribute to a spirit of compromise and conservatism in art. At worst, such a program could lead to attempts at political control of culture. "The arts are a sitting duck for any politician who feels the need of making personal headlines," he observes. This is the intellectual spear-tip of the argument against any program of direct federal aid to the arts.

Advocates of direct federal aid argue that such fears are exaggerated. Senator Ralph W. Yarborough, for example, has testified that "federal aid will not lead to regimentation. There was not an effort that I ever heard of to interfere with paintings that were done by artists in W.P.A. days." Yet the danger cannot be so easily dismissed. In point of fact, the Senator is mistaken. Indeed, one does not need to reach back to the 1930's. As recently as 1959 the chairman of a House committee bitterly condemned many of the paintings selected by the U.S. for display at the Moscow Fair. He charged that half of the 67 painters represented were or had been at one time connected with the Communist movement.

There was plenty of controversy about the character of the painting produced under the short-lived federal arts project in the W.P.A. days, but this was nothing compared with Congressional agitation over the subsidies to the federal theater. Political pressures forced Elmer Rice's play *Judgment Day* off the boards for a time. A North Carolina Senator charged that the plays produced by the federally subsidized theater were "spewed forth from the gutters of the Kremlin." On another occasion a play was closed because it was critical of Fascist Italy at a time when we were not yet at war.

Then there was the case of Congressman J. Parnell Thomas who criticized a play for allegedly trying "to prove that all politicians are crooked." Mr. Thomas himself later went to prison for eight and a half months for padding his government payroll and taking kickbacks, but that did not help the playwright whose work he had attacked.

Congressional guardians of public virtue grew alarmed about sex as well. Everett Dirksen, the present minority leader in the Senate, termed the output of the federal theater "salacious tripe." The GOP National Committee, citing such titles as *Bill of Divorcement*, asked: "Could any more suggestive or salacious titles be found for plays to parade before the American public? Are the people of this country to be taxed to support such vulgar and villainous activities?"

Exactly what is villainous or vulgar remains, of course, a matter of dispute. Recently Congress once again proved its utter inability to refrain from comment on artistic mattters when federal funds are involved. A performance of a modern dance called *Phaedra* was staged in West Germany by the Martha Graham Company under the sponsorship of the State Department's cultural exchange program. Thereupon two members of the House, Peter H. B. Frelinghuysen and Edna Kelly, both of them intelligent and sophisticated enough to know better, publicly denounced the work for being "erotic." Angry reference was made to male dancers leaping about in loincloths. Miss Graham's comment was terse and to the point: "I feel as if I had been pawed by dirty hands."

The pressures under which a Congressman operates sometimes becloud his judgment. We can be certain that Senator Jacob Javits, who is the chief Senatorial sponsor of arts legislation, no more wants to control or dictate artistic standards in the United States through the subsidy program he endorses than he wants to get up on a stage and dance *Phaedra*. He is a staunch liberal and a civil libertarian. Yet he grew exercised many years ago when the Fellows of American Letters, a group chosen by the Library of Congress, awarded a major literary prize to Ezra Pound, who, the reader will recall, was an outright fascist and anti-Semite during World War II. It was the then-Representative Javits who first proposed a Congressional investigation of the award. He was quoted as saying: "We are not so much interested in Pound himself as we are in the minds and characters of those who could make such an award under such circumstances." Senator Javits would probably be the first to agree on sober consideration that the "minds and characters" of people are not a fit subject for Congressional inquiry, especially in the arts.

Dredging up this ancient quote, which perhaps was garbled by the press, is not intended to embarrass one of our better law-makers, but merely to give pause to those who brush aside impatiently the argument of Mr. Lynes that a program of federal subsidy to the arts might bring with it unhealthy political pressures.

Nor do opponents of federal subsidy take comfort from our happy experience with the use of public funds for support of culture at the city, county or state level. They point out that there are thousands of such jurisdictions, but only a single federal government. They consider it altogether too big and powerful to be "just another" partner in a system of plural patronage. Moreover, while it may leave decision-making to the experts in science or other fields, the experiences just recounted inspire no confidence that it would do so in the arts, where every man tends to be his own expert, Congressmen included.

Sophisticated advocates of federal aid are, of course, familiar with most of these arguments. They reply that the entire experience of the arts under government subsidy in Western Europe proves that state financial aid need not entail undue political pressure. They cite studies of state-supported opera houses and theaters on the Continent, and of the Arts Council of Great Britain, the government agency responsible for patronage in

England, as evidence that political pressure is not a major problem.

Beyond this, they argue that even though the federal government channels money into hospitals and colleges, there are no serious signs of an effort to dictate to them from Washington. A careful study published by the Brookings Institution under the title *Effects of Federal Programs on Higher Education*, points to other problems that stem from federal subsidies. It reports "the tendency of government programs to make increased administrative demands." It raises the serious danger "that the spontaneous and willing redirection of academic effort to areas of national interest will lead to the essential nationalization of our greatest universities." It urges university officials to be ever vigilant against the threat of political pressures, saying, "We are not inclined to dismiss the danger of federal control as a myth. . . ." Yet, in the end, it concludes that, "The ultimate danger, political dictation of what should be taught and who should teach it, is generally conceded to have been remarkably absent during the great postwar expansion of federal programs." Moreover, it finds, "The dominant sentiment of the academic community today unquestionably favors an expansion of federal aid to education."

Proponents of federal aid to the arts argue that federal inclusion in the patronage partnership could actually have the effect of freeing the artist or director from presently troublesome pressures. "There is no question about the fact that single patrons or groups of patrons have had a very strong influence upon the artistic policies of the institutions," John MacFadyen, former director of the New York State Council on the Arts, has testified. "I do not think you have to ask many conductors why they perform the repertoires they perform. They would say almost unanimously, 'It is because my major contributors want it that way.'" The implication is that federal subsidy grants might help buffer the artist against the present line-up of patrons.

Finally, there are those who insist that even if there is a danger of political interference by the federal government, the risk is worth taking. Artists and arts institutions are always subject to pressure and must always be vigilant and ready to battle for their integrity. In words attributed to Prof. Henry Steele Commager:

"Of course government intervention [in the arts] is dangerous; government is dangerous; life itself is dangerous."

Having answered, to their own satisfaction, the objections raised by Mr. Lynes, they shift to the offensive. The federal government, they charge, has failed to offer conscious recognition to the arts. It pumps money into science and heaps honors on mathematicians and astronauts, but it refuses even to think seriously about the place of art in American life. The time has come, John Kenneth Galbraith has said in debating Russell Lynes, for the government to recognize formally that "the artist is a first class citizen . . . and that art is . . . one of the great and respectable resources of society."

Not only does the federal government fail to recognize the arts in this light, it actually handicaps them, for the non-existence of federal subsidies to arts institutions places them at a decided disadvantage in the private philanthropic market-place, so long as other types of non-profit institutions do receive federal subsidies. For example, John MacFadyen has testified that in many communities fund raisers for the arts "are told . . . to lay off for a while because there is an opportunity to build a hospital with a matching federal grant, and therefore, one cannot give so much to the symphony orchestra or the theatre or the opera." The point is echoed by Arlan R. Coolidge, president of the Rhode Island Fine Arts Council, when he says: "We are subsidizing . . . so many things that formerly were local and private that an unfair burden is placed on those activities which must succeed or fail on the basis of private benefactions." In short, if we are going to subsidize hospitals or colleges or other enterprises by offering private donors the stimulus of matching federal funds for every dollar they contribute, it is unfair not to offer the same incentive to cultural donors.

There is, one might add, another injustice, too. It is, after all, our declared policy to hasten the spread of new technology throughout the economy. The federal government actively subsidizes research, much of which is translated into new and more highly efficient techniques of production. It offers businessmen tax credits and accelerated depreciation of capital investments. But every step toward automation and higher productivity in the economy at large pushes the arts back a step in terms of their peculiar handicraft economics. For, as the Law of the Inefficiency of Art tells us, the more the cost of production of other products declines, the more the relative cost of production of art rises. The further we advance into the age of technological efficiency, the wider the disparity grows. To the degree that the federal government encourages this process, it can be said to have a moral obligation to compensate for the side-effects on art.

But the primary argument raised by advocates of direct federal aid to the arts rests on the claim of economic need. This case has been stated—and overstated—frequently. The fact that deficits are climbing across the board in the non-profit sector of the culture industry—not merely in a few institutions, not merely in one or two of the artistic disciplines, but almost universally—is offered as evidence that the present system of plural patronage can no longer keep up with the aggregate need. John D. Rockefeller, 3rd, a cautious exponent of federal aid, has argued that only with federal patronage "will we be able to close the final gap between our present resources, comprising actual income and private philanthropy, and the costs of operating our institutions."

Others are less cool and careful. Herman Kenin, president of the American Federation of Musicians, has stated categorically that "serious music cannot survive much longer in the United States without assistance from government." Soprano Risë Stevens has gone so far as to present a schedule. Without federal subsidy, she has claimed, "opera could die as an art form in this country within ten years, while ballet and symphony could wither to a much lesser scale." Senator Javits has charged that subsidies are necessary because "the concentration of the visual and performing arts in ever-narrowing circles in the big cities where much of our nation's wealth is centered is leading to cultural starvation."

There is, unfortunately, a cry-wolf tone about such arguments. We have heard them for many years and the arts, thank goodness, seem always to outlive their pallbearers. We are further today from "cultural starvation" than ever in our past; moreover, instead of becoming concentrated in "ever-narrowing circles" the arts in America are today undergoing a quite revolutionary decentralization. Similarly, there is simply no data to substantiate Miss Stevens' tenebrous timetable.

Such arguments contradict the factual evidence, and for this reason they are unconvincing. Yet the fact that a good many first-class American artists are poorly rewarded and that many high-quality cultural institutions have a hard time attracting the patronage they need cannot be shrugged off. A problem does exist. Those who wish to solve it, however, do not help matters by distorting or over-dramatizing the truth. To ask whether the federal government "must" give subsidies to non-profit arts institutions to keep them from perishing is to frame the question negatively, to obscure the central issue with theatrics. The issue is not whether the federal government "must" give subsidies or watch its non-profit cultural institutions perish. The issue is whether the federal government "should" make such subsidies available to foster the further growth and improvement of the arts.

What makes it difficult for so many intelligent Americans to make up their minds about this is the inconvenient fact that neither the pros nor the cons have a monopoly on truth or logic. Almost everyone, regardless of the side he may have chosen on this issue, can agree that it would be nice if the Living Theatre, or the Metropolitan Opera, or the Cleveland Symphony Orchestra, or the Art Institute of Chicago, had more money. The conflict arises when one side claims the way to accomplish this is to make direct federal grants and the other insists that such grants invite bureaucracy and political interference.

The controversy therefore is not so much over principle as it is over practicalities. Thus, if practical mechanisms can be found for channeling money into the arts economy without at the same time inviting bureaucratic or political interference, then there is a way to resolve the controversy.

Such mechanisms do exist. There are things the federal government can do to help the arts without in the least endangering their freedom. For example, as this is written it appears almost certain that Congress will authorize the creation of a national advisory council on the arts to be an agency of the White House and to be chaired by the President's Special Consultant on the Arts. This body will, no doubt, consist of artists, arts administrators and representatives of various organizations and unions. It will have only the power to conduct studies and to make recommendations for federal policy on matters affecting the arts. It will have no power to make grants or distribute subsidies of any kind.

Even so, the council can, if it goes about its work intelligently, make a definite contribution to the arts. It should, of course, routinely study legislative proposals in other fields to see how, if at all, they may affect the arts. It should report to the President its views on such legislation. It should searchingly examine existing federal programs to see how they might legally be adapted or administered so as to provide maximum assistance to the arts.

Such a council should, for example, examine carefully a number of the proposals that would copyright material now in the public domain—such as the symphonies of Schubert or the plays of Shakespeare—to raise money that might be distributed to composers, dramatists, or other artists through a variety of non-government channels. It should study the possibility of broadening present federally-financed scholarship programs to make possible the award of funds for the advanced training of artists in the few fields—such as orchestral string playing—where shortages exists.

More imaginatively, the council might explore the possibility of attacking the economic problems of artists and arts institutions at the level of distribution cost—i.e., transportation. The federal government now subsidizes airlines. Would it be possible to add a sum to the existing subsidy in return for which airlines would agree to offer cut-rate prices for travel by professional artists, the definition of that term to be worked out not by the government, but by the airlines and the major arts organization in this country? Any reduction in the cost of transport would give a great boost to the process of decentralization; it would facilitate the dissemination of the highest-quality performing talent to communities that now rely chiefly on amateur institutions for live theater, dance, or music.

Whether or not this proposal could be put into practical operation, the council should give extended consideration to the principle of subsidizing others in return for the assurance that they will pass along the benefits of such subsidies to the arts. The principle offers an excellent way to keep the political snout of government out of aesthetics while at the same time channeling money into the arts economy. The council must not be afraid to use its imagination, to entertain fresh and novel ideas from whatever source. That the federal government has not done more for the arts cannot be attributed to a failure of will alone, but to a failure of imagination as well.

The creation of an advisory council in the White House is, however, a modest step forward at best. There is much more that the federal government can and ought to do for the arts without endangering their freedom. This is not the place to spell out a fully elaborated program for federal action. But a start can be made. Here, then, as a suggestive sample, are three proposals. They are listed in the order of increasing importance. Two of them involve major legislation that could release very large sums of patronage money for the arts. One of the proposals is, on its surface at least, relatively unorthodox. Yet all three are moderate enough, and safe enough, to command the support of all reasonable men who wish to see the arts expand and flourish without interference by the federal government.

First: The looseness of public discussion of this entire issue arises from the absence of comprehensive and reliable statistics about the non-profit sector of the culture industry. The federal government should create without delay a small office the sole function of which would be to compile precisely the kind of data about the arts economy that we now lack. By refining certain existing census and Internal Revenue statistics, by adding a few questions to existing forms, a mass of information could be quickly drawn together. This data would be invaluable not only to arts administrators, who at present are forced to base practical decisions on intuition rather than information, but also to Congress itself. Moreover, the task is nicely non-political. It involves no threat of control of culture, no invasion of privacy. Best of all, it is so inexpensive that it could probably be undertaken right away by one of the existing agencies without any special appropriation from Congress.

Second: Recognizing the reality of the danger of political or bureaucratic interference in the process of artistic decision-making, the principle should be established that the United States government will make absolutely *no grants* to independent arts institutions—directly or through the States—*to underwrite operating expenses or the costs of artistic production.*

Proposals for a national arts foundation that would distribute funds to foster experiment, innovation or (in the words of one bill) "productions of . . . new works and existing works . . . which have substantial artistic or historic significance" are on the wrong track. They ask the government to make decisions in a field in which it has vested political interests. As soon as federal money is used to underwrite a play, a musical program, a ballet or other artistic presentation, the Congress of the United States has not only the right, but the duty, to ascertain how that money is being spent. This idea is an open invitation for a Congressional committee, now or in the future, to make sure that the works produced are politically or morally "suitable" to be financed by public funds. It is an open invitation for a witch hunt in pursuit of artists who made the mistake of belonging to leftwing organizations in their youth, or who happen to be homosexuals, drunks, or otherwise "different" from the mass of taxpayers.

This does not mean, however, that all subsidy programs should be blindly opposed. For there is one approach to subsidy of the arts that is not only useful, but safe. This is the bricks-and-mortar route: the provision of money, not for operating expense or artistic production, but for the construction of better stages, exhibition halls, theaters and concert auditoriums. Such a program, in the words of Supreme Court Justice Arthur J. Goldberg, "poses the minimum danger of government interference with the arts themselves."

Justice Goldberg, whose comments date from the time when, as Secretary of Labor, he helped settle a dispute at the Metropolitan Opera, would go so far as to permit the government to subsidize maintenance as well as construction of new facilities. This is unwise. Allowing the federal government to maintain (or contribute to the maintenance) of arts facilities could, in the end, place them almost as deeply under federal control as Mr. Tynan's plan for letting the government hold them "in trust." But there is nothing whatever the matter with allowing the federal government to contribute to the costs of construction.

The case in favor of construction subsidies is a strong one, from many points of view. To begin with, the federal government is already in this business—and without visible harm to the arts. Attention has been called earlier in this book to the way in which urban renewal funds have helped build Lincoln Center and other arts facilities. Federal money flows into arts construction through other, less known pipelines as well. In Detroit, for example, a museum addition is being financed through the accelerated public works program of the Department of Commerce. Such subsidies, however, are almost accidental.

Congress should pass a Cultural Facilities Construction Act that would make money available through the States on a matching basis for the building of new and better stages, concert halls and exhibition galleries.*

Unfortunately, both Senator Javits and Roger L. Stevens, whom President Johnson chose as August Heckscher's successor, favor exactly the opposite approach. They argue for subsidies toward operating and production expenses and they oppose bricks-and-mortar money on the mistaken assumption that there is no need for new physical facilities. Mr. Stevens has testified in the Senate that "except in Washington and New York . . . physical plants throughout the country are not too bad at all." This was not the conclusion of Mr. Heckscher after many months of criss-crossing the country and visiting arts institutions. In his final report to President Kennedy, he wrote: "A major obstacle hindering the development of the performing arts throughout the country is the lack of proper facilities." That opinion deserves respect.

The great surge of construction of new arts facilities that we

---

* Such a program could be imaginatively designed so that if a non-profit arts institution—a museum, for example—so desired, it could receive aid in constructing rental apartments or other profit-generating structures in connection with its basic facilities. A leading problem for arts institutions today is their lack of income-producing endowment funds. They do not have a backlog of money or property that will produce income for them. A carefully-thought-out program of bricks-and-mortar subsidies could help them in this respect, too.

have witnessed in recent years is a response to generations of neglect. But it has not yet begun to fill the need. Moreover, while arts groups are busy building and renovating all over the country, the process puts an economic strain on them. Were the federal government to make modest grants available for this purpose on a matching basis, arts institutions would have more money to devote to improving the quality of the services they render. At the same time, such a program would overcome the disadvantage that arts groups now face when they compete for private patronage against institutions that do receive subsidies. A construction program would have precisely the effect that Hill-Burton had in the field of medicine: it would unloose a flow of non-federal patronage.

Beyond all this, construction subsidies are likely to face less political resistance than any other proposed subsidy program. The arts lack an effective lobby in Washington. But, if they want help from government, they are going to have to build one, and they are going to have to learn to play the game of political coalition. A movement in favor of construction subsidies could attract wide support, particularly from the construction industry and the building trades unions—two lobbies to reckon with in Washington.

In short, for the immediate future, there is a relatively simple way for the federal government to offer economic assistance to the arts in a practical, simple, and—above all—a safe manner.

Third—and final: In the long run, however, the federal government can do incomparably more—more than has been dreamed of—for the arts through imaginative manipulation of the machinery of taxation than it can in any other way.

It is essential to grasp this. A construction program, a bureau of statistical research, the creation of an advisory council, are all important. But they are simply picayune in comparison with what can and should be done by tuning the dials of the tax machine.

No program of front-door subsidies, even if limited to bricks-and-mortar, even if buffered by use of the States as intermediaries in the distribution of funds, can ever be as problem-free and pressure-free as back-door subsidy based on tax incentives to artists and patrons. The tax method allows patronage decisions to be made by millions of individuals and thousands of organizations, thus encouraging maximum cultural variety and offering maximum freedom for the artist. It entails the least amount of bureaucracy. And in terms of cold cash on the barrelhead, skillful use of the tax method can be made to yield far more money for the arts than Congress is ever likely to grant in the form of direct subsidies.

The time has come for those who are interested in the economic problems of the arts to take a fresh and radical look at the many possibilities of fiscal action. Cultural organizations, to the degree that they have shown any interest at all in taxation, have limited their attention to minor specifics. They have not approached the entire tax system with an eye to manipulating it broadly for their own self-interest. To propose this may sound coldly opportunistic. Any other approach is innocent. In the precise words of one of the nation's leading tax experts, "taxes . . . are a changing product of earnest effort to have others pay them." They have been deftly exploited by oil millionaires, Hollywood moguls, and Greek shipowners. They already play a very heavy part in financing culture. It will cost the federal government money, but taxes can and should be made to yield far more money for art than they do at present.

By working with other forces more politically potent, arts institutions and organizations could, over a period of years, greatly expand the economic assistance they now receive as a result of the tax regulations. They could assist and win wide backing for their case by making plain that the tax concessions they ask are in lieu of the direct operating subsidies that other national governments grant. They could win support for such a position from groups that would never side with them in a battle for outright subsidies of any kind. Lacking the credentials of an accountant or tax attorney, I cannot begin to detail all the possibilities of a fiscal program for the arts. It is enough, perhaps, to stimulate the imagination of those who have more expert knowledge. With that end in mind, the following proposals are outlined.

We begin by seeking ways to stimulate donations from business and foundations. Corporations do not as yet give anything like the full five per cent of pre-tax net income that they are permitted to deduct from their taxes. Their aggregate philanthropy can, however, be sharply increased. For example, present restrictions bar deductibility of sums given during years when the company shows a deficit. Some corporate donors wish to make a gift to an orchestra, museum, or other cause even in a year when they may be temporarily or insignificantly in the red. The restrictions should be lifted. In short, it should be made easier for a company to contribute.

More important, the incentive to give should be strengthened. One way to do this is to permit corporate donors to take the first 25 per cent of their gift off the top of their tax bill—i.e., as a tax credit rather than as a deduction. The difference is illustrated by what happens when the fictional Acme Corporation makes a $1,000 gift to the Center City Ballet. Under present law, if the corporation is in the 50 per cent bracket, as most large companies are, the gift of $1,000 costs it $500. In other words, the company gives $500, and the government matches it. Under the tax credit arrangement, the first $250 of the company's contribution would be subtracted from the company's tax bill. The remaining $750 would be deductible in the normal fashion. This would change the proportions so that making a $1,000 contribution would cost the company $375 and the government $625. Under such a stimulus, the corporation is encouraged to give more. Clearly, the percentages involved and the exact method used can vary widely. The essence, however, is to spur increased corporate contributions by offering a greater bounty for each dollar donated.

In the case of foundations, the government can actually stimulate giving at no cost to itself. Some foundations receive more in gifts or earn more from invested income each year than they disburse in the form of philanthropic contributions. Between 1960 and 1963 alone foundation assets mushroomed by $3 billion. Foundation giving to all causes—and inevitably to cultural causes—could be stimulated by a tax provision that foundations must disburse at least a certain percentage of each year's receipts. This might slow the rate of asset accumulation, but it would pump more money into the arts economy at a time when it is needed.

Tax regulations can make an even more fundamental contribution to the arts—indeed, a qualitative contribution—in the field of individual patronage. One of the long-term trends in patronage has been the proliferation of collective patrons. At one time all patronage emanated from individuals. Today, as the last chapter made plain, patronage funds come from corporations, foundations, local organizations, and government at the city, county and state level. The artist or arts institution that seeks money must, in every instance but one, confront a committee. Whether it is making its "pitch" to the contributions committee of a corporation, the board of a foundation, the budget bureau of a municipality, or to a state legislature, the appeal must be understood and acted upon by a committee—a collective.

There are, however, some artistic programs, some experiments, some seemingly wild enterprises, that simply cannot be sold to a committee. They need the sympathetic help of the individual patron, given as he is to whim, caprice, and daring. It is for this reason that the most important contribution the federal government can make to the arts would be to provide greater incentives to individual patrons. Encouraging the individual to give helps assure support for the unconventional, the new, the worth-trying-though-likely-to-fail. To expect federal subsidies to underwrite innovation or "way-out" artistic enterprises is naive. The same is true of city, county, or state subsidies. Dealing directly with the taxpayers' money, politicians have neither the right nor the wisdom to risk it foolishly. Corporations will measure a proposal according to their own self-interest; they cannot be expected to endanger their prestige or their product image by playing the patronage game against long odds. Even foundations, despite the brave show they make of being 'seed money' providers, worry too much about failure. Moreover, making a presentation to a foundation is often a complicated and costly job for a small arts institution, especially when the likelihood is great that, after lengthy consideration by a faceless committee, the request will be turned down. In short, if we wish to encourage the spirit of experiment and risk-taking, the attitude of playfulness that is essential to art, we must enlarge the base of individual, as against collective, patronage.

The best and most direct way to do this is to build on the tax deduction that the government already allows an individual for charitable contributions. Individuals are now permitted to claim a deduction for contributions up to 30 per cent of their adjusted gross income. Clearly, only a reasonably wealthy person can afford to contribute 30 per cent of his income to worthy causes. Raising this limit might have some small effect on wealthy donors. A far better method would be to retain the present limitation, and, as in the case of the corporation, add a 25 per cent tax credit for contributions.

At present, the donor who contributes $100 to his local museum building fund is permitted to deduct that much from his adjusted gross income. If he is in the 30 per cent bracket, it actually costs him $70; the government makes up the other $30. Under the tax credit arrangement, the individual donor could deduct $25 not from his adjusted gross income, but from his actual tax bill. He could then deduct the remaining $75 in the ordinary way. The result would be that he saves $47.50 instead of $30, and the government's share of the contribution rises, thus increasing the dollar-for-dollar incentive to give. As in the case with the proposed corporate tax credit, the percentage—even the method—is less important than the result: motivating the individual donor to part with more of his money. Such an approach could send a surge of new money into the arts without putting the government into the business of making aesthetic judgments.

Lastly, the tax approach could also be used to launch a direct attack on the chronic problem of artists' income. Most artists receive the bulk of their income from two sources: payments made to them by the non-profit institutions that employ them; and royalties on creative works such as novels, plays, or musical compositions. Once again a tax credit or similar expedient could be used. Permitting artists to subtract 25 per cent of all royalty earnings from the top of the tax bill would be of immense help to the young author whose first novel brought him a grand total of $1,800 or the composer whose parlous finances were dissected earlier in this volume. By allowing the artist a 25 per cent credit on royalty income from creative works, the government would give a direct economic stimulus to creative production. The sums involved here could not be large, but the help would be significant; and no government agency would have to go into the business of deciding which artists should or should not receive direct grants.

Since painters and sculptors do not ordinarily receive much

royalty income, but earn by selling their works outright, the same principle could simply be applied to income earned from the sale of works of art. And, for those musicians, singers, dancers or actors who are paid in wages or salaries, the principle could be extended by permitting them a special deduction (not a credit) of 25 per cent of any income earned from a non-profit institution. The second violinist who earned $4,000 last year with a mid-western orchestra would, under this arrangement, simply have to report and pay taxes on $3,000. The saving would amount to a few hundred dollars, depending upon his overall tax bracket. It would be money in his pocket just as surely as if he had won a pay raise or as if the government were suddenly to provide him with a small annual stipend.

It is obvious that all such schemes are highly complex. They have ramifications that we have not begun to consider. My object, however, has not been to present a neat and complete package, a panacea for the arts. Rather, it has been to call attention to the kinds of ingenious manipulation to which the tax laws are amenable. Perhaps this or that proposal is impractical. No matter. The principle remains. Imaginative fiscal policy is the best and simplest way to assist the arts economically without entangling the federal government in aesthetic issues in which it has no place. The slogan of the Living Theatre in its last-ditch struggle was "Art before taxes." What is proposed here is more constructive and practical: "Art through taxes."

Vast changes in the ecology of art are reflected in these pages. We have seen how art in a society of affluence moves to a more central position in society. We have trained a microscope on the culture consumer, a new breed today, forerunner perhaps of a new kind of American. We have examined his character, his interests, and his motivations—more complex and creditable than his critics understand. We have also looked at the rise of the university as a producer and distributor of art, and the rise of new organizational forms, a movement toward rationalization of the arts. Finally, in the part just concluded, we have examined the age-old interlock of artist and patron. We have seen the emergence of a uniquely American system of plural patronage. We have proposed ways for the federal government to fit into that system without snarling the arts in a tangle of political pressures.

The changes we have described are neither trifling nor transient. A great shift in the locus of art in American life has taken place. At the same time, innumerable smaller alterations are transforming the architecture of the culture industry. These changes come at a moment when the computer is entering the stream of human history, at a moment when the potential intelligence of the machine, indeed the potential creativity of the machine, makes it necessary to reexamine the meaning of art in human life.

What will the shrinkage of work mean for the human psyche, so deeply wedded to the gospel of toil? How does a man in a leisure-filled world structure his personality? Around what cluster of values? The decline of work creates a vacuum in which other values, once the property of a special elite, sprout. Aesthetic discrimination, for example, becomes more important. Art takes on new relevance.

Masses of Americans are now for the first time culture consumers. Nor does this imply a passive posture toward art. For some there is amateur involvement. For others there is a quality of alert response that is anything but passive. The potential impact of art on their lives is deeper and subtler than it may seem on the surface. What, however, is their impact on art? Does the rise of a mass base doom art to mediocrity? What is the relationship of quantity to quality in culture? What has been happening to the standards by which we judge excellence? Can cultural excellence survive in an affluent and democratic society? It is to such troublesome questions that we must turn in our final chapter.

PART FOUR

Epilog

"Now that the masses take baths every week, how can one ever distinguish the gentleman?"

Vogue magazine, 1892

14

Excellence For What?

THE CULTURE CONSUMER STANDS ACCUSED OF A HEINOUS CRIME: THE subversion of taste in America. He is charged with being a secret agent of mediocrity. We are told that he has entered our gates, overrun the guards posted by the elite, and caused the destruction of our standards of excellence.

To prove the case against him, it must first be established that a crime has occurred. The prosecution must therefore demonstrate that American taste has, in fact, been deteriorating. Witness Number One is our old friend Mr. Harold C. Schonberg of *The New York Times,* who, in between exposing the culture explosion as "phony" and hailing the new "renaissance," testifies flatly that: "The American public has become coarser in its taste."

Before this testimony can be compared with other statements by the same witness, the prosecution hustles him off the stand and reminds us of the similar conclusion drawn by Randall Jarrell, by Marya Mannes, by such critics of the mass media as Hannah Arendt and Ernest van den Haag. He calls up again that resounding phrase heard earlier in Congressional testimony: "Cultural starvation!"

This is not all. A certain Mr. Albert Bush-Brown, author and president of the Rhode Island School of Design, is sworn in to testify that "the proliferation of musicals, melodramas, miserable art classes, community cultural centers, and supermarket galleries is reducing our standards for performance." Daniel Catton Rich, an art expert and museum director, reminds us that museums were once criticized for being the "attics of civilization" but, he charges, "at the pace we are going . . . they may soon become the cocktail lounges or drive-ins of our day . . . today we are often expending nine-tenths of our energies to see how much and how fast we can make the public fall in love with us."

The prosecution now explains the so-called Law of Raspberry Jam—that the wider culture is spread, the thinner it must become. In support of this "law" he cites eminent authority. He asks the rhetorical question posed by the historian Rostovtzeff: "Is it possible to extend a higher civilization to the lower classes without debasing its standard and diluting its quality to the vanishing point?" He answers with de Tocqueville's assertion: "In aristocracies, a few great pictures are produced: in democratic countries, a vast number of insignificant ones."

We are now ready for the chief witness, Dwight Macdonald, author of *Masscult & Midcult*, the essay that has become the manifesto of contemporary culture elitists. Mr. Macdonald, a bespectacled man with a gray goatee and a look of amused intolerance, is, perhaps, less fierce than he tries to sound, but his contempt for the culture consumer is boundless.

Macdonald begins by lamenting that the rise of democracy since 1750 has wiped out the elite audience for culture, with the result that by today the audience in the United States "has changed from a small body of connoisseurs into a large body of ignoramuses."

Ignoramuses, of course, have a hard time distinguishing good from bad even when the two are polarized and clearly labeled. What makes matters worse, Macdonald contends, is that today cultural goods are no longer polarized. At one end of the spectrum is High Culture. At the other end is Mass Culture, or, as he dubs it, "Masscult"—the lowbrow junk churned out by the mass media. But instead of clean open space between the two, there now exists "a whole middle culture" exemplified by works like Hemingway's *The Old Man and The Sea* or Archibald MacLeish's *J.B.*, as well as by magazines like *Horizon, Harper's,* the *Atlantic,* and the *Saturday Review*. This middle culture—inevitably abbreviated and elided by Macdonald into "Midcult"—is far more dangerous to High Culture than the out-and-out vulgarity of the Beatles or the Beverly Hillbillies because "it pretends to respect the standards of High Culture while in fact it waters them down and vulgarizes them." And the culture consumer of today, being an unregenerate rube, allows himself to be conned, thus contributing, according to Macdonald, to the progressive debasement of our standards of excellence.

"A tepid ooze of Midcult is spreading everywhere," Macdonald warns, his voice rising. "Institutions like the Museum of Modern Art . . . once avant garde and tiny, are now flourishing and respectable," he tells us. A sure sign of decay.

Only radical surgery can now save the arts. This, Macdonald says, is the total excision of Midcult. Culture must be polarized once more. "The problem of vulgarization has become acute," he declares. "I see only two logical solutions: (a) an attempt to integrate the masses into high culture; or (b) a contrary attempt to define two cultures, one for the masses and the other for the classes. I am for the latter." In short, something analogous to the pre-1750 status quo must be restored.

The case against the culture consumer is thus completed. Rube and ignoramus that he is, the arts must be saved from his embrace.

One could dismiss the proposal for a return to elitism as obvious nonsense, if the Masscult-Midcult thesis had not become chi-chi in certain intellectual circles in the United States, especially among liberals in the culture establishment. The premise that only an elite can maintain standards of excellence in the arts is, of course, a trite one. It gained wide currency in the early part of the nineteenth century when the decline of the landed aristocracy and the emergent evils of industrialism cast a golden glow over the past. We hear critics of that era inveighing, in words that Macdonald himself might use, against the "lowering of standard that must necessarily arise from the extending of the circle of judges; from letting the mob in to vote." What is new, therefore, is not the basic premise of the theory, but the fancy catchphrases in which it is swaddled and the peculiar stridency with which the neo-elitists present their arguments.

A generation ago one might have found within the culture establishment a solid block of liberal and radical intellectuals who viewed with regret, rather than satisfaction, the fact that most Americans were indifferent to the arts. These intellectuals did not for a moment doubt their own qualifications for membership in an elite, but they were benevolent elitists, as it were, who genuinely wished their own passion for painting, music, theater and the other arts might be shared by the broad public. This was, after all, the democratic ideal, from Whitman on. Culture, they would have agreed, shouldn't be the monopoly of the few.

One would have expected then that this wing of the critical establishment would have welcomed the extraordinary rise of public interest in the arts. Instead, most of its members have allied themselves wholeheartedly with the elitist position. We are thus treated to the curious spectacle of formerly radical intellectuals marching in lockstep with conservative trustees of the most tradition-encrusted museums and orchestras to defend the arts from the new culture public.

This *volte face* has been explained in various ways. Sociologist Daniel Bell has observed that the rise of the welfare state, the amelioration of the worst economic problems of capitalism, and the disenchantment with Communism left the radical critic with nowhere to go. "Having defined a role for himself as critic," Bell writes, "the radical intellectual . . . turned his attention to the quality of American life." There followed the spectacular rise of television, and the cranking out of sociological and literary treatises about the mass media became a major academic industry. This is not to suggest, of course, that all the mass media critics are disillusioned ex-radicals or liberals, or that television and the mass media are above criticism. It helps, however, to explain the strident polemic quality of much of the criticism.

There is perhaps another reason, too, why so many older intellectuals and art lovers, regardless of political persuasion, have suddenly warmed to the elitist line. This, I believe, is their sense of violated exclusivity. I noted at the beginning of this book my own memories of a time when the Museum of Modern Art was quietly my own, when the galleries were uncrowded and I could feel an affinity with those few other visitors wandering its silent corridors. Our common presence set us not only apart from other Americans, as I suggested earlier, but also—so we liked to think—above them. At one time a relative handful of Americans had the theaters, concert halls, and museums of the nation pretty much to themselves. Today they have difficulty fighting their way through the crowd and they can no longer claim a spurious superiority simply because they can show the stub of a ticket. Once only they could discuss music or poetry in knowing terms. Today one's neighbor may well be playing *Death and the Maiden* on his high-fidelity set and discussing it in a sophisticated way.

Obviously, for those who were raised under the *ancien régime* this is unsettling. It undermines their sense of superiority. Their exclusivity has been rudely violated. And so Mr. Macdonald laments that the Museum of Modern Art has grown from a tiny avant-garde institution into flourishing respectability, adding that "something seems to have been mislaid in the process." Something has been mislaid. But it may have more to do with self-esteem than with art.

Finally, the elitist line appeals to all those who sentimentalize the past and secretly hate the present. When a poet despairs of the so-called "appalling taste of the age," we have a right to ask whether there is not, concealed within his charge, an abhorrence of our age that has little to do with aesthetics. Such people need to be reminded of all the aesthetic atrocities committed in the past, even during so-called golden ages and even by the most cultivated of aristocratic elites. Closer to home, when they fulminate, for example, against the alleged decline of American musical taste, they need to be reminded that half a century ago the Schola Cantorum, conducted by Walter Damrosch, closed a Carnegie Hall concert with a ballad by Percy Grainger, for which the orchestra was augmented by a volunteer band of forty mandolins, guitars, and banjos. All hail to the past!

This is not to argue that the present is the best of all possible worlds, or that the present level of cultural attainment in the United States is all anyone might desire. There are striking defects. There are sickening concerts and bumbling plays aplenty. Many of the paintings hanging in shopping centers or theater lobbies deserve to be hacked to shreds. Our landscape is cluttered with Taj Mahal pizza stands, as someone once remarked, and despite the intermittent enthusiasm of certain crtics and experts, we are not living in the middle of a renaissance. Yet the picture is not nearly as bleak as the elitists paint it, and there is ample evidence that matters are improving rather than getting worse.

Let us take the matter of performance standards. If the so-called Law of Raspberry Jam were operating, the growth of the culture public should cause a decline in the levels of technical accomplishment in the arts. As the audience expands beyond the circle of "cognoscenti" it should become less discriminating, less demanding of the artist. This lowering of standards, this general slackening, should be followed by a corresponding decline in the technical excellence of performance. Musicians, for example, should be playing more sloppily today than they were before the great expansion in the culture public.

If we attempt to check this theory against reality we find that the exact reverse is true. Exquisitely polished performances are commonplace today among the millions of LP records sold each year. These recorded performances, with flaws edited out and special qualities intensified electronically, are technically more perfect than anything one could hear at a concert twenty years ago, perhaps better than one can hear "live" today. Millions of Americans are now listening to these technically flawless performances, either on their own high-fidelity sets or over the radio, and, unless our elitist friends wish to argue that exposure to excellence debases taste, we must conclude that the ready availability of these recordings is creating better, more skilled and discriminating listeners. Moreover, when a culture consumer has heard first-rate performances on records, the chances are he will demand more, not less, of the musicians he hears "live" in the concert hall. Second-rate playing is far less likely to pass unnoticed today than it did in years gone by.

This finding is confirmed by talking with professional musicians, many of whom have commented publicly on the heightened sophistication of the culture consumer today. Moreover, they will tell you that the technical levels of production, as well as consumption, have been elevated. That is, not only is the listening more skilled and demanding, but the playing is better. They report that even the young musicians streaming from the conservatories are equipped with truly remarkable technical polish.

Foreign musicians visiting here have expressed surprised admiration, too.

The same, in perhaps a lesser degree, is also true of the other arts. Television may choke the airwaves with banality and there are plenty of meretricious movies. But even in bad television plays the level of acting, singing, or dancing is often undeniably excellent. I would not press the point as far here as in the case of classical music, but audiences today will stand for a lot less ham than twenty years ago. Television and the movies make it possible for most people today to see and hear, at least occasionally, some of the world's most technically expert actors, dancers, and singers. The high-quality performances conveyed electronically today help determine the criteria that viewers take with them to their seats in a legitimate theater or concert hall. In this sense, it can be argued that the culture consumer, at least with respect to performance standards, is much harder to please than his grandparents were.

Technical standards, of course, are not everything. Another factor to consider in estimating the quality of artistic life is the degree of receptivity of the audience to diversity and complexity. Here, too, there is evidence of definite improvement. Kurt Adler, for example, the general director of the San Francisco Opera, has noted that "There has been a tremendous change in public taste in the last ten years. The contrast is evident in the growing appeal of modern works and novelties." This finding is confirmed again and again by artists. Phyllis Curtin, the soprano, reports with a touch of wonderment: "In an unsophisticated town nowadays I find I'm able to do Alban Berg, Fauré, Pergolesi—exciting programs." Peter Ustinov, the actor, has commented on the unexpectedly high level of sophistication he found while touring the Midwest some years ago. Artur Rubinstein has been quoted as saying that "Small towns throughout America are more receptive to fine music than old cities in France." Again and again, critics who manage to leave their desks in New York for a tour of what used to be called the hinterland come back to report in tones of shocked surprise that the audience is no longer composed of hayseeds.

When art critic Emily Genauer returned from a trip to Iowa

a few years ago she was moved to write: "There couldn't be any doubts, from the questions the students threw at me, that not only were they familiar with the last word in modern art, but that they had no predisposition to accept anything simply because it *was* the last word." Brooks Atkinson, reporting on the first few months of operation of the Tyrone Guthrie Theatre in Minneapolis, wrote: "The greatest success this year has been the audience. It has been not only consistently large but attentive and responsive."

Far from being passive or bovine, our culture consumers are quite often alert, active, and possessed of definite opinions. Pickets march outside the theaters where *The Deputy* is playing. Booing breaks out when Bernstein plays John Cage's offbeat work *Atlas Eclipticalis*. Among aficionados of the art film a fierce debate is raging over the merits of the so-called New American Cinema Group. Culture consumers argue vehemently over James Baldwin's *Blues for Mister Charlie*, and when the Lincoln Center Repertory Theatre choses its program badly, the audience makes its displeasure painfully known. The responsiveness of the audience is discernible to anyone who spends time in the concert halls, theaters, or museums. Oliver Daniel, writing in the *Saturday Review*, comments: "A growing and enthusiastic audience is making possible some exceedingly lively events. The reaction to what is being heard is often as noisy and controversial as much of the music itself."

The vivacity and sophistication of the new culture public is reflected in a general improvement in the diversity and quality of cultural programming. In theaters one now finds examples of Ionesco being performed in North Carolina and Anouilh in Ohio. A report on the musical scene in New York observes: "The concert repertory is being enriched with music of chronological periods and combinations of instruments that were not formerly heard on standard programs." This same richness is carried all over the country by the recitalists who, to their delight, are finding it increasingly possible to do better, more profound and less standardized programming. In the visual arts, too, there is a general movement toward diversity and richness. In the words of Alfred Barr, director of collections of the Museum of Modern Art, the rise of the culture consumer is not "compromising art of integrity and conviction. A wide range of art is being produced simultaneously, from the exactly representational to the highly abstract. And I find work of quality in all areas." This observation is echoed by the art critic who after a swing through the galleries felt moved to point out that "Variety is not only the spice of art, but also, in a civilization so many-sided that it demands a multitude of expressions, the surest sign of good health." And one of the nation's leading dance critics, Allen Hughes, reports: "If New York is currently the dance capital of the world, as it seems to be, it is because . . . we are producing more dance works of vitality and, perhaps, durability than anyone else." This assertion drew criticism on the grounds that it was chauvinistic, but no one denies that the American dance scene is full of exciting ferment today.

A similar ferment is present, though frequently overlooked or denied, in the theater. The hoary charge that American plays are not being written or that young dramatists are ignored has less and less sting to it. A recent issue of the *New Yorker,* for example, listed 28 plays or musicals under its "Off Broadway" heading. The play-goer that week could choose from among works by Shaw, Pirandello, Euripides, Calderón, Molière, Genet, Gide or Gorky. But he also had his choice of seventeen works by Americans, at least seven of which were by young or little-known dramatists, including LeRoi Jones, Edward Albee, and Lewis John Carlino. Uptown on Broadway James Baldwin's play was being performed and Lincoln Center audiences were watching *After The Fall* by Arthur Miller.

If the Law of Raspberry Jam were true, if "a tepid ooze of Midcult is spreading everywhere," the decline of American standards of excellence should be visible to foreigners. Historically, of course, Europeans have looked down their noses at American culture—and with justification. This contempt should be more marked now than ever before, if the elitist theory had any basis in reality. Yet, it turns out, the exact opposite is true. Europeans are being forced to revise their traditional attitude toward the arts in America.

The most dramatic proof of this has been the emergence of New York as the unrivaled world capital of painting and sculpture. Foreign buyers now trek to American galleries much as Americans used to go to Paris and London. American painters, sculptors, and architects during the 1950's began to walk off with armloads of top prizes at the Venice Biennale and at other great international competitions. By the mid-1950's the English critic Lawrence Alloway announced that "New York is to mid-century what Paris was to the early 20th century: it is the center of Western art." In London by 1960 the conservative Tate Gallery had announced plans to open a special room devoted to a newly formed permanent collection of American work. Even more startling was the rapidity with which abstract expressionism, for better or worse an American development, swept the studios of the world. So complete was its triumph that when H. Harvard Arnason, now a vice president of the Guggenheim Museum, traveled through Korea in 1959 he found artists in wattle huts discussing the latest developments on the New York scene. Arnason told of his astonishment when, after giving a lecture, one of his listeners stood up and delivered a long discourse in Korean, punctuated by the names of Jackson Pollock, Robert Motherwell, and other American painters. More recently Pop Art has begun to win foreign imitators.

In music, foreign applause for American performers since the end of the war has been lavish. When Leontyne Price sang in Italy, it was said that "at last we have heard the true Aïda." The triumph of Van Cliburn in Moscow is too well publicized to need description. Grace Bumbry and dozens of less-well-known singers and instrumentalists have also been cheered by Europe's leading critics. In contrast, praise for American composers has been grudging, but even here a change is noticeable. American avant-garde compositions are receiving more and more performances abroad, and recently the famed Internationale Ferienkurse für Neue Musik at Darmstadt acknowledged the importance of the work being done here by appointing Milton Babbitt, one of our leading innovative composers, to its faculty. A similar story could be told about the theater. Plays by Americans are being produced all over the world—not only the works of O'Neill, Miller, and Williams, but also those of a whole new crop of talented young dramatists like Albee and Gelber.

Perhaps the ultimate tribute paid by other nations to the upsurge of the arts in the United States since the end of the war is the persistent migration of their artists to our shores. They come now not as refugees, but as students and participants. Recent years have seen a continuing flow of artists from other countries who come to settle or to spend prolonged periods studying artistic developments here. In music, avant-garde composers like Mario Davidovsky, an Argentine, Bulent Arel, a Turk, Halim El-Dabh, an Egyptian, and Luciano Berio, an Italian, have come to visit or work at Columbia and Princeton where American composers are conducting exciting experiments with electronic composition. Gunter Grass, the German novelist, author of *The Tin Drum,* has announced his desire to spend a period in the United States because, as he put it enthusiastically, "Here you have everything." The number of foreign painters and sculptors who visit here is enormous. Many, having once made contact with the vital ferment here, decide to stay or to spend a substantial part of their working time here. Oyvind Fahlstrom of Sweden, Richard Smith and Peter Stroud from England, the French painters D'Allegret and Arman, the Italian painter-playwright Giordano Falzoni, Tinguely, the Swiss experimenter, and Mellehi from the United Arab Republic are only a few. Instead of homing instinctively for Paris or Rome, they are drawn to New York.

In a speech not long ago August Heckscher said: "We live in the midst of a brilliant society, alive with creative impulses, rich in individual geniuses. Whatever one may think of this or that particular play or book, or exhibition, the total effect is dazzling." He reminded his audience that a century ago supercilious and carping Englishmen used to taunt us by asking: "Who reads an American book? "Today," Heckscher replied, "nobody could ask that question. '*Who* reads an American book? Who waits to see a new building by one of America's top architects? Who watches for trends in American painting or music?' The answer is, the whole world. . . ." Mr. Heckscher is not given to exaggeration.

One of the precious ironies of the present situation has to do with the place of the avant-garde in American cultural life. That foreign artists are increasingly attracted to the United States, is an historic reversal. Thirty or forty years ago the movement was all in the other direction. Europe was the True North. It was there that the really provocative innovation was being done. At the same time, the American public was so cruelly indifferent to art, and so hostile to aesthetic experiment, that many of our freshest, most daring talents sought refuge in Paris or Rome. The Hemingways and Fitzgeralds, the hundreds of expatriate poets and painters, created a special tradition of their own in rebellion against the suffocating cultural climate in the United States. Those who could not afford the price of a transatlantic ticket clustered in the artistic ghetto in Greenwich Village.

The critical establishment, sympathetic to the artist and eager to display its own superior cultivation, bludgeoned the American public mercilessly for its insensitivity. Americans were berated for being bigoted, reactionary, and blind, for not recognizing native talent and for condemning the avant-garde to exile.

Since then a remarkable change has crept over us. Culture consumers in the United States, perhaps more than anywhere else on earth, have become curious and open-minded about innovation in the arts. New developments in the theater or in painting are quickly seized upon. The mass media popularize them. Crowds fill the galleries and theaters, eager to know what the experimenters are up to.

This has brought about a change in the pattern of artistic exile. There are still expatriates. James Jones, Mary McCarthy, and William Saroyan find Paris more comfortable than the United States. American painters and sculptors like David Porter and Lee Bontecou still find it useful to spend a period in Rome. But going abroad today is less a matter of exile than a grasping of opportunity offered under the Fulbright scholarship program. It is less and less a flight from an uncongenial environment. It is more and more the enactment of a ritual "bit." And the hard fact is that the exciting work being done by Americans today, in all the arts, is done at home, not abroad.

Any reasonable observer, remembering the cultural history of our recent past, might be expected to regard all this as an expression of healthy change. We now appear to be secure enough or sophisticated enough to tolerate, even encourage, creative experiment. Yet the congenital carpers in the critical establishment today are quite as unhappy as before. Yesterday they lambasted the culture consumer's resistance to the avant-garde; today they damn his receptivity to it. Thus novelist Harvey Swados laments in *Contact* magazine that the new mood of acceptance means that "the avant garde is on its way out." For Mr. Macdonald the funeral is already over. He grumbles, "'The old avant garde has passed and left no successors." And Leslie Fiedler complains that "Anti-fashion becomes fashion among us at a rate that bewilders critics and writers alike." He frets that "Nobody will find so many staunch friends and supporters as the man who labels himself an outcast or an enemy of society." He knows whereof he speaks; Mr. Fiedler's own successful career as a critic has been based entirely on his pose as a literary outlaw.

What is wrong about all these criticisms is the definition of avant-garde that underlies them. The implied definition is fuzzily romantic. It confuses two things that have no inherent relationship with one another: innovation and public response. The function of an avant-garde is to advance the technical frontiers of art, to broaden or narrow the scope of its content, to hone its cutting edge. This is innovation; it is brought about through painstaking experiment, trial and error. This process of development has gone on since the first cave painter drew his first bison. Without an avant-garde willing to conduct experiment, the process of artistic development would come to a halt.

This, however, has no necessary connection with the romantic mode of behavior popularized 120 years ago by Murger as *la vie de bohême*. It has no essential relationship with sensationalism, irresponsibility, or offensiveness. Yet it is precisely these elements that critics like Mr. Fiedler lump into their definitions of avant-garde. They conceive it to be the function of the avant-garde to shock and offend. "Truly experimental art aims at *insult*," writes Mr. Fiedler. This is a debatable point. Truly experimental art poses new problems or seeks new means of expression. If it offends, it does so incidentally. The offense is a by-product, a side-effect. Setting out in advance to "offend" is as artificial as setting out self-consciously to have a good time—and as futile. What really offends or insults Mr. Fiedler, who is a more reasonable fellow than his bully-boy writing suggests, is that the avant-garde can no

longer *"epater le bourgeois"* for the simple reason that the bourgeois is no longer easily shocked or offended.

What does not occur to those who secretly hanker for the good
old days when bohemians could behave like bohemians and have
the fun of agitating the rubes, is that the change we have undergone is a tribute to the increased sophistication, education, and
sensibility of the culture consumer. The artist finds it more difficult to generate a cheap thrill by giving the reader a glimpse of
female nipple or by depicting a homosexual or a dope addict on
stage. The ability of the consumer to discriminate more
finely makes all the gross tricks of the past seem cheap and easy.
This does not mean that advanced work is impossible. It does
mean the consumer is ready for a real advance. It means that the
entire level of subtlety, complexity, and profundity in art must
be raised. Thus, far from causing a decline in standards of excellence, the culture consumer is, if anything, presenting a direct
and healthy challenge to the artist to elevate them.

The keening we hear about the death of the avant-garde needs
to be received with a dry and skeptical eye. The avant-garde of
Murger's era may have had to carry its protests into the streets.
The contemporary culture consumer, in the United States at least,
makes this unnecessary. It may be that fewer artists are trying to
"epater le bourgeois" today than a generation ago. This does not
mean that an active and energetic avant-garde is not busily at
work pressing outward against the frontiers of art. This avant-
garde spends less time railing against society and more time at the
easel, the practice bar, or the sound synthesizer. It is quite as
likely to be found at any one of a hundred university campuses
as it is in Greenwich Village. The "garde" is less noisy, perhaps,
than it was, but it is no less alive and avant, and foreigners appear to be aware of this even if many of our own critics, frozen
into the clichéd postures of the past, are not.

A final irony remains to be dealt with. Thus, when the culture
consumer is not cudgeled for his alleged passivity, he is attacked
for his activity as an amateur. The charge is that he is an amateur
dabbler, that he grinds out shabby pictures, or blows false notes
on his English horn, or does a hopelessly crude job of playing

Willy Loman with the local community theater. Painters are annoyed that amateur works are exhibited and sometimes even purchased. Professional musicians think the increase in amateur playing has taken jobs away from them. Others are disturbed because they believe that the increase in amateur production contributes to that critical blur that Macdonald decries. Amateurism, they charge, pulls down public standards of excellence.

The allegation that the rise of amateur activity in music, painting, the dance or the other arts will tear down our standards of excellence is repeated in many forms. It is so widely accepted in certain quarters that it is treated as *prima facie* evidence of cultural decline. In Mr. Schonberg's article attacking the supposed phoniness of the culture explosion a great point is made that of our 1,250 orchestras the majority are amateur. Again and again the figures on cultural growth are brushed aside as insignificant on grounds that so much of that growth is at the amateur level.

These criticisms miss the point. They totally misunderstand the relationship between amateurism and professionalism. This relationship is not inherently antithetical; it is mutually reinforcing. Guided sensibly, there is no reason why our burgeoning amateur movement cannot lend positive support to professionalism in this country.

First, it must be noted that while much of the amateur work is just that and nothing more, some of it is of near-professional quality. Many of our so-called amateur orchestras play as well as some of the so-called professional orchestras abroad. The truth is that skilled amateurs can sometimes equal, even on occasion outshine, professionals. The occasional high quality of amateur performance around the country pleasantly surprises even exacting critics. Allen Hughes, in *The New York Times*, after a visit to an amateur ballet company in Dayton, Ohio, asks: "Would you have guessed that there are four girls in Dayton and probably more that can dance Anton Dolin's *Pas de Quatre* quite commendably?" Similar expressions have come from critics in the other disciplines. Each time it is treated as a revelation.

Second, the amateur movement provides an excellent grassroots training ground for artistic talent. Mr. Hughes continues his report on Dayton: "Can you scoff at a ballet company that on a single random weekend had a dance-film viewing (Martha Graham and Maurice Bejart . . .), a lecture demonstration on stage make-up . . . and a master class in ballet taught by [Tatiana] Grantzeva . . . ?

"Is a Pavlova, a Nijinsky or a Fokine about to emerge in Dayton? Probably not. They seldom emerge anywhere. But if a native talent of that quality should appear there, it could find much, if not all of the training it would need to make it flourish . . . and if this fact is true about Dayton, it is obviously true of other regions throughout the country." The same is roughly true in the other arts as well.

Third, the existence of a broad amateur movement in the arts reinforces professionalism by building the culture public, not only quantitatively but also qualitatively. The ballet again provides an excellent example. According to a survey conducted by Doris Hering of *Dance* magazine, many amateur dance companies go out of their way to create larger and more informed audiences for professional performances. At the simplest level, they serve to keep interest high in the ballet, publicizing the arrival of touring professionals, urging women's clubs, music groups, and others to buy tickets for the professional events. Many amateur organizations go far beyond this, however. Before a professional company arrives in their community, the amateurs discuss the repertoire. Some amateur groups maintain dance libraries so that their members may study the peculiar history and traditions of the visiting professionals. Miss Hering writes: "Several, like the Detroit City Ballet, the Cornish Ballet in Seattle, and the Ballet Royal Concert Group of Orlando, conduct post-performance discussions; even requesting their dancers to prepare written reports on what they have seen." Finally, there are amateur companies that go on to perform the works just presented by the professionals. "In other words," *Dance* magazine concludes: "the regional [amateur] ballet companies and the community groups surrounding them are a special breed of self-starting advance agent—an advance agent who works diligently and without pay. That's a far cry from the competitors they are thought to be." It is a far cry, too, from the debasers they are charged with being.

Not all amateur groups set out quite as consciously as these to build appreciation for professional-caliber work. Nevertheless, many do, and even where, as in painting, amateurism is less organized, it is reasonable to suppose that the very act of amateur creation heightens aesthetic sensitivity. The man who has tried to compose a picture on a canvas, however poor his ability, comes away with at least a slightly improved understanding of what the professional artist is about. The rise of amateurism can play a positive and invigorating role in the arts as it has in many other fields. Those near-sighted defenders of excellence who condemn amateurism out of hand need to be asked whether American professional basketball is poorer because there is a hoop in every schoolyard. Or, lest this homely example shock their easily-injured sensibilities, the question can be phrased another way: Has widespread amateur participation in chess in Russia appreciably lowered the professional ability of its Grand Masters? The answer is obvious. Russian chess mastery over a period of many years is precisely a product of grassroots appreciation, amateur participation, and a whole elaborate system of organizations and competitions at every level of skill from the most primitive to the world's finest.

The attack on amateurism, like the direct attack on the culture consumer, is based less on fact than on fear. Cultivated art lovers of long standing, treasuring their seniority like old-time members of the plumbers' union, fear the arrival of the newcomer. They are told that they are an elite and that the elite is now threatened. They lash out, always careful to announce as their purpose not the retention of status or privilege, but the defense of excellence. But what exactly is meant by the term "elite"?

Two definitions are relevant. In one sense, the word denotes a wealthy and powerful aristocracy, bound together by kinship ties and leisured enough to have developed superior sensibility. This, one may presume, is what is meant when the elitists refer to pre-1750 European history. If this is the meaning of the word elite, then no one can sensibly argue that art or excellence is dependent upon it. This kind of elite passed away in most European countries by the middle of the last century, leaving behind only vestigial traces of its pomp and power. Yet the death of this elite as an important cultural force did not kill art. Far from it. The years since the decline of this elite have seen the production of vast quantities of durable art in Europe. The romantic rebellion, the rise of impressionism in painting and music, naturalism in the novel and play, the whole concatenation of movements and schools of modern art—all these developed without benefit of the elite, if by that we still mean something approximating a feudal aristocracy. Clearly, art is not dependent upon any elite in this sense of the word, and few elitists would go so far as to suggest the contrary, although in their writing they consistently senti- mentalize the pre-democratic past.

The other, more meaningful sense in which the word elite is used in connection with art has nothing directly to do with so- cial class or economic or political power. It refers to qualities such as intellect. Thus we find that Macdonald, while he spends much time arguing the merits of the old-fashioned pre-1750 elite, slips in a footnote suggesting that what he really means now when he says the "classes" should monopolize High Culture is that an "intellectual elite" should do so. Here, of course, the term is based on a natural, rather than a sociological, differentiation.

No two human organisms are similarly gifted in sensory ca- pacity, in intelligence, in the ability to abstract, in the talent for fantasy. Some individuals are marvelously equipped, by nature and training, to appreciate the exquisite pleasures of painting. Others are more responsive to music, dance, or drama. Often the individual with a passion for one of the arts is ill-equipped to appreciate the others. Everyone has met, at one time or another, the passionate music lover whose home is filled with the sound of chamber music, who attends concerts regularly, who plays an instrument himself, but whose visual taste, as expressed in the pictures he hangs on the wall, is simply ludicrous. We have run into the drama lover who can critically enjoy the latest plays and the Greek classics, but who is totally illiterate about music.

Such variations reflect differences in training and physiology, and they mean that there has never been a "cultural elite" in the sense of a single all-purpose elite with super-powers of appreciation, but rather a series of largely unrelated elites, each operating in another artistic discipline. If this is what is meant by elite, then the fear that the culture explosion will wash it (or them) away is groundless. Such distinctions among culture consumers will continue to exist so long as human differences endure. There will always be superior appreciators.

The issue posed by the elitists, therefore, after all else is rinsed away, is whether art should address itself solely to the elite in each discipline, whether it should ignore everyone else, whether, in short, there should be a re-polarization into High Culture for the elites and Crap for the rest of humanity.

Such a proposal overlooks the immorality of condemning the mass of mankind to eternal inferiority by destroying precisely that "middle culture" that makes it possible for the individual to gain skill and taste as he ascends toward connoisseurship. It asserts that the culture consumer is uneducable, unredeemable—a slur that reality refutes. Moreover, such a proposal, for all its seeming solicitude for art, overlooks the real danger to art today, the danger of meaninglessness. In the words of Norman Podhoretz, the proposal "condemns high culture to an eternal isolation, and loneliness that would finally end in sterility, desiccation and mandarinism."

Were such a proposal put forward in the name of snobbery it would receive short shrift. Instead, it is put forward in the name of "excellence." The word has achieved the status of a shibboleth. Like motherhood and flag, it is unassailable. It is the safest of all slogans to hide behind. And yet, excellence by itself has no meaning. We may speak of the excellence of organization of the Auschwitz extermination camp or the excellent efficiency of the H-bomb as a weapon of genocide. The question always remains "excellence for what?"

Is the purpose of art to serve a circle of connoisseurs alone— Mr. Macdonald's "cognoscenti"? Is its sole object to intensify the understanding or delight of a handful? If this is all, then it is difficult to justify the expenditure of social resources on its behalf. The creation of art, music, drama, dance or literature involves not merely financial expense, but a whole series of complex social arrangements to make it possible. Why should a society maintain these arrangements, why should it spend a penny to support the artist or disseminate his goods, if the benefits of art must be restricted to a few? And if it be argued that its benefit "trickles down" through these few to the rest of society, there is ample historical ground to contest the assertion. The French masses who made the revolution that overthrew the old order received very little of the culture that flourished alongside their physical and spiritual agony. Against the idea that art must be fenced off from the mass of humanity is the not unreasonable counter-concept that it should be an organic part of society, radiating into the lives of millions. Thomas Mann, through the words of Leverkuhn in *Doctor Faustus*, argued that art would be "completely alone, alone unto death, unless it finds a way to 'the people,' or, to put it less romantically, to human beings." If and when that happened, Mann, through Leverkuhn, declared, art would "once more see itself as the servant of a community, a community welded together by far more than education, a community that would not *have* a culture, but which perhaps would *be* one." This is certainly an objective worth pursuing.

The elitist contention that no democracy has ever produced a high-quality culture is irrelevant. It is a non-sequitur to assume that what *has* not been done *cannot* be done. It is a contention born of fear and of a secret yearning for the simplicities of the past. It forgets that we approach the challenge with great resources. It ignores the remarkable progress we have already made. We are not yet enjoying the exhilaration that perhaps comes of living through a genuine renaissance. But we may well be laying the material and human basis for one. That we are attempting to do this in a democratic fashion, that we are about to test the alleged incompatibility of art and democracy, should be for us a source of pride, not shame.

Benjamin Franklin, who founded both the first American subscription library and the American Philosophical Society, wrote: "The first drudgery of settling new colonies . . . is now pretty well over; and there are many in every province in circumstances that set them at ease and afford leisure to cultivate the finer arts . . ." Today it might be said that the first drudgery of providing for the material well-being of most Americans is also, historically speaking, pretty well over, and that a maturing nation is beginning to concern itself with the quality of existence. This is the meaning of the rise of the culture consumers.

Acknowledgments

THIS BOOK COULD NOT HAVE BEEN WRITTEN WITHOUT THE HELP OF about 200 men and women—painters, musicians, actors, managers, patrons, arts administrators, businessmen, foundation executives, educators and others—who allowed themselves to be questioned by me, giving freely of their time and knowledge. They were unfailingly courteous, supplying me not only with their own comments and the names of other people to interview, but also with letters, memoranda, programs, and other not-readily-available documentation. It is impossible to thank each of them individually. I hope the book will prove useful and illuminating and thereby, in some measure, express my gratitude.

In addition, a few individuals went so far beyond the call of friendship or duty in permitting me to sharpen my ideas through extended discussion with them over a period of many months, that I must single each of them out for public thanks. The first is my wife, Heidi, to whom this book is dedicated, and who was and is far more than a patient spouse. The book was read by her —or to her—chapter by chapter, often paragraph by paragraph. Her perceptive and forthright comments provided a running critique that compelled me, at each step, to clarify and condense. She has been a good editor and tough-minded intellectual companion.

Several friends have also been especially helpful. Lawrence A. Mayer, Associate Economist, *Fortune* magazine, assisted in straightening out some of the early kinks in those sections that deal with economics and culture. Dr. Donald F. Klein, Research Associate in psychiatry, Hillside Hospital, applied his fine intelligence not merely to those chapters that describe the character and motivations of the culture consumer, but to the entire manuscript. Ralph Burgard, director, St. Paul Council of Arts and Sciences, and R. Philip Hanes, Jr., a Winston-Salem businessman who is one of the driving forces behind the arts council movement in the United States, were both unusually patient with my repeated requests for information and special insight. Herman A. Slotoroff, C.P.A., was kind enough to read the part of the book that deals with taxation and to give his expert advice.

It goes without saying, however, that I, alone, am responsible for the point of view of the book and for any errors that may have crept into the text.

Finally, I must thank *Fortune* magazine for assigning me to do the article entitled "The Quantity of Culture" that appeared in the November, 1961, issue of that magazine, thus starting the train of circumstance that led to this book. Some passages from that article are, with *Fortune's* permission, embodied in the present text. Similarly, some parts of this book have appeared, in another form, in *Show* magazine.

Notes

MUCH OF THIS BOOK IS BASED ON FIRST-HAND INTERVIEWS AND ON ORGANI-zation memos, reports, unpublished correspondence, mimeographed documents and other sources that are not readily accessible to the public. I shall therefore list only published materials that are conveniently available and items of special interest regardless of availability. I shall omit items of secondary importance that are hard to locate. In the case of works listed in the Bibliography, I shall avoid repeating titles by referring to them by number in the Notes. Thus in the Notes [1] will stand for the first item in the Bibliography, *The Lords of Creation* by Frederick Lewis Allen.

CHAPTER ONE

Miss Mannes is quoted from *The New York Times Magazine*, July 9, 1961.

The Randall Jarrell piece appeared in the *Saturday Evening Post*, July 26, 1958. See also his article "A Sad Heart at the Supermarket" in *Daedalus*, Spring, 1960.

Mr. Macdonald will appear again in this book. It should be made explicit that I consider him an asset to the American scene, witty, provocative and, at least sometimes, insightful. I take issue here only with his elitist views as spelled out in the essay "Masscult & Midcult" which appears in *Against the American Grain*, a collection of Mr. Macdonald's work [36].

Mr. Schonberg's *Saturday Evening Post* article "debunking" the culture explosion appeared in the July 13, 1963, issue. The item in which he leaped to the rostrum appeared in *The New York Times*, February 18, 1962.

CHAPTER TWO

The historical section of this chapter leans heavily, though not exclusively, on [62].

An account of the American Art Union is to be found in [35].

For the story of the Chautauqua movement see [18].

Book sale figures are from the American Book Publishers Council, Inc.

Library data come from the Office of Education, U.S. Department of Health, Education and Welfare.

A comment about the American Symphony Orchestra League: of all the national associations in the arts, the A.S.O.L. is the strongest, the most businesslike, and the most interested in collecting statistical data about its members. It is headquartered in Vienna, Virginia.

Statistics on the number of amateur musicians and on musical instrument sales are based on annual estimates released by the American Music Conference, an organization supported by the musical instrument manufacturers.

August Heckscher's comment on "numbers" appeared in a special Lincoln Center Supplement published by *The New York Times Magazine*, September 23, 1962.

CHAPTER THREE

The low estimate of the size of the culture public is extrapolated from [91], p. 31.

The high estimate is from a press release issued by the Stanford Research Institute in announcing its Long Range Planning Service Report No. 140, July, 1962, entitled "The Arts and Business."

Figures on museum attendance are from Otto Wittmann's testimony before a U.S. Senate subcommittee. [83], pp. 152–156.

Data on the characteristics of the culture consumer are drawn from:

"Minneapolis Symphony Poll," conducted November 11, 1955, and available only from the Minneapolis Symphony Orchestra.

"Marketing Study of American Artist Subscribers," available from *American Artist* magazine. This is based on a survey conducted in 1963 by the Mark Clements Research Company.

"Analysis of the Guthrie Theatre Audience," prepared for the Minnesota Theatre Company Foundation by the Twin Cities Marketing and Research Department, Batten, Barton, Durstine and Osborn, Inc., in December, 1963.

Thomas Gale Moore surveys of the Broadway audience, reported in *Arts Management*, December, 1963.

"Who's Who in the Audience," *Playbill* magazine. Survey conducted by Lionel D. Edie & Co. covering the period October, 1960, to October, 1961.

"*Show* Survey of Subscribers," conducted by Erdos and Morgan between November 12, 1962, and January 2, 1963.

"A Household is a Market," 1963, *Saturday Review*, based on the Simmons study entitled, "Selective Markets and the Media Reaching Them."

"The *Bravo!* Magazine Audience," prepared for *Bravo!* by Richard Manville Research, Inc.

"The People Next Door," conducted for *Harper's* and *Atlantic* by Erdos and Morgan. Dated September, 1962.

Figures on income distribution are from [38], p. 29.

Comments on Jewish participation are drawn from *The Reconstructionist*, January 25, 1963, p. 22.

The Demby quotes are from interviews and from a report prepared by his company for the author.

CHAPTER FOUR

Figures on the number of children receiving musical instruction are from the American Music Conference annual reports.

Max Lerner is quoted from [32], pp. 260–261.

Many of these quotes are to be found in [24], a useful anthology.

The Riesman-Roseborough quote is to be found in [52], p. 114.

For mobility material see [65].

The Stanford Research Institute materials quoted in this chapter are from "Consumer Values and Demand," Long Range Planning Service Report No. 81, December, 1960.

The article by Prof. Mauser appeared in the *Harvard Business Review*, November–December, 1963.

The article by Edward T. Chase in *Atlantic* appeared in the April, 1962, issue.

The *Business Week* reference is to the issue of February 1, 1964, p. 50.

Machlup, see [37], p. 374.

Peter Drucker's comments on the "knowledge industry" are to be found in *The New York Times Magazine*, January 12, 1962.

CHAPTER FIVE

The testimony of the American Symphony Orchestra League is reprinted in that organization's newsletter dated February–March, 1963.

The events in Detroit are reported in an article by me in *Show* magazine, June, 1962. Most of the information is based on interviews. The statistical passage on the character of industry in Detroit is based on data supplied by the city's Chamber of Commerce.

CHAPTER SIX

The data on the campus construction boom are culled from a variety of sources including *The New York Times, Architectural Record, Architectural Forum, Arts Management,* and *Back Stage.*

For the names of artists and where they appeared, see the annual music calendar prepared by the President's Music Committee.

The U.C.L.A. material is drawn from *Arts Management*, September, 1962.

Material on the University of Michigan relationship with the Association of Producing Artists is based on *The New York Times*, October 3, 1962, and on unpublished correspondence.

The McNeil Lowry quote appears in *The New York Times*, August 12, 1962.

The reference to the University of Mississippi is based on accounts in *The New York Times*, April 9–11, 1963.

The reference to Baylor University is based on material in the *Christian Science Monitor*, March 18, 1963.

The quote from Harold Taylor appeared in *Arts in Society*, June, 1962.

CHAPTER SEVEN

The Henry Ford quote is from [5], p. 141.

Mr. Struthers is quoted in *Business Week*, December 1, 1962, p. 28.

E. B. Weiss's proposal was reported in *Advertising Age*, July 22, 1963, p. 3.

The typical ad referred to appeared in *Newsweek*, September 3, 1962. Others like it can be found in *Time, Business Week,* and other periodicals.

All references to the Stanford Research Institute study in this chapter are to the report entitled, "The Arts and Business"; see notes for Chapter Three, above.

John Kenneth Galbraith is quoted from *Horizon*, September, 1960, p. 40.

Mr. Buechner is quoted from *Museum News*, October, 1962.

Devereux Josephs is quoted from a speech he made on November 11, 1963, the text of which appears in *Musical America*, December, 1963, p. 160.

The position of the Council of Trent is to be found in [23] volume 2, p. 64.

The review of the Whitney Museum's exhibition of company-owned art appeared in *Commonweal*, May 20, 1960, p. 214.

Harold Taylor and Karl Shapiro are quoted from *Arts in Society*, Fall–Winter, 1962–63, pp. 12, 21.

Herbert Read is quoted from [50], p. xi and p. 9.

Herbert Blau's remarks are in *Arts in Society,* Fall–Winter, 1962–63, p. 42.

The Josephson quote about Frick appears in [25], p. 346. Mr. Josephson, himself, is quoting someone else, although he does not say who it is.

CHAPTER EIGHT

Figures on the numbers of arts councils are derived from various issues of *Arts Management,* and from interviews with officials of Community Arts Councils, Inc., including Ralph Burgard, and with R. Philip Hanes, Jr., who maintains in Winston-Salem, N.C., the most complete library and research file on the arts council movement in the United States.

The St. Paul data are largely based on interviews and correspondence with Ralph Burgard.

The survey of Chambers of Commerce appeared in the June, 1962, *Arts Management.* Other data on arts councils and their building activities are to be found in a survey in the November, 1963, issue of the same newsletter.

Mr. Slayton's speech is quoted in the newsletter of the American Symphony Orchestra League dated July-September, 1962.

The history of the Lincoln Center project is to be found in the special Lincoln Center Supplement published by *The New York Times Magazine,* September 23, 1962, p. 14.

See also the first annual report of Lincoln Center, dated 1963.

For charges against Lincoln Center, see an article by Joan Peyser in *Commentary,* May, 1961, p. 411; also a piece by Percival Goodman in *Dissent,* Summer, 1961, p. 333.

The McNeil Lowry quote on the shortage of arts managers appears in *Arts Management,* August, 1962.

CHAPTER NINE

The study referred to is *College Student Images of a Selected Group of Professions and Occupations* by Donald D. O'Dowd and David C. Beardslee. Wesleyan University, Middletown, Conn., April, 1960.

The Slonimsky quote is from *A Thing Or Two About Music* by Nicolas Slonimsky, p. 50.

The American Federation of Musicians survey is reported in *Business Week,* August 19, 1961, and in the mimeographed text of a speech by Herman Kenin, president of the union, dated April 18, 1961.

The Philadelphia Orchestra contract is reported in *Arts Management,* September, 1963.

Figures on the concert management business are drawn from an article by me in *Show,* May, 1963. They were originally based almost entirely on interviews with industry executives.

The survey of composers' earnings is reported in *The New York Times,* October 1, 1961.

Data on employment of artists are drawn in part from [73].

Figures on increase in number of artists are from U.S. Census Bureau, reported in *The New York Times,* October 8, 1963.

CHAPTER TEN

Figures on the book industry are from [39]; *Atlantic,* October, 1947; bulletins of the American Book Publishers Council, Inc.; and *Show,* September, 1962.

Book profits data are from *Forbes,* October 15, 1963; figures for trade publishers are from interviews.

Record manufacturer figures are from the Record Industry Association of America; interviews with executives of RCA Victor and Columbia Records; the CBS Annual Report for 1962; and *Fortune,* July, 1963.

Orchestra deficit figures are from [29], pp. 36–52. The reference on page 151 to national expenditures of $30,000,000 annually for orchestras differs from the $26,000,000 figure cited on page 16 in that it includes college and university orchestras. These are specifically excluded from the $26,000,000 figure.

The quote from the American Symphony Orchestra League is from its newsletter dated March–April, 1961.

Figures on deficits of specific institutions are usually based on interviews with officials of those institutions.

Data on Museum of Modern Art are from that institution's 1962–63 annual report and from its publication *Today and Tomorrow.*

The study of 52 art museums is reported in "Museum Report No. 4," published by the American Association of Museums, January, 1963.

CHAPTER ELEVEN

Figures on what it would cost to attend symphony concerts, the Museum of Modern Art, or the Metropolitan Opera are extrapolated from annual reports, interview data, and other materials cited earlier.

CHAPTER TWELVE

A brief summary of the history of patronage appears in [44]. This book also includes a survey of state support of the arts in other countries, and a history of the federal government's involvement with the arts up through the early years of the W.P.A. arts programs.

The Dürer quote is to be found in [61], p. 165. The book is a scholarly, but readable, social history of painting "from antiquity to the French Revolution."

For material on the tycoon-patrons see [4], [9], [34], [41].

On the number of millionaires, see *New Republic*, March 3, 1958, p. 8.

For figures on American philanthropy see [74].

On the San Francisco hotel tax, see [88].

For data on state activities in the arts, see issues of *Arts Management* and annual reports of the New York State Council on the Arts.

The account of the differences between the Robert Joffrey Ballet and the Rebekah Harkness Foundation are drawn from newspaper accounts, including *The New York Times* of March 18, 1964. Spokesmen for the Foundation believe that the Foundation was unfairly treated in some news accounts.

CHAPTER THIRTEEN

The Living Theatre's battle with the Internal Revenue Service was reported in the *Village Voice*, October 24, 1963; and in *The New York Times* on the following dates: October 18–19–20, 1963; January 23, May 14–15, 1964.

The view that federal aid to the arts would coincide with a Moscow plot is reflected in testimony before the U.S. Senate. See [83], p. 250.

Mr. Tynan's proposal is to be found in *Musical America*, December, 1963, p. 156.

The Lipton quote is from *The New York Times*, April 6, 1963.

Pollack's remarks are to be found [83], p. 157.

The Treasury estimate of tax savings by contributors is to be found [67], p. 23.

The figures on private philanthropy lean heavily on [74].

Figures for European national expenditures on subsidies to the arts are from [81].

Larry Rivers on government aid is from *The New York Times*, April 28, 1961.

Mr. Richards on the dangers of federal aid is drawn from [75], p. 178.

Mr. Lynes' sensible attack is to be found in *The New York Times Magazine*, March 25, 1962, p. 84.

Senator Yarborough is on record: [83], p. 119.

On the Martha Graham affair, see *Newsweek,* October 28, 1963, p. 68; also letter in *The New York Times,* September 23, 1963.

The quote from then-Representative Jacob Javits appeared in the *New York Post,* August 9, 1949.

References to the study published by Brookings are to [42], pp. 280–288.

John MacFadyen is quoted from his testimony before the U.S. Senate. [83], p. 117.

For Mr. Galbraith's remarks, see [84].

Arlan R. Coolidge's comments are from [83], p. 131.

Mr. Rockefeller is quoted from *The New York Times,* June 23, 1963.

Senator Javits on "cultural starvation" will be found in [83], p. 103.

The quotation from a bill for a national arts foundation is from S.165, printed in [83], p. 8.

Roger L. Stevens' remarks about physical facilities for the arts are found in [83], p. 194. Mr. Heckscher's exactly opposite findings appear in [67], p. 14.

CHAPTER FOURTEEEN

Mr. Schonberg on the coarsening of public taste: *The New York Times,* May 28, 1961.

Albert Bush-Brown's remarks are in [83], p. 77.

Daniel Catton Rich's warning is to be found in *Museum News,* March, 1961, p. 36.

Macdonald: see [36], pp. 18, 37, 54, ix, x. By all means read the entire essay.

Re: "letting the mob in to vote . . ." see [60], p. 39.

Daniel Bell's response to Mr. Macdonald is in *Studies in Public Communication,* Autumn, 1962. Among other things, Mr. Bell's sharp eye has noted internal evidence in the various versions of "Masscult & Midcult" that tend to contradict the notion that public taste is declining. The point is too complicated to spell out here without quoting at length. But for anyone who enjoys an "inside" literary-academic joke I recommend the Bell footnote on p. 15.

Kurt Adler's comments on the new public appear in *The New York Times,* August 28, 1963.

Mr. Arnason's experiences in Korea are described in *The New York Times,* November 20, 1959.

August Heckscher's quote about "Who reads an American book?" is from a speech given November 11, 1963, the text of which will be found in *Musical America*, December, 1963, p. 150.

On the alleged disappearance of the avant garde: Mr. Swados' remark is from *Contact*, April 1963. Mr. Macdonald's appears on p. 56 of *Against the American Grain* [36]; Mr. Fiedler's is from the *New York Herald Tribune Magazine*, May 17, 1964.

The *Dance Magazine* report on amateur companies is in its December, 1962, issue.

Norman Podhoretz's comment on elitism is from *Show*, December, 1962, p. 43.

Benjamin Franklin's words are from "A Proposal for Promoting Useful Knowledge among the British Plantations in America," a handbill issued May 14, 1743, in which he urged the establishment of the American Philosophical Society.

Bibliography

Books:

1. Allen, Frederick Lewis. *The Lords of Creation*. New York: Harper & Bros., 1935.

2. Amory, Cleveland. *Who Killed Society?* New York: Harper & Bros., 1960.

3. Barzun, Jacques. *Music in American Life*. Gloucester, Mass.: Peter Smith, 1958.

4. Beer, Thomas. *The Mauve Decade*. Garden City, N.Y.: Garden City Publishing Co., 1926.

5. Behrman, S. N. *Duveen*. New York: Vintage Books, n. d.

6. Bell, Bernard Iddings. *Crowd Culture*. Chicago: Henry Regnery, 1952.

7. Blau, Peter M. and Scott, W. Richard. *Formal Organizations*. San Francisco: Chandler Publishing Co., 1962.

8. Calverton, V. F. *The Liberation of American Literature*. New York.: Charles Scribner's Sons, 1932.

9. Curti, Merle. *The Growth of American Thought*. New York: Harper & Bros., 1943.

10. De Grazia, Sebastian. *Of Time, Work & Leisure*. New York: Twentieth Century Fund, 1962.

11. Eliot, T. S. *Notes Towards the Definition of Culture*. New York: Harcourt, Brace & Co., 1949.

12. Fischer, Ernst. *The Necessity of Art*. Baltimore: Penguin Books, 1963.

13. Freedman, Morris. *Confessions of a Conformist*. New York: W. W. Norton, 1961.

14. Gaunt, William. *The Aesthetic Adventure*. New York: Harcourt, Brace & Co., 1945.

15. Graña, Cesar. *Bohemian versus Bourgeois*. New York: Basic Books, 1964.

16. Griffith, Thomas. *The Waist-High Culture*. New York: Grosset & Dunlap, 1959.

17. Guerard, Albert L. *Art for Art's Sake*. New York: Schocken Books, 1963.

18. Harrison, Harry P. and Detzer, Karl. *Culture Under Canvas*. New York: Hastings House, 1958.

19. Hauser, Arnold. *The Social History of Art*. New York: Vintage Books, n. d. (4 vols.).

20. Heckscher, August. *The Public Happiness*. New York: Atheneum, 1962.

21. Hindemith, Paul. *A Composer's World*. Garden City, N.Y.: Anchor Books, 1961.
22. Hoggart, Richard. *The Uses of Literacy*. Boston: Beacon Press, 1961.
23. Holt, Elizabeth G., ed. *A Documentary History of Art*. Garden City, N.Y.: Anchor Books, 1957, 1958 (2 vols.).
24. Josephson, Eric and Mary, eds. *Man Alone*. New York: Dell Books, 1962.
25. Josephson, Matthew. *The Robber Barons*. New York: Harcourt, Brace & World, Inc., 1962.
26. Keezer, Dexter M., ed. *Financing Higher Education 1960–70*. New York: McGraw-Hill, 1959.
27. Keller, Suzanne. *Beyond the Ruling Class*. New York: Random House, 1963.
28. Knight, Arthur. *The Liveliest Art*. New York: New American Library, 1957.
29. Lang, Paul Henry, ed. *One Hundred Years of Music in America*. New York: G. Schirmer, Inc., 1961.
30. Larrabee, Eric and Meyersohn, Rolf, eds. *Mass Leisure*. Glencoe, Ill.: The Free Press, 1958.
31. Laski, Harold J. *The American Democracy*. New York: Viking Press, 1948.
32. Lerner, Max. *America as a Civilization*. New York: Simon & Schuster, 1957.
33. Lowenthal, Leo. *Literature, Popular Culture, and Society*. Englewood Cliffs, N.J.: Prentice-Hall, 1961.
34. Lundberg, Ferdinand. *America's 60 Families*. New York: Citadel Press, 1946.
35. Lynes, Russell. *The Tastemakers*. New York: Grosset & Dunlap, 1954.
36. Macdonald, Dwight. *Against the American Grain*. New York: Random House, 1962.
37. Machlup, Fritz. *The Production and Distribution of Knowledge in the United States*. Princeton, N.J.: Princeton University Press, 1962.
38. Miller, Herman P. *Rich Man, Poor Man*. New York: Thomas Y. Crowell, 1964.
39. Miller, William. *The Book Industry*. New York: Columbia University Press, 1949.
40. Myers, Bernard S. *Problems of the Younger American Artist*. New York: The City College Press, 1957.
41. Myers, Gustavus. *History of the Great American Fortunes*. New York: Modern Library, 1937.
42. Orlans, Harold. *The Effects of Federal Programs on Higher Education*. Washington, D.C.: The Brookings Institution, 1962.
43. Ortega y Gasset, Jose. *The Dehumanization of Art*. Garden City, N.Y.: Anchor Books, n. d.

44. Overmyer, Grace. *Government and the Arts*. New York: W. W. Norton, 1939.
45. Packard, Vance. *The Status Seekers*. New York: David McKay, 1959.
46. Parrington, Vernon Louis. *Main Currents in American Thought*. New York: Harcourt, Brace & Co., 1930.
47. Pieper, Josef. *Leisure the Basis of Culture*. New York: Pantheon Books, 1964.
48. Read, Herbert. *Art and Society*. New York: Pantheon Books, n. d.
49. ———. *The Tenth Muse*. New York: Grove Press, 1958.
50. ———. *To Hell with Culture*. New York: Schocken Books, 1963.
51. Reitlinger, Gerald. *The Economics of Taste*. London: Barrie & Rockliff, 1961.
52. Riesman, David. *Abundance for What?* Garden City, N.Y.: Doubleday & Co., 1964.
53. Rosenberg, Bernard and White, David Manning, eds. *Mass Culture*. Glencoe, Ill.: The Free Press, 1960.
54. Rosenberg, Harold. *The Tradition of the New*. New York: Grove Press, 1961.
55. Schultz, Theodore W. *The Economic Value of Education*. New York: Columbia University Press, 1963.
56. Sinclair, Upton. *Mammonart*. Pasadena, Calif.: Published by the Author, 1925.
57. Taylor, Harold. *Art and the Intellect*. New York: The Museum of Modern Art, 1960.
58. Tocqueville, Alexis de. *Democracy in America*. New York: Vintage Books, n. d. (2 vols.).
59. Weber, Max. *From Max Weber*. New York: Oxford University Press, 1961.
60. Williams, Raymond. *Culture and Society*. Garden City, N.Y.: Anchor Books, 1960.
61. Wittkower, Rudolf and Margot. *Born Under Saturn*. New York: Random House, 1963.
62. Wright, Louis B. *The Cultural Life of the American Colonies 1607–1763*. New York: Harper & Row, 1962.

Reports and Other Documents:

63. *The American Imagination,* a critical survey of the arts from the *Times Literary Supplement*. Published in the U.S. by Atheneum Publishers, 1960.
64. "The American Reading Public," *Daedalus,* Winter, 1963.
65. "America's Tastemakers," a new strategy for predicting change in consumer behavior. Published by Opinion Research Corp., Princeton, N.J., 1959.
66. "Analysis of the Guthrie Theatre Audience," prepared by Batten, Barton, Durstine and Osborn, Inc., Minneapolis, 1963.

67. "The Arts and the National Government," report to the President submitted by August Heckscher, Special Consultant on the Arts, May 28, 1963. U.S. Senate Document No. 28, 88th Congress, First Session.

68. "The Arts and Public Patronage," by Sir William Emrys Williams. Published by the Arts Council of Great Britain, London, 1958.

69. "Bricks and Mortarboards," a report on college planning and building. Educational Facilities Laboratories, Inc., 1964.

70. "The Canada Council Annual Report 1962-63," The Canada Council, Ottawa, 1963. Contains a statement of the Canadian government's philosophy of arts patronage.

71. "The Changing Shape of the American Class Structure," by Kurt B. Mayer. Social Research, Winter, 1963.

72. "The Debate on Cultural Standards in Nineteenth Century England," by Leo Lowenthal and Ina Lawson. Social Research, Winter, 1963.

73. "Economic Conditions in the Performing Arts." Hearings before the Select Subcommittee on Education of the House Committee on Education and Labor; 87th Congress, First and Second Sessions.

74. "Giving USA," annual reports on philanthropy in America; issues from 1958 to 1964. Published by The American Association of Fund-Raising Counsel.

75. "Government and the Arts." Hearings before a Special Subcommittee of the Committee on Labor and Public Welfare. U.S. Senate, 87th Congress, Second Session, August 29–31, 1962.

76. "Greater St. Louis Arts Survey." Summary of Questionnaire Findings, Booz, Allen & Hamilton, Chicago, 1963. A pioneer attempt to collect economic and sociological data on non-profit institutions on a national basis.

77. "The Higher Dialectic of Philanthropy," by Arthur Vidich. Social Research, Winter, 1963.

78. "Lincoln Center, Emporium of the Arts," by Percival Goodman. Dissent, Summer, 1961.

79. "Mass Culture and Mass Media," Daedalus, Spring, 1960. Symposium participants include Hannah Arendt, Ernest van den Haag, Randall Jarrell, Edward Shils and Stanley Edgar Hyman.

80. Modernity and Mass Society, by Daniel Bell. Studies in Public Communication, Autumn, 1962. Published by University of Chicago Press.

81. "Money for the Arts," by Henry Lee Munson. A report on state support of the arts in seven European countries. H. L. Munson & Co., Inc., New York, 1962.

82. "Music and Records Survey Among Readers of Harper's Magazine and The Atlantic Monthly." Harper-Atlantic Sales Inc., New York, 1962.

83. "National Arts Legislation." Hearings before the Special Subcommittee on the Arts of the Committee on Labor and Public Welfare. U.S. Senate, 88th Congress, First Session, October 28–November 1, 1963.

84. "The Nation's Future," transcript of NBC Television program, February 11, 1961. Debate on federal aid to the arts: John Kenneth Galbraith *vs.* Russell Lynes.

85. "The New Man in the Arts," by Jacques Barzun. *Arts in Society,* January, 1958. Published by University Extension Division, University of Wisconsin. A discussion of amateurism.

86. "New York State Council on the Arts Annual Reports." Published by the N.Y.S.C.A., New York.

87. "Night and Day in Richmond, Va.," a report on the feasibility of a cultural center in Richmond, by William A. Briggs; Richmond, February, 1962. Contains tables on arts center construction and financing all over the United States.

88. "Partnership in the Arts," public and private support of cultural activities in the San Francisco Bay Area, by Mel Scott. Report published by the Institute of Governmental Studies, University of California, Berkeley, 1963.

89. "The Shorter Work Week and the Constructive Use of Free Time." Proceedings of the Eighth Annual AFL-CIO National Conference on Community Service Activities, New York, 1963.

90. "A Permanent Classical Repertory Theatre in the Nation's Capital," by Zelda Fichandler. Washington, D.C., 1959.

91. " A Study of Cultural Change in the United States." Kenyon & Eckhardt, Inc., New York, 1962.

92. "A Study of Voluntary Support for Public Higher Education," prepared by G. A. Brakeley & Co., Inc., New York, 1963.

93. "Subsidy Makes Sense," by Hope Stoddard. Published by the American Federation of Musicians, New York, n. d.

94. "Survey of Arts Councils." American Symphony Orchestra League, Vienna, Va., 1959.

95. "Wingspread Conference on the Arts," papers and discussion reported in *Arts in Society,* Fall–Winter, 1962–63. Published by University Extension Division, University of Wisconsin. Participants include Harold Taylor, Karl Shapiro, Herbert Blau, and Kenneth Burke.

Index

A

About the Author

ALVIN TOFFLER achieved international recognition with his study of social and psychological change, *Future Shock*. A former associate editor of *Fortune* Magazine, he has written for scores of periodicals, ranging from *Horizon* and the London *Observer* to the *Annals of the Academy of Political and Social Science*. He is the editor of two collections, *The Schoolhouse in the City* and *The Futurists*. He is a contributing editor of *ARTnews* and a member of the board of directors of Composers and Choreographers Theatre. At the New School for Social Research, Mr. Toffler taught the "Sociology of the Future"—one of the first such courses in the world. Later he served as a Visiting Professor at Cornell University and a Visiting Scholar at the Russell Sage Foundation. His works have won many awards here and abroad, and he holds honorary degrees in letters, science, and law. He is married, has one daughter, and does much of his writing at home in Ridgefield, Connecticut.

VINTAGE POLITICAL SCIENCE
AND SOCIAL CRITICISM